I LIFT UP MY
SOUL

I LIFT UP MY SOUL

DEVOTIONS TO START
YOUR DAY WITH GOD

CHARLES F. STANLEY

THOMAS NELSON
Since 1798

NASHVILLE   DALLAS   MEXICO CITY   RIO DE JANEIRO

Published in Nashville, Tennessee, by Thomas Nelson. Thomas Nelson is a registered trademark of Thomas Nelson, Inc.

Thomas Nelson, Inc., titles may be purchased in bulk for educational, business, fund-raising, or sales promotional use. For information, please e-mail SpecialMarkets@ThomasNelson.com.

Library of Congress Cataloging-in-Publication Data

Stanley, Charles F.
    I lift up my soul : devotions to start your day with God / Charles F. Stanley.
    p. cm.
    ISBN 978-1-4002-0289-8
    1. Devotional calendars. I. Title.
BV4811.S8155 2010
242'.2—dc22   2010020906

Printed in the United States of America

11 12 13 14 QG 5 4 3 2

To You, O Lord, I lift up my soul.

PSALM 25:1

Wake Up to a New Day with the Lord

SCRIPTURE READING: PSALM 143:8–12
KEY VERSE: PSALM 143:8

Cause me to hear Your lovingkindness in the morning,
For in You do I trust;
Cause me to know the way in which I should walk,
For I lift up my soul to You.

What is it you crave first thing in the morning? Does a steamy, fresh-brewed cup of coffee or tea catch your attention? Does your morning seem incomplete without your usual cereal or plate of eggs? Do you feel as if you can't make it out the front door without reading the morning paper or watching one of the cheerful morning shows?

In Psalm 143:8, David wrote, "Let me hear Your lovingkindness in the morning; for I trust in You; teach me the way in which I should walk; for to You I lift up my soul" (NASB). David saw the necessity of seeking God to direct his steps. He looked to God for guidance for the needs of each day.

A sign of spiritual growth is longing to be with the Lord in a time of Bible study and prayer each day. Whether in the morning or at night, is there a time in your day when you spend time with the Savior? Is it a time that you guard jealously?

Henry Ward Beecher said, "The first hour of the morning is the rudder of the day."

Nothing, not even coffee, will begin your day like time alone with God. Seek Him so that you may grow closer to Him. Go into His presence so that you may sing for joy and be glad all your days (Ps. 90:14). When you make plans to meet God, He will place an intimate joy within your heart. Then you will learn to hunger for His Word.

Father, give me a hunger for Your Word. Let me hear Your lovingkindness
in the morning. I lift up my soul to You.

(PATHWAYS TO HIS PRESENCE)

The Goodness of God

SCRIPTURE READING: LUKE 18:18–23
KEY VERSE: PSALM 86:5

You, Lord, are good, and ready to forgive,
and abundant in mercy to all those who call upon You.

Concerning the goodness of God, Henry Thiessen explains, "In the larger sense of the term, the goodness of God includes all the qualities that answer to the conception of an ideal personage; that is, it includes such qualities as God's holiness, righteousness, and truth, as well as His love, benevolence, mercy, and grace."

The rich young ruler called Jesus "Good Teacher," but the Lord was quick to reply, "Why do you call Me good? No one is good except God alone" (Luke 18:19 NASB). Faithfully, Jesus was doing exactly what the Father had sent Him to do: point men and women to their heavenly Father. He also was involved in training people to seek God not out of fear, but out of a desire to know and experience His goodness and mercy.

In *The Pursuit of God*, A. W. Tozer concludes, "Right now we are in an age of religious complexity. The simplicity which is in Christ is rarely found among us. In its stead are programs, methods, organizations and a world of nervous activities which occupy time and attention but can never satisfy the longing of the heart."

Often we seek Him because we have heard that He is "good." But we stop at this point and miss learning about the deeper goodness of God. Make sure that as you discover more about God's goodness, you also take time to grow in your devotion to Him.

Lord, let me grow in my devotion toward You. I wait each day for a divine encounter with You.

(SEEKING HIS FACE)

The Call of Faith

SCRIPTURE READING: GENESIS 12:1–9
KEY VERSE: HEBREWS 10:23

Let us hold fast the confession of our hope without wavering, for He who promised is faithful.

Suppose you plan a wonderful surprise vacation for your family or friends. The big day finally comes. The car is loaded, everyone has taken care of all those last-minute details, and your tank is full of gas. Everyone piles in the car and fastens seat belts in anticipation of the trip.

Finally someone asks the fateful question, "Hey, where are we going?" And you say with great authority, "Well, I don't know exactly." After the bewildered looks and cries of dismay, probably the only one left in the car with you is the dog, and he isn't looking too certain either. People simply don't make big trips without knowing where they're going—unless God asks them to. And that is precisely what God asked of Abram and his family: "Go forth from your country, and from your relatives and from your father's house, to the land which I will show you; and I will make you a great nation, and I will bless you, and make your name great" (Gen. 12:1–2 NASB).

God gave Abram some very important information, but He did not hand him a road map. Why? He wanted Abram and Sarai to trust Him for the journey. Abram did not know where they were headed, but he knew their future was blessed, more than he could conceive.

Are you letting God take you in His direction, or are you still insisting on a travel plan?

Lord, take me in Your direction. Help me learn to walk by faith. I know my future will be blessed, more than I can imagine. No travel plan is necessary for my journey—I need only You as my Guide.

(ON HOLY GROUND)

Satisfying Your Heart

SCRIPTURE READING: COLOSSIANS 3:12–17

KEY VERSE: COLOSSIANS 3:15

Let the peace of God rule in your hearts, to which also you were called in one body; and be thankful.

Wasn't life simpler when you could plunk down a quarter and get a steamy cup of java? Now, to buy coffee, you must make a hundred different decisions. Would you like a latte, cappuccino, espresso, macchiato, or frappuccino? Flavored with mocha, caramel, vanilla, amaretto, or hazelnut? Would you like it caffeinated or decaf? Tall or grande? The options are endless and create a sense of satisfying whatever your heart desires. It is natural for situations to go from simplicity to chaos when the heart is involved.

However, Scripture has an indictment for the heart, as Jeremiah 17:9 reveals: "The heart is deceitful above all things, and desperately wicked; who can know it?"

Sometimes the reason circumstances become more complicated is because the simplest answers are challenging to the heart. Even though you really do know what to do, the decision would take a great deal of courage and commitment. As you wait to find a solution that caters to the whims of your heart, answers become increasingly difficult to find.

The only answer is for God to direct you. As Colossians 3:15 teaches, "Let the peace of God rule in your hearts." Is it Christ who rules your heart and directs your path? His is the greatest satisfaction your heart will ever know.

Lord, my heart wanders as it wills. I give it to You, so that You may guide it around the pitfalls of its own longings.

(PATHWAYS TO HIS PRESENCE)

Your Talents

SCRIPTURE READING: LUKE 19:12–27
KEY VERSE: LUKE 19:17

*He said to him, "Well done, good servant; because you were faithful
in a very little, have authority over ten cities."*

An essential ingredient for success in the personal or corporate realm
is productivity. Businesses must be profitable if they expect to survive.
Employees must work hard and wisely if they are to progress.

Although the believer's identity and security in Christ should never
be confused with his performance (the Father unconditionally loves and
accepts him), God expects him to be productive in the use of his natural talents and spiritual gifts. This is clear in the parable of the talents,
where the industrious servant is rewarded and the indolent worker is rep-
rimanded for his lack of initiative and effort.

The fear of failure is perhaps the greatest obstacle for many Christians.
We flunk a course, flub an assignment, disappoint a boss, and decide we
must not be made of the right stuff. What heresy! Failure is never final in
God's eyes. Look at David, Moses, Mark, and others who blew it but still
found great favor with God. All God desires is that you learn from your
mistakes and trust Him to help you.

A productive, satisfying life can be your experience. There will be
unexpected lapses and momentary pauses as you seek to maximize your
talents, but in the end, you will hear God say, "Well done, my good servant" (Luke 19:17 NIV). This is reward enough.

*Father, I praise You that failure is never final in Your eyes. Remove my
fear of failure and replace it with divine confidence. Help me learn from my
mistakes.*

(ON HOLY GROUND)

The Life of God

Scripture Reading: John 11:1–45
Key Verse: John 10:10

The thief does not come except to steal, and to kill, and to destroy. I have come that they may have life, and that they may have it more abundantly.

Think about your best friend for a moment. Try to remember your very first meeting. What if your best friend had handed you a long list of dos and don'ts, telling you any violation would lessen his care for you? Obviously your relationship would never have progressed. Who would want such a friend?

Yet many Christians act as if this is their view of Jesus. But He did not hand you a list of conditions when you accepted Him. What He gave you was His life.

In the New Testament, there are several Greek words for life. *Bios* (origin of *biology*), generally translated, means "lifestyle." Another Greek word for life is *zoe*, which means "life as God has it."

In John 10:10, Jesus said, "I came that they may have life, and have it abundantly" (NASB). In John 11:25, He stated, "I am the resurrection and the life" (NASB). In both cases, Jesus used the word *zoe*. How awesome to hear from our Lord Himself that the "life as God has it" is within us, a magnificent gift of His unconditional love.

Since you have this life, His life, you already have the very best. He dwells within you to encourage and empower you. As long as you are within God's will, sustaining energy will flow through you from His eternal wellspring. Within His will, you'll never tire of living for Jesus.

Father, help me walk in Your will so that sustaining energy from Your eternal wellspring will flow through me.

(Seeking His Face)

Your Best Friend

SCRIPTURE READING: JOHN 15:12–17
KEY VERSE: PROVERBS 18:24

A man who has friends must himself be friendly,
but there is a friend who sticks closer than a brother.

Do you remember having a best friend as a child? This person went everywhere with you, from recess in the schoolyard to adventures around the neighborhood. You had small fights and squabbles occasionally, but you stuck by each other when difficulties came along.

As an adult, you may have a friend like this today, but you are certainly aware that such friends are rare indeed. The blessing of a friend who understands your deepest thoughts and needs and loves you through the hard times is a gift from the Lord. It is important to recognize, however, that the best friend in the entire world can still let you down at times. It is not a cliché to state that Jesus is your only true Friend.

Joseph Scriven, an Irishman born in 1819, discovered this truth in a powerful way. The night before he was to be married, his beloved fiancée drowned. Grieving deeply, Scriven decided to move to Canada and begin a new life, dedicated entirely to letting the Lord use him in others' lives. Out of this experience and several others, he penned the words to the favorite hymn "What a Friend We Have in Jesus."

Can you imagine writing this poetry after going through such pain? Scriven saw the Lord's faithfulness. He knew firsthand that when all earthly supports and emotional props disappear, Jesus is there to love and comfort eternally.

Jesus, You are the best Friend I will ever have. Thank You for Your
faithfulness and this wonderful relationship we share.

(INTO HIS PRESENCE)

Encouraging Sagging Saints

SCRIPTURE READING: 1 CORINTHIANS 16:10–21
KEY VERSE: HEBREWS 6:10

God is not unjust to forget your work and labor of love which you have shown toward His name, in that you have ministered to the saints, and do minister.

Stephanas. Fortunatus. Achaicus. Aquila. Priscilla. Although names not on the tip of your tongue, these people were instrumental in the formation of the early New Testament church. Paul mentioned their indispensable labor in his parting instructions to the church at Corinth. Without defining their specific contributions, he remarked that their ministries refreshed and revitalized believers, including himself.

The local church today frequently errs in the notion that its pastor and staff members are the sole nucleus for the work of the gospel. They have vital functions, but the saints themselves share and participate in the growth of Christ's body.

Your name may not be on the bulletin. You may not be a deacon or elder. But you have been equipped with spiritual gifts to strengthen the saints. A note with a brief word of encouragement, a phone call to someone in your Sunday school class, lunch with a discouraged parent, a small gift to someone in need—these are discreet but practical and encouraging ways to lift the spirits of sagging saints.

Ask God to show you how you might refresh fellow workers. Let Him lead you in appropriate ways to demonstrate His gentle love: "God is not unjust so as to forget your work and the love which you have shown toward His name, in having ministered and in still ministering to the saints" (Heb. 6:10 NASB).

Dear God, teach me to be an encourager and a source of hope to others. Show me how to refresh my fellow workers, demonstrating Your love in appropriate and practical ways.

(ON HOLY GROUND)

God's Plan for Your Future

Scripture Reading: Jeremiah 29:11–14
Key Verse: Jeremiah 29:11

"I know the thoughts that I think toward you," says the LORD, "thoughts of peace and not of evil, to give you a future and a hope."

Are you aware that God knows exactly where you are and what you are doing right now? What about tomorrow, or the next day, or the next? God is just as aware of what you will be doing at 10:42 a.m. on any random morning five years from now as He is mindful of what you are doing now.

Contrary to secular thought, we are not bouncing around haphazardly through time and space. The same God who created the universe and everything in it also has a specific plan for every single person on earth. Because He is the God of yesterday, today, and tomorrow, He alone knows the ultimate outcome of each decision we make. Therefore, only God can be trusted to guide our daily steps as we seek to follow Him.

The Lord revealed through Jeremiah, "For I know the thoughts that I think toward you . . . thoughts of peace and not of evil, to give you a future and a hope" (Jer. 29:11). These two things—hope and the expectation of a bright future—are in short supply these days. However, we have the assurance of almighty God that He already has a plan to provide us with both.

In Christ, the hope for our eternal future is secure. However, God is still intimately interested in your day-to-day living as well. Invite Him into your decisions; only He knows how to get you where He wants to take you.

Father, I am so thankful that You are interested in my day-to-day living. I invite You to guide me in every decision and get me where You want to take me.

(PATHWAYS TO HIS PRESENCE)

Personal Intimacy

SCRIPTURE READING: PSALM 142:1–7
KEY VERSE: PSALM 142:5

I cried out to You, O LORD:
I said, "You are my refuge,
My portion in the land of the living."

The goal of a married couple is not just to stay married but to develop a personal intimacy that touches body, soul, and spirit. Likewise, the goal of a believer is not just to be a Christian but to cultivate an intimate, devoted relationship with the heavenly Father.

In both instances, honest, sincere, and consistent communication is the key to such oneness and nearness. The Christian experiences that process through a deepening, growing, expanding experience of praise, worship, and prayer.

God's goal in intimacy is not just to answer your petitions, hear your complaints, or solve your problems. Although He does address each of these needs, they are only a part of the Lord Jesus Christ's ultimate purpose—oneness and union with Him.

God wants you to know Him; to enjoy Him; to live continually in the light of His favor, wisdom, and truth. He desires a genuine relationship with you, His child. Daily worship and prayer are where you and the Father are drawn into intimate relationship—where His love for you and your love for Him become the bedrock of your faith.

Make it your goal to know God intimately. Learn to worship and praise Him . . . then watch your prayer life move into a new dimension.

Heavenly Father, my goal is to know You intimately. Teach me how to worship. Teach me how to pray.

(INTO HIS PRESENCE)

Joyful in All Things

SCRIPTURE READING: PHILIPPIANS 2:15–18

KEY VERSE: PHILIPPIANS 4:4

Rejoice in the Lord always. Again I will say, rejoice!

Jesus often instructed those He healed to go to the temple and offer a sacrifice to God. In doing so, the people were acknowledging God's mighty work while giving praise to Him instead of just focusing on the healing itself.

There was a release of joy and praise as the people went before God, thanking Him for what He had done. Joy is foundational to the Christian life. The Bible teaches us to be joyful in all things.

Can this mean that even when we fail to see God's miraculous hand at work in our lives, there is joy? Yes. Imprisoned and away from those he loved, the apostle Paul wrote, "Even if I am being poured out as a drink offering . . . I rejoice and share my joy with you all" (Phil. 2:17 NASB). It is possible to be joyful, even if your world seems to be coming apart at the seams.

Because of Christ's love and devotion to you, you can be joyful in times of disappointment, heartache, and personal loss. Joy is not based on your circumstances; it is based on a Person—the Lord Jesus Christ.

When you feel sorrowful, take your sacrifices of praise to Him. Let His arms of encouragement engulf you and hold you close. Joy is not just external; it lives deep within your heart.

Thank You, Lord, that I can be joyful in times of disappointment, heartache, and personal loss. Your joy is not just external. It lives within my heart.

(SEEKING HIS FACE)

The Eternal Adventure

SCRIPTURE READING: 1 JOHN 5:6–13

KEY VERSE: 1 JOHN 5:9

If we receive the witness of men, the witness of God is greater; for this is the witness of God which He has testified of His Son.

When someone testifies about something—a product, an event, another's character—the testimony is only as strong as the character of the person giving it. And when it comes to God, there should be no question about what He says. His words are truth.

But there is an even greater benefit to knowing God. As we draw near to Him, we learn that He not only provides the guidance we need at every turn in life, but He also gives us clear direction on how to accomplish His plan for our lives.

John wrote, "If we receive the witness of men, the witness of God is greater; for this is the witness of God which He has testified of His Son . . . and this is the testimony: that God has given us eternal life, and this life is in His Son" (1 John 5:9, 11). The assurance of our salvation is based on God's Word. We do not have to be afraid that one day we will fall from His grace. This cannot happen to those who have accepted Christ as their Savior. God's love is eternal. There is never a moment in time when He turns His love in another direction. It is always focused on us.

He provides us the assurance we need through what He has testified about His Son. The moment we accept God's Word as truth and receive Christ as our Savior, we are saved. The eternal adventure begins with great assurance!

Thank You for salvation and assurance. Thank You, Lord, that Your love is forever focused on me.

(PATHWAYS TO HIS PRESENCE)

The Dedication of Your Life

SCRIPTURE READING: PSALM 138:1–8

KEY VERSE: GALATIANS 6:9

Let us not grow weary while doing good, for in due season we shall reap if we do not lose heart.

Julian of Norwich (1343–1413) lived through plagues, poverty, and war. But a serious illness brought her into a new awareness of God's personal love. In *I Promise You a Crown*, a compilation of her writings by David Hazard, she wrote:

> It had come to me that nothing can keep us from knowing the joy of heaven while we remain under the cross—that is, in humble obedience to God no matter what is sent to us. . . . I will tell you what faith showed me in its light. In my struggle, I saw the terror that lies in forsaking the power of the cross. For in making our soul submit, as Jesus submitted, we are remade into the image of Christ. This will never happen if we seek only earthly blessings. When I understood this, I did not want to look up, as if I had already achieved a place in heaven among the blessed. I knew that to do so would make my soul proud and arrogant in itself. And so I made my choice.
>
> And I can tell you this: I would rather have remained in my terrible pain until the Day of Judgment than to try to come into heaven by any other means than the Way of Jesus. The light of faith had shown me He had bound this bundle of suffering to me. And faith showed me He would unbind me when suffering had done the work of His will in perfecting me.

Let the dedication of your life be set on pleasing Jesus above all else.

Dear heavenly Father, I rededicate my life to You today—to serve Your purposes, fulfill Your plans, and please You above all else.

(INTO HIS PRESENCE)

The Power Within

SCRIPTURE READING: 1 CORINTHIANS 1:26–31

KEY VERSE: 1 CORINTHIANS 1:27

God has chosen the foolish things of the world to put to shame the wise,
and God has chosen the weak things of the world to put to shame the
things which are mighty.

God has equipped you for every good work. The presence of the Holy
Spirit is His guarantee that no matter what you face, He is committed to
providing the power and strength you need to accomplish the task, get
through the hurt, and end up victorious in Him.

D. L. Moody had only a fifth-grade education, but he became one of
the greatest evangelists of our time. He was never ordained to the ministry, yet God used him to lead thousands to the saving knowledge of Jesus
Christ. The book *More Than Conquerors* tells us: "During the nineteenth
century when mass media consisted of only printing presses and public
oratory, more than 100 million people heard or read the gospel message
of D. L. Moody. The evangelist spoke to at least 1.5 million people in
London during four months in 1875, long before radio and television."
God chooses to work through those who seem unqualified so He can
shame those who rely on their own abilities (1 Cor. 1:27–29).

There is only one way God can be glorified in your life, and that
is through your willingness to lay aside your talents, skills, and personal
desires in order to follow Him in obedience. Sacrifice and submission lead
to a life of tremendous hope, freedom, and eternal joy. D. L. Moody could
do nothing apart from the Savior, and what he did through the power of
the Holy Spirit can never be duplicated.

O Lord, thank You for equipping me for every good work. Your presence is
my guarantee of success. Help me accomplish the task, get through the hurt,
and end up victorious in You.

(ON HOLY GROUND)

This Grace in Which You Stand

SCRIPTURE READING: EPHESIANS 2:1–10
KEY VERSE: EPHESIANS 2:5

Even when we were dead in trespasses, [God] made us alive together with Christ (by grace you have been saved).

There are times when we say words that we wish we could take back. Or perhaps we do something in such a way that we wish we could retrieve our actions and correct them. As these moments mount, we wonder how much longer our favor with God will last. We seek His forgiveness, but we wonder if we are in danger of exhausting God's grace for our lives.

The truth is this: you cannot exhaust the grace of God. He loves you, even when you act unlovable. He does hold us accountable for our words and actions. When our words or actions hurt another, we need to admit what we have done and ask God and the person we have hurt to forgive us.

Humility is a sign that God's grace is flowing unhindered through us. Realize also that grace is a gift—something God gives us and something we should give others. When you are hurt by another's actions or words, remember the grace that God has extended to you. Forgive and allow God to restore your relationship with the other person. God desires to transform our lives by the realization that His grace never ends. We are saved by grace (Eph. 2:5), and we are called to live grace-filled lives.

When was the last time you thanked God for His grace toward you? Take time to do this, and extend grace, love, and acceptance to another today.

Lord, thank You for Your grace extended to me. Help me to extend grace, love, and acceptance to someone today.

(PATHWAYS TO HIS PRESENCE)

Through Troubled Waters

SCRIPTURE READING: PSALM 18:1–6

KEY VERSE: ISAIAH 43:2

When you pass through the waters, I will be with you;
And through the rivers, they shall not overflow you.
When you walk through the fire, you shall not be burned,
Nor shall the flame scorch you.

At six weeks of age, Fanny Crosby lost her eyesight. The tragedy came at the hands of a man claiming to be a physician. Her entire life was spent in physical darkness because of his mistreatment, and yet she lived in the eternal light of God's blessed hope.

She could have become bitter and angry, but she didn't. Instead, biographers have written that in reality her blindness did not slow her down. In her youth she played with other children, participated in sports, and traveled. Good-natured humor was a vital part of her life. Laughter filled her household. Most of us remember her deep affection for Christ through the many songs she wrote.

At one point when questioned about the incident that altered her life, she answered, "Although it may have been a blunder on the physician's part, it was no mistake on God's. I verily believe it was His intention that I should live my days in physical darkness, so as to be better prepared to sing His praises and incite others so to do. I could not have written thousands of hymns."

You may be facing troubled times and wonder if you will ever be happy again. No matter what has happened, God is able to take the trial and turn it into a blessing. Nothing is too formidable for Him. When you pass through troubled waters, He will be with you (Isa. 43:2).

You will be with me, no matter what I face today. Thank You, Lord!

(INTO HIS PRESENCE)

Banishing Boredom

SCRIPTURE READING: PSALM 37:1–7
KEY VERSE: PSALM 37:4

Delight yourself also in the LORD,
and He shall give you the desires of your heart.

A subtle thief of contentment is boredom. Have you ever felt that a day was so dull that you just wanted to go to bed and wait for another one? Everyone goes through emotional periods of feeling listless or lifeless. But a chronic sensation of boredom may be a sign that you are lacking much-needed spiritual freshness.

Carole Mayhall comments on boredom in *When God Whispers*:

Boredom can rob a person of joy. Apathy may not sink my boat, but it can becalm me and cause despair as the wind is taken out of the sails of my life. . . .

Three things will bring rejoicing to our souls: (1) God's very presence, (2) His world around us, and (3) people! God's promise to be present with us always can bring comfort and delight. So can the complexity and variety of His creation: a flower, the misty rain, the billowing clouds. Sometimes we may have to look hard into some of the people we encounter, but as we ask, God will help us delight in them, too. These are the three pools of delight we can bathe in when we're young and strong, old and feeble, or incapacitated or ill.

Anytime. Anyplace. Any condition. I'll probably have to remind myself often when dullness of soul creeps over me, but the truth is that God provides no excuse for boredom!

If you're feeling burned-out and unexcited by life, ask the Lord for His renewal today.

Lord, You have filled my life with Your exciting wonders. Renew my spirit and help me to see them.

(SEEKING HIS FACE)

Freedom and Assurance

SCRIPTURE READING: EPHESIANS 5:1–7
KEY VERSE: 1 JOHN 4:16

We have known and believed the love that God has for us. God is love,
and he who abides in love abides in God, and God in him.

"Halo effect." "Teacher's pet." Regardless of what we call it, it is that phenomenon where a person can seemingly do no wrong. As long as the person stays within the parameters of defined protocol, he receives heaps of praise.

Many people may never have experienced this situation within a classroom or work-related setting, but we can experience the same dynamic in our relationship with God. Instead of fearing that we will get punished for our next words or actions, freedom pervades our spirits. We come to the understanding of what the Bible means when it says, "God is love" (1 John 4:16 NASB). And as we do this, we realize that it is not God's intention to restrict our beings, but rather to free us to do His will and fulfill all the desires He has placed in our hearts.

Paul wrote, "Therefore be imitators of God as dear children. And walk in love, as Christ also has loved us and given Himself for us, an offering and a sacrifice to God for a sweet-smelling aroma" (Eph. 5:1–2). When such freedom is given to us because of God's incredible love, we realize that we can trust Him with assurance.

As we walk according to His prescribed ways, we will experience freedom like we have never known—and we will learn to trust Him with everything.

Thank You for freedom to do Your will, Lord. Thank You that I can trust
You with complete assurance.

(PATHWAYS TO HIS PRESENCE)

The Gift of Forgiveness

SCRIPTURE READING: MATTHEW 18:21–35

KEY VERSE: LUKE 6:37

Judge not, and you shall not be judged. Condemn not, and you shall not be condemned. Forgive, and you will be forgiven.

"That's it. I've had it. No more chances," the girl said in exasperation. For the umpteenth time, her good friend had done something that greatly annoyed her.

After she dealt with the situation, the conflict would not leave her mind. The issue of repeat offenses made her think about the time that Jesus explained to Peter what unlimited forgiveness really means. We can easily become weary of forgiving, but it is essential to our spiritual health.

Jesus calls us to this kind of forgiveness. The girl shares the common feeling that there's a limit to human patience. She is right. There is a limit to your emotional resources when you do not rely on Jesus to do the job of forgiving. Peter thought he was being gracious by suggesting the number seven as the maximum. Then Jesus blew apart his limited thinking (Matt. 18:22).

When Jesus died on the cross to pay for sin, He didn't pay only for a select few. He paid for all of them, in full—no limitations, reservations, or exceptions. As you deal with personal relationships and people who have hurt you (sometimes repeatedly), you can draw on the unlimited account of His forgiveness.

You do not have to be concerned with protecting your rights and feelings because Jesus is in charge of taking care of you. You can never run out of love, the ingredient of forgiveness.

Thank You, Lord, for dying to pay for all sin. Help me draw on the limitless account of Your forgiveness as I deal with others.

(INTO HIS PRESENCE)

Renewing Your Mind

SCRIPTURE READING: ROMANS 12:1–2
KEY VERSE: ROMANS 12:2

Do not be conformed to this world, but be transformed by the renewing of your mind, that you may prove what is that good and acceptable and perfect will of God.

Wouldn't it be wonderful if the moment Jesus became your Savior, He lifted out your old mind and gave you a brand-new one, a kind of heavenly transplant?

You wouldn't struggle with thinking old thoughts. No more sinful images would crowd your prayers. You wouldn't be able to conjure negative words to say, and you would be able to forgive others easily. But God did not choose to do this. Instead, He wants you involved in the process of transformation, step-by-step.

Paul urged us: "Do not be conformed to this world, but be transformed by the renewing of your mind, so that you may prove what the will of God is, that which is good and acceptable and perfect" (Rom. 12:2 NASB).

The gradual change involved in renewal is not the same for everyone, so there is not a set formula for replacing the old with the new. The Lord knows exactly what your trouble spots are, however, and He will make you sensitive to areas of your thought life that need His attention.

What you must do continually is to choose truth over error and deliberately set your mind to the task of meditating on His Word. That way, when old falsehoods try to ruin your thinking, you will be alert to the patterns and ready to replace them with God's unchanging truth.

Father, help me to choose truth over error and set my mind to meditate on Your Word. Make me alert to replace false patterns with Your wisdom.

(SEEKING HIS FACE)

The Light of God's Word

SCRIPTURE READING: HEBREWS 4:12–16
KEY VERSE: HEBREWS 4:12

*The word of God is living and powerful, and sharper than any
two-edged sword, piercing even to the division of soul and spirit, and
of joints and marrow, and is a discerner of the thoughts and intents of
the heart.*

Many Christians' lives are like the proverbial digital clock. They have a
power source from which to draw, but like the unset blinking clock that
flashes 12:00—12:00—12:00, their Christian walk is stuck in neutral.
They feel no real sense of purpose.

Whether you are resetting a digital clock or traversing the difficult
terrain of life, your most essential obligation is to read the instructions.
The only way to know the proper course of action is to see what the
expert designer says about each step in the process.

God gave us one instruction manual: the Holy Bible. There is no way to
navigate life in a way that glorifies God or edifies yourself and others unless
you know what God has to say. If you have cyclically gotten away from His
Word throughout your life only to come back later, ask yourself why you
keep returning. It's because it's much easier with the instruction manual.

There are two reasons that people wander from God's Word. They
may be ignorant of its precious truths and overwhelmed by its magnitude
and complexities (as with many new believers), or they simply lay it aside
and endeavor to make it in life in their own wisdom.

This start-and-stop approach stymies proper growth and, as with the
blinking clock, leaves Christians emitting only an intermittent light.

*Keep my light brightly shining, Lord, as it is illumined by Your truth. I want
to live my life with Your divine instruction manual as my guide.*

(INTO HIS PRESENCE)

Your Great-Commission Role

SCRIPTURE READING: MARK 16:15–20
KEY VERSE: MARK 16:15

He said to them, "Go into all the world and preach the gospel to every creature."

Have you ever considered your role in the Great Commission? Before He ascended to the Father, Jesus commanded His disciples: "Go into all the world and preach the gospel to all creation" (Mark 16:15 NASB).

With such a broad-reaching command, we somehow tend to think its implications are limited. We often read over this passage and think it applies only to certain chosen servants. Surely Jesus means someone else. Jesus knows whom He's picked out to fly overseas.

We've all had similar thoughts. But the Great Commission is not exclusionary. His assignment isn't only for preachers and missionaries. He intends for all of us to fulfill His commandment wherever we are. You can obey Him while standing at your backyard fence. Or at a social gathering. Or at the mall. Or by getting on your knees or opening your wallet.

God knows your particular situation and how you can best fulfill His commission. Perhaps He wants you to pray for a particular missionary family. Perhaps He wants you to witness to a sibling, neighbor, or friend. Ask God to make clear your Great-Commission role, and be willing to break free from your comfort zone if needed. God may not ask for your presence in a faraway land, but He may want you to pray for someone or give financially.

God, please show me my role in the Great Commission. I am willing to break free from my comfort zone to touch the lives of others.

(SEEKING HIS FACE)

Vision Without Boundaries

SCRIPTURE READING: LUKE 24:46–53
KEY VERSES: LUKE 24:52–53

They worshiped Him, and returned to Jerusalem with great joy, and were continually in the temple praising and blessing God.

Four stirring, motivational forces were behind the disciples' desire to proclaim the gospel message: (1) their personal experience with the Lord; (2) the promise of Christ's presence with them; (3) the promise and the coming of the Holy Spirit; and (4) the memory of the way Jesus dealt with those who were hurting. Theirs was a vision without boundaries.

However, their ministry certainly did not begin that way. There was a time on the Sea of Galilee when doubt and confusion ruled their minds. That was until Jesus stood up in the boat and commanded the waves and the winds to be still.

There was a night when all but one deserted our Savior, and that one was frightened and overcome with sorrow. The disciples wanted to believe Christ was the One promised by God, but their vision was shortsighted—much like ours at times.

Jesus knew the Father's plan reached to eternity. It was His destiny to become the Lamb of God who would take away the sins of the world. No boundaries erected by man or Satan could stop the plan of God.

The same God who raised Christ from the grave is alive in every believer. Never place boundaries on the vision God brings: "He who began a good work in you will perfect it until the day of Christ Jesus" (Phil. 1:6 NASB).

What a wonderful, glorious Friend, Master, and Savior we have in Jesus.

Dear heavenly Father, remove every boundary that limits Your work in my life. Expand my spiritual borders. Give me vision without boundaries.

(ON HOLY GROUND)

People God Picks

SCRIPTURE READING: 1 CORINTHIANS 1:26–29
KEY VERSES: 1 CORINTHIANS 1:26–27

For you see your calling, brethren, that not many wise according to the flesh, not many mighty, not many noble, are called. But God has chosen the foolish things of the world to put to shame the wise.

God rarely picks people who are extremely qualified to do His work. Rather, He often chooses those who, from the world's perspective, are weak and less than qualified yet have a deep hunger to know Him.

The reason God takes this route is simple. As long as we claim a certain degree of self-adequacy, our dependence on God is hampered, and we are tempted to think that we have something of value to offer Him. The only things we can offer the Lord are our hearts and humble awareness of His greatness and power.

You may reason that the apostle Paul was an adequate messenger of the gospel. He was, but not on his own. It wasn't until he met Jesus Christ on the Damascus road that he was faced with the severity of his inadequacy. In accepting Christ as Savior and Lord, Paul positioned himself for great potential.

If you are tempted to think, *God is certainly fortunate to have me in this position; look at all I can do for Him,* more than likely you are headed for trouble. It is true that God created us with certain abilities and talents, but never to make us strong or adequate in our own eyes.

God is your strength. And He alone deserves all the glory and honor from every good thing you do. Give Him praise for your life today.

Dear God, You are my strength. You deserve the glory and honor from every good thing I do.

(SEEKING HIS FACE)

Christlike Maturity

SCRIPTURE READING: LUKE 2:41–52
KEY VERSE: EPHESIANS 4:13

Till we all come to the unity of the faith and of the knowledge of the Son of God, to a perfect man, to the measure of the stature of the fullness of Christ.

People's perspectives on Jesus seem to shift with the seasons. During Christmas, Jesus is seen as a tiny infant, nestled in blankets and housed in a barn. At Easter, Jesus is seen as beaten and broken, or as the shimmering victor over death. The perspective that is traditionally excluded, however, is one very important segment of His life: His youth.

Luke 2:41–52, the only biblical account of the adolescent Jesus, reveals something surprising, in that He was increasing in wisdom. This shows that Jesus—who was fully God—was experiencing growth! Prayer, Scripture study, and the use of His gifts were bringing about maturation in the Son of Man. Jesus was sinless and perfect, yet He still experienced maturity. How much greater is the need for that growth in sinful man!

Ephesians 4:13 calls all believers toward Christlike maturity, unified as one body through faith in Jesus. Are you experiencing that growth? Are you utilizing your spiritual gifts in such a way as to strengthen the body of Christ and to increase your personal development? Pray for God's help as He directs you into the fullness of the Christian life.

Lord, let me use my spiritual gifts to strengthen others around me. Draw me into a deeper relationship with You so I can increase in wisdom and knowledge.

(PATHWAYS TO HIS PRESENCE)

Are You a Good Listener?

SCRIPTURE READING: JAMES 1:21–25
KEY VERSE: JAMES 1:22

Be doers of the word, and not hearers only, deceiving yourselves.

Are you a good listener? One young man became so perplexed over his inability to remember, he decided to tape much of what was told to him. He even went so far as to keep a tape recorder in the car to record his thoughts and prayers to God. In our fast-paced world, many of us may find ourselves desiring to follow his example.

However, the mind's ability to remember, process, and code information is amazing. Yet researchers tell us we use very little of the brain's capacity to think, reason, and recall past events. Even if you feel that you are a poor listener, God can change that.

Your brain is like a muscle; the more you use it, the stronger it becomes. Memorizing Scripture increases your ability to think and reason. Doctors agree that when you force the brain to activity, even if it has been injured, it will seek a way to get the task done. Truly we are fearfully and wonderfully made (Ps. 139:14 NASB).

An important part of being a good listener is making sure you have a teachable spirit. If you have a closed mind to God's Word, or if you are passive in your spiritual outlook, chances are you will retain very little of what God is saying.

Ask the Lord to make you sensitive to His voice. Plan your spiritual activity to include times spent in prayer and seeking His will for your life. If your greatest desire is to know Him, He will give you the desires of your heart (Ps. 37:4).

Father, make me a good listener. Give me a teachable spirit that is open to Your Word. Make me sensitive to Your voice. Deliver me from spiritual passivity.

(ON HOLY GROUND)

Mustard-Seed Faith

SCRIPTURE READING: MARK 11:23–26
KEY VERSE: MATTHEW 17:20

Jesus said to them . . . "If you have faith as a mustard seed, you will say to this mountain, 'Move from here to there,' and it will move; and nothing will be impossible for you."

Mary Damron refuses to stare at her mountain, not even the impoverished one she calls home. Mary is from the poor coal-mining hollows of West Virginia, but she is rich beyond measure.

In his book *Living Beyond the Limits*, Franklin Graham devotes a chapter to Mary, who is a walking testimony of the life-changing power of faith in Christ. In 1994, Mary learned that Graham needed gift-filled shoe boxes to distribute to the war-scarred children of Bosnia. Instead of focusing on her struggling Appalachian family, Mary traversed her community, asking for donations from churches and groups.

The day after Thanksgiving, she delivered to Graham twelve hundred shoe boxes in a twenty-ton truck. A year later, Mary delivered more than six thousand shoe boxes in time for Christmas. Her devotion and uncanny faith resulted not only in Graham's sending her to Bosnia to help deliver gifts, but also in President Bill Clinton's honoring her at the White House. Mary boldly asked the president for permission to pray for him, and she did.

The story of Mary Damron can be duplicated by anybody. She started small, with a mustard seed of faith and a mountain-sized heart for Jesus. And just as He will do for you whenever you are within His will, He made sure nothing stopped Mary's twenty-ton truck full of shoe boxes.

Lord, give me mustard-seed faith to move mountains. Use me for Your glory!

(INTO HIS PRESENCE)

Overcoming Obstacles to Victory

SCRIPTURE READING: JOSHUA 6:1–20
KEY VERSE: JOSHUA 6:5

It shall come to pass, when they make a long blast with the ram's horn, and when you hear the sound of the trumpet, that all the people shall shout with a great shout; then the wall of the city will fall down flat. And the people shall go up every man straight before him.

It was huge, and it stood in their way. As Joshua looked at the wall of Jericho, he realized that taking the city was no small task, especially with the seemingly impenetrable fortifications that stood before him.

However, God promised Joshua that Israel would triumph, and Joshua believed Him. Joshua 6:5 records God's command: "It shall come to pass, when they make a long blast with the ram's horn, and when you hear the sound of the trumpet, that all the people shall shout with a great shout; then the wall of the city will fall down flat. And the people shall go up every man straight before him."

For generations to come, the children of Israel would ask about the onslaught at Jericho, to which their parents would respond that it was by shouts and trumpet blasts that the walls were destroyed, because the power of God was with them. No battering-ram technology, no modern warfare strategy was necessary—only obedience. The lesson for you remains that God has a way for you to overcome every obstacle by His power. It may not be what you expect, but it is exactly what is needed.

As Theodore Parker prayed, "Give me, Lord, eyes to behold the truth; a seeing sense that knows the eternal right; a heart with pity filled, and gentlest truth; a manly faith that makes all darkness light."

Lord, You are the Creator, the Innovator in the face of the impossible. I give You all my obstacles, for I know that You alone can overcome them.

(PATHWAYS TO HIS PRESENCE)

Made for Praise

SCRIPTURE READING: PSALM 19
KEY VERSES: PSALM 19:1–4

The heavens declare the glory of God; and the firmament shows His handiwork. Day unto day utters speech, and night unto night reveals knowledge. There is no speech nor language where their voice is not heard. Their line has gone out through all the earth, and their words to the end of the world. In them He has set a tabernacle for the sun.

Our Maker designed all creation to be to the praise of His glory. The tiniest pebble and the tallest mountain bear testimony to God's power and love. Warbling birds, chirping crickets, and croaking frogs all lend their special voices to the chorus.

Those who appreciate nature and the wonders of the environment from a godless perspective cannot fathom their real message. God intended the majesty of creation, even though its manifestations are now flawed by sin, to point us to Him (Rom. 1:20).

Have you ever been outdoors on a clear night in an open space, where there are no artificial lights to get in the way? You cannot count the thousands of stars in the sky. In that moment outside, your feelings of awe may well up so strongly inside, you are unable to speak.

Psalm 8:1 is a wonderful prayer: "O LORD, our Lord, how majestic is Your name in all the earth, who have displayed Your splendor above the heavens!" (NASB).

God, I praise You, the Maker of heaven and earth. Thank You for the majesty of creation, which points us to You.

(ON HOLY GROUND)

The New You

SCRIPTURE READING: 1 CORINTHIANS 15:21–22, 45
KEY VERSES: ROMANS 7:24–25

O wretched man that I am! Who will deliver me from this body of death? I thank God—through Jesus Christ our Lord! So then, with the mind I myself serve the law of God, but with the flesh the law of sin.

Trying to live a victorious Christian life while fighting yourself is a losing proposition. But experiencing Christ's triumph on a consistent basis against the power of sin makes the abundant life feasible.

The Bible speaks of it this way. Before you were saved, you were "in Adam." That means you were totally apart from Christ, separated from His life, dead to His presence. You were an enemy of the cross.

Once saved by a supernatural act of God, you were placed "in Christ." That means you are now entirely pleasing to the heavenly Father. You are totally accepted in the Beloved because your old sin nature (what you were before Christ) has been crucified with Christ.

Even more, the triumph of Christ over sin is now available to each of His children. Since you are in Him, all of His divine resources—His Word, His Spirit, His power—are yours to conquer the power of sin that indwells you but is no longer your master or your identity.

For the Christian, it is Christ and you against the power of sin, not Christ and you against you and sin. Your victory over dominating habits, treacherous passions, and emotional strongholds is entirely possible, for Christ is in you and for you.

Christ is in me and for me! I have authority over all the power of sin. Thank You for this freedom, dear Lord.

(INTO HIS PRESENCE)

People in Process

SCRIPTURE READING: MATTHEW 13:3–9, 18–23
KEY VERSE: MATTHEW 13:23

He who received seed on the good ground is he who hears the word and understands it, who indeed bears fruit and produces: some a hundredfold, some sixty, some thirty.

The seed and the soil are inseparably linked in nature's cycle of growth. A good seed must lodge in good soil if there is to be a harvest.

Jesus' parable of the soil and seed is familiar to most of us. His message is clear; it is the condition of the soil, not the content of the seed or the actions of the sower, which governs a person's response to the gospel of Christ.

This should bring a sigh of relief to many fervent evangelicals who wonder why people don't instantly and enthusiastically embrace Christ as Savior when the gospel is presented. There is no need to burden yourself with thoughts such as, *If only I had remembered that fourth point.* Nor should you run out and enlist in yet another study course in evangelism.

The seed, God's Word, is always good. It is the soil—the person's heart, personality, will, and emotions—that must be prepared to receive Christ.

God works by His Spirit through people and circumstances to attract men and women to faith in Christ. Evangelism is a process, and sharing your faith is part of the equation. But don't despair when the feedback is negative. When the conditions are right, faith will blossom.

Precious Lord, work by Your Spirit to attract those around me to Christ. When the timing is right, help me share the gospel in such a way that faith will blossom.

(ON HOLY GROUND)

A Taste of Heaven

SCRIPTURE READING: REVELATION 21:1–8
KEY VERSE: REVELATION 7:11

All the angels stood around the throne and the elders and the four living creatures, and fell on their faces before the throne and worshiped God.

Some dear saints long for a glimpse of heaven. The apostle John had this very experience. Momentarily, God allowed John to taste the goodness of His heavenly presence while remaining on earth. What an honor for a faithful servant of the Lord Jesus Christ.

Heaven is a place of worship and praise. The overwhelming scene that opened before John's eyes was one of true glory. John wrote: "When I saw [Jesus], I fell at His feet as dead. But He laid His right hand on me, saying to me, 'Do not be afraid; I am the First and the Last. I am He who lives, and was dead, and behold, I am alive forevermore. Amen. And I have the keys of Hades and of Death'" (Rev. 1:17–18).

The emotion that swept through John as he saw the risen Savior and Lord was one of awesome fear and worship. It was not fear as we experience it in everyday life. Instead, it was a reverent fear that recognized the power and strength of almighty God.

When you are called to stand in God's presence, life on earth and all its troubles will seem small and insignificant. There will be only one issue at hand—the need to bow down and worship the Savior.

You can enjoy a taste of heavenly worship here and now. Enter God's presence with a grateful heart as you meditate on the goodness of His affections toward you.

Thank You for Your goodness to me, Lord. As I enter into Your presence to worship today, give me a taste of what awaits me in heaven.

(INTO HIS PRESENCE)

The Lifeline to Freedom

SCRIPTURE READING: JAMES 1:12–17
KEY VERSE: JAMES 1:12

Blessed is the man who endures temptation; for when he has been approved, he will receive the crown of life which the Lord has promised to those who love Him.

Satan cannot have your soul, so he wants nothing more than to ruin your fellowship with the Lord and to sidetrack your walk and your witness.

James, Jesus' half brother, described the destructive progression Satan sets in motion through temptation: "But each one is tempted when he is carried away and enticed by his own lust. Then when lust has conceived, it gives birth to sin; and when sin is accomplished, it brings forth death" (James 1:14–15 NASB).

We can be carried away and lured to go beyond the limits of our God-given desires and interests. Our own lust can conceive and give birth to sin. But this birth is not one involving life. Rather, it brings forth death.

Jesus, however, is a God of hope. While it sometimes seems as if Satan is throwing everything in his formidable arsenal at us, we can trust in God's Word and believe Him when He tells us that He is faithful. He will never allow us to be tempted beyond what we are able, in His power, to withstand. God will always give us the opportunity to escape. He always honors His Word. And He is always trustworthy.

The key to overcoming temptation is simple obedience. At times, that may seem impossible. But keep in mind that what is impossible with man is possible with God (Matt. 19:26). The Bible says that He will make a way of escape (1 Cor. 10:13). The lifeline to freedom forever will be there. It is simply a matter of whether we are willing to grab hold.

Dear Lord, I thank You that You will not allow me to be tempted beyond what I am able. Thank You that the lifeline to freedom is available to me today as I reject temptation.

(PATHWAYS TO HIS PRESENCE)

The Trustworthiness of God

SCRIPTURE READING: PSALM 89:1–9
KEY VERSE: HEBREWS 13:8

Jesus Christ is the same yesterday, today, and forever.

Sometimes we find ourselves in deeply threatening situations where we can't see how God can possibly carry out His promises of being with us always or sustaining us through difficulties. Yet, as we read in Psalm 89, David, in spite of the many times he felt his life was threatened and feared he had lost everything, said with conviction, "For I have said, 'Lovingkindness will be built up forever; in the heavens You will establish Your faithfulness'" (v. 2 NASB).

So, too, God's loyalty to us is everlasting. His promises are trustworthy. God sees beyond the here and now to what was and what will be.

In this one truth, we find our reason for hope and for unwavering confidence. God's unchanging nature teaches us that even when we feel unlovely, we are beautiful to Him. There is nothing we can do to change His love for us. It is unconditional, and it flows freely from His throne of grace.

Do you trust Him? Have you experienced a strong assurance that comes from placing your faith in His unfailing ability? Roll the burden of your heart onto Him.

Lord, my confidence is in You. My peace comes from the assurance that You know what is best, do what is best, and provide Your best.

(PATHWAYS TO HIS PRESENCE)

Be Like a Bird

SCRIPTURE READING: MATTHEW 6:25–34
KEY VERSE: MATTHEW 6:34

Do not worry about tomorrow, for tomorrow will worry about its own things. Sufficient for the day is its own trouble.

You're sitting by a tree in the middle of a meadow, taking in the pleasant country sights and sounds. Suddenly you see a bird rush past you, feathers all in a fluff. He has a daily schedule under one wing and a cell phone in the other. He's looking all over the ground frantically, with his beak poking wildly at the dirt. You hear him mutter, "The bug crop better be good next February, or I'll lose my nest egg for sure!"

Can you imagine such a ridiculous scene? Of course not! Birds aren't people, and they're not capable of worry or anxiety. That's why Jesus used them as an example of how you are to trust Him for your needs: "Look at the birds of the air, that they do not sow, nor reap nor gather into barns; and yet your heavenly Father feeds them. Are you not worth much more than they?" (Matt. 6:26 NASB).

God knows worry is a waste of precious time. You can't change your circumstances anyway. Worry is a useless activity that robs you of the peace of trusting in His provision. Jesus said, "Seek first His kingdom and His righteousness, and all these things will be added to you. So do not worry about tomorrow; for tomorrow will care for itself" (Matt. 6:33–34 NASB).

When you recognize God's control over your life, you are able to let go of the need to manage things yourself. Be like one of His little birds and place yourself entirely in His care.

Lord, help me let go of the need to manage things myself. I want to be like one of Your little birds. I am placing myself entirely in Your care.

(SEEKING HIS FACE)

Something Worth Thinking About

SCRIPTURE READING: EPHESIANS 2:1–7
KEY VERSE: MATTHEW 26:41

Watch and pray, lest you enter into temptation. The spirit indeed is willing, but the flesh is weak.

Controlling your thoughts can be difficult, especially if you open the door to thoughts that are not in keeping with the thoughts of Christ. Many people say, "Well, that's not my problem. I don't think about sinful material or things that would compromise my relationship with God." But they overlook their negative thoughts and feelings toward themselves and others.

Hidden within the vast resources of our minds is a tremendous ability to store and retrieve data. The brain is so complex that scientists still do not know all its capabilities. However, one thing is clear: we view ourselves in light of what we believe to be true. If we construct a negative belief system concerning who we are, then we will act negatively. Thus, the old adage, "Winners never lose and losers never win," is true. Not because winners win and losers lose, but because of how each group views itself.

For the next week, refuse to react to any negative thought about yourself or others. If your inner self says you are ugly, look in the mirror and tell yourself, "I am a child of God, and He loves me just the way I am"—end of discussion!

God will never belittle or embarrass you. He leads you to His altar of forgiveness so that you can experience His glorious love and care on a personal basis. It is there that He gives you a totally new beginning. Now, that's worth thinking about!

Father God, I praise You that I am Your child and You love me just the way I am. I am a winner!

(ON HOLY GROUND)

The Pattern of Life

SCRIPTURE READING: EPHESIANS 4:1–15
KEY VERSES: EPHESIANS 4:14–15

*That [you] . . . speaking the truth in love, may grow up in all things
into Him who is the head—Christ.*

The pattern Jesus gave us to live by is one of love. Paul wrote, "I . . .
implore you to walk in a manner worthy of the calling with which you
have been called, with all humility and gentleness, with patience, showing
tolerance for one another in love" (Eph. 4:1–2 NASB).

As a believer, live each day in such a way that your life honors the
Lord, who saved you through His mercy and grace. This means to live in
a "manner worthy" of your calling. How did Jesus call you? Did He come
to you with a list of demands, requiring you to fulfill each one before He
would consider caring for you? No. He came to you in love.

Redemptive love brought Him to earth so that you might receive
eternal salvation. Love was all the motivation He needed to be crucified
at Calvary.

His love watches over you, protects you, plans your future, and encourages you not to give up in times of sorrow and discouragement. You will
spend eternity in the radiant goodness and greatness of His blessings, all
because He chooses to love you.

Love that is from God is humble and gentle. It loves with the surety
of Christ. Someone today is hurting because he thinks God could not
possibly love him. You know the truth about His love; will you tell him?

*Thank You, Lord, that I know the truth about Your love. Help me to share
it with others.*

(SEEKING HIS FACE)

Eternal Friendship

SCRIPTURE READING: LUKE 10:1–9

KEY VERSE: PROVERBS 18:24

A man who has friends must himself be friendly,
But there is a friend who sticks closer than a brother.

Jesus did not send His disciples out alone. He sent them two by two. This is a strong indication that God intends for us to need the help and companionship of others. Ecclesiastes 4:9–10 tells us,

Two are better than one,
Because they have a good return for their labor.
For if they fall, one will lift up his companion.

Friendship softens us and makes us easier to live with. God uses the presence of friends to remind us of Himself. Often the avenue of blessing begins with a friend. But beyond our earthbound friendships is the love of Christ, who is our dearest Friend. Through His Spirit, we receive the gift of His friendship.

The Holy Spirit instructs us in the ways of God, provides discernment, shouts a warning when we get off course, and provides a deep, residing sense of peace to all who have learned to rest in Christ. But the Spirit's greatest goal is to lead us into an intimate relationship with the Lord Jesus Christ.

Nothing comes close to the friendship you can have with God through the Holy Spirit. In the Greek language, He is our Comforter— the One who has been instructed to come alongside us whenever we are hurting, lonely, or fearful.

Jesus told His disciples, "I will never leave you." He meant it. The Holy Spirit is Christ living in you, your eternal source of friendship.

Lord, thank You for Your eternal friendship. I will never be alone. You are always with me.

(INTO HIS PRESENCE)

God's Plan for Your Life

SCRIPTURE READING: ROMANS 1:14–16
KEY VERSE: ROMANS 1:16

I am not ashamed of the gospel of Christ, for it is the power of God to salvation for everyone who believes, for the Jew first and also for the Greek.

In his book on world missions, *In the Gap*, David Bryant shares a letter from a young student whose spiritual eyes had been opened to the importance of a missionary spirit:

> What really hit home to me the most was the fact that God wants us to live beyond the getting of things in life. Even as a Christian, I could see myself becoming an average college graduate, concerned only about getting through, getting out, and getting a job. I was feeling boxed in by my career in special education because preparing for it was taking too much of my time and energy.
>
> But as God spoke to me about being part of the great adventure of life by being a World Christian I started to see my career through God's eyes. I can see now that a career in special education is significant only as it relates to God's total plan for life as a World Christian.

Perhaps you, too, have felt "boxed in" by career or family. These are not liabilities at all, since work and family are integral parts of God's plan. Be sensitive to how God may want to use you to reach out to your coworkers and neighbors. Seek out information from your local church about the need for prayer and financial support for missions.

God's plan for your life is bigger than you can ever imagine.

Dear heavenly Father, give me a missionary spirit. Make me a World Christian. Open my spiritual eyes to new opportunities to become involved in Your divine plan.

(ON HOLY GROUND)

No Condemnation

SCRIPTURE READING: ROMANS 8:1–11
KEY VERSES: ROMANS 8:1

There is therefore now no condemnation to those who are in Christ Jesus.

Heaping condemnation upon our own heads rarely solves our problems. Perhaps our insensitivity toward someone was wrong. Or maybe we made a mistake, offending someone in the process. Guilty feelings—real or contrived—have a way of taking the life out of us.

They divide our minds, drain our energy, cause us to punish ourselves, and stir up feelings of insecurity. Following our rebirth in Christ, the guilt of our past sins is taken away. But guilty feelings—conviction from the Holy Spirit—return when we sin against God. However, we must learn to be a repentant people, understanding how to accept the forgiveness of God in our lives.

No matter how mired we are in our sin, God will cleanse us when we ask. There might be consequences associated with our actions, but the sin is not held against us. God has forgiven us, and we must accept it, refusing to condemn ourselves any longer.

Like the woman caught in the act of adultery, we must learn to accept God's forgiveness. Regardless of how dirty and guilty she felt, Jesus wiped away her sin. He simply told her to go and sin no more (John 8:10–11).

I stand before You free from condemnation. Thank You, Lord, for wiping clean my sins. I will not look back.

(PATHWAYS TO HIS PRESENCE)

The Deepest Form of Intimacy

SCRIPTURE READING: LUKE 11:1–4
KEY VERSES: MATTHEW 6:14–15

If you forgive men their trespasses, your heavenly Father will also forgive you. But if you do not forgive men their trespasses, neither will your Father forgive your trespasses.

In Luke 11, Jesus provided a rich pattern for prayer. Yet we know He never prayed this prayer because He was sinless and, therefore, did not have to ask forgiveness. However, He used these words to teach us how to pray.

Jesus was specific about the need for forgiveness. Even though God has provided a way through His Son for your eternal forgiveness, there is still a need for you to acknowledge your sinfulness whenever you yield to temptation.

Forgiveness is crucial to your spiritual growth. Remember the words of Jesus on the cross, "Father, forgive them, for they do not know what they do" (Luke 23:34).

Prayer that comes from the heart involves responsibility: "Father, I love You, and I choose to do Your will even when it seems difficult and unbearable." It always honors God for who He is. Jesus taught us to pray: "Hallowed be Your name." He went on to show us how to present our requests to the Father by praying, "Give us day by day our daily bread" (Luke 11:2–3).

Recognize that God is your sovereign Provider. He loves you unconditionally and wants you to experience His goodness, no matter what comes your way. His daily bread for you is His Word, and He gives it as a source of encouragement and hope.

Prayer changes you and leads you into the deepest form of intimacy, time spent with your loving heavenly Father.

Father, give me a heart to do Your will even when it seems difficult and unbearable. Change me as I wait before You today.

(INTO HIS PRESENCE)

At the Feet of Jesus

SCRIPTURE READING: LUKE 10:38–42
KEY VERSE: LUKE 10:42

One thing is needed, and Mary has chosen that good part, which will not be taken away from her.

Can you imagine what it was like to sit at the feet of Jesus? Mary of Bethany knew. So did Peter and James and John. They all knew what it was like to be in the presence of Eternal Love. Yet even though Jesus was with them, they still did not have the fullness of God that we enjoy today through the presence of the Holy Spirit.

You may be thinking, *That was fine for Mary and the others, but I am so easily drawn away by temptation. I love God, but there are so many other things that grab my attention. What does He think of me, and how can I be sure He will accept me when I come to Him?*

God will never turn you away. Those who followed the Savior knew this because they witnessed His love and acceptance each day. Mary was at the Savior's feet because she chose to be there. God's love drew her, but she decided to go to Him. The same was true for John and Peter and the others.

There always will be temptations vying for our hearts, but we must decide who or what we love the most. When it comes to God and the things of this world, there is only one choice.

Those who find themselves at the Savior's feet choose humble devotion over worldly prestige, power, and fame. Love is never complex when it comes to God. He loves us without hesitation, and this is what He longs for from us in return.

Thank You for Your love and acceptance, Father. I am grateful that You never turn me away.

(INTO HIS PRESENCE)

Giving Love

SCRIPTURE READING: 1 THESSALONIANS 3:11–13
KEY VERSE: 1 THESSALONIANS 3:12

May the Lord make you increase and abound in love to one another and to all, just as we do to you.

How freely do you love others? Do you give love without needing or expecting love in return? While each of us desires love, it is far more rewarding to give rather than receive.

In a note to a friend, Amy Carmichael wrote:

A few minutes ago I read words that sum up my desires for you: 1 Thessalonians 3:12 [KJV], "The Lord make you to increase and abound in love one toward another." This poor world is a cold place to many. I pray that no one who comes to us may ever feel chilled here, but rather that all chilliness may melt, melted by the blessed glow of heavenly love. Don't let us ever be afraid of being too loving. We can never love enough.

So I pray, "Lord, keep us free to love. Never let the slightest shade of suspicion to shadow any heart. Help each to think the best of every other. Through all the chances and changes of life, hold all together in tender love. Let nothing quench love. Let nothing cool it. Keep every thread of the gold cord unbroken, unweakened, even unto the end. O my Lord, Thou Loving One, keep my beloveds close together in Thy love forever."

How you love others reflects the love you have for Jesus. Be patient in love, willing to receive little or no thanks for something you have done in love for another, and quick to forgive. Remember, no act of love, including forgiveness, is ever wasted.

Lord, help me remember that no act of love is wasted. Help me increase and abound in love.

(PATHWAYS TO HIS PRESENCE)

Unconditional Love

SCRIPTURE READING: 1 JOHN 4:13–21
KEY VERSE: ROMANS 5:8

God demonstrates His own love toward us, in that while we were still sinners, Christ died for us.

God is not afraid to love us just the way we are, with all our flaws and shortcomings. He is secure in who He is. Therefore, He loves us unconditionally and without regard to our failures.

He created us not to live apart from His love but to be partakers of His holiness. However, He knows that there will be times when we look and act unholy. Our misguided actions do not erase or stop the love of God. Sin can separate us from His blessings and intimate fellowship, but there is never a time when God withholds His love.

In loving us, God knows that we can never give back to Him what He has given to us, but He does require us to love one another with the same love that He has demonstrated toward us.

In his book *Mighty Is Your Hand*, David Hazard paraphrases the words of Andrew Murray,

> In our life with people, the one thing on which everything depends is love. The spirit of forgiveness is the spirit of love. Because God is love, He forgives. Consequently, it is only as we are dwelling in the love of God that we can forgive as God forgives.
>
> Our love for others is the evidence of our love for God. It is our grounds for confidence before God in prayer. It is our assurance that our prayer will be heard (1 John 4:20).

Let your love for God be a symbol of love and forgiveness to all you meet.

Lord, let Your presence shine through my life as a symbol of Your unconditional love and forgiveness.

(INTO HIS PRESENCE)

The Source of Lasting Love

SCRIPTURE READING: LUKE 15:11–24
KEY VERSE: PSALM 5:11

Let all those rejoice who put their trust in You;
Let them ever shout for joy, because You defend them;
Let those also who love Your name
Be joyful in You.

When was the last time you heard the words *I love you?* Many have the opportunity to hear them every day. Countless others go weeks, even months, never hearing these words.

In *The Friendship Factor*, Alan Loy McGinnis reports,

> In 1925 a tiny sanitarium for mental patients was established on a farm outside Topeka, Kansas. At a time when the "rest cure" was in vogue in psychiatry, a team of physicians were determined to create a family atmosphere among their patients.
>
> The nurses were given specific directions on how they were to behave toward specific patients: "Let him know that you value and like him." "Be kind but firm with this woman—don't let her become worse . . ."
>
> Menninger Clinic, using such "revolutionary" methods, has become world famous. Karl Menninger, summing up, said: "Love is the medicine for the sickness of mankind. We can live if we have love."

God told us from the very beginning that in love—His love—we find the answer to all our needs as well as healing for our broken souls.

When your heart is anchored to the heart of Jesus Christ, you will find Him near and always eager to confirm His personal love for you. The love of the world will pass away, but God's love is guaranteed never to fade. He is the Source of all true, lasting love.

Dear God, I thank You that in Your love I find the answer to all my needs and healing for my broken soul.

(INTO HIS PRESENCE)

Nehemiah's Pattern

SCRIPTURE READING: NEHEMIAH 1:1–11

KEY VERSE: NEHEMIAH 1:11

O Lord, I pray, please let Your ear be attentive to the prayer of Your servant, and to the prayer of Your servants who desire to fear Your name; and let Your servant prosper this day, I pray, and grant him mercy in the sight of this man.

Nehemiah received word about the city of Jerusalem and how it had been ravaged by war. Jerusalem's walls lay in ruins. In Old Testament times, the walls surrounding a city were extremely important. They were a formidable means of protection from enemy attack. Any hope Jerusalem had for future survival depended on getting its walls put back in place. The thought of Jerusalem being open with no way of defense caused Nehemiah to cry out to God.

From the moment Nehemiah heard of Jerusalem's fate, he set his heart on seeking God for a solution. He was ready, if necessary, to return to the city and work on the walls.

Most of us know Nehemiah's story. God granted him favor in the king's presence. He returned to Jerusalem to lead in the rebuilding of the city's walls. The crucial point in this story is found in the prayers of Nehemiah. He held nothing back before God. He was honest about his love and desire for the city. There was a brokenness within his heart that God could not resist.

Do you want God to use you? Follow the pattern of Nehemiah. Humble yourself and confess your need to Him. Then be willing to go when He opens the door. God blesses those who are willing to be used by Him.

Lord, I love You. I am willing to go where You open the door as long as You go with me.

(SEEKING HIS FACE)

The Cure for a Heavy Heart

SCRIPTURE READING: 1 PETER 2:1–10
KEY VERSE: 1 PETER 2:9

You are a chosen generation, a royal priesthood, a holy nation, His own special people, that you may proclaim the praises of Him who called you out of darkness into His marvelous light.

Praise seems to be a natural part of what we want to do when things are going our way. But on the days when the dishwasher breaks or the children are sick or the mechanic gives you bad news about the car, it is much more difficult to be effusive with thanksgiving.

God understands how your emotions are built; He made them. He also knows the cure for a heart weighed down by concerns and irritations—praise.

Praise focuses your attention upon God. When you take a long and deliberate look at the character and ways of the Lord who loved you enough to die for you, your eyes are naturally shifted away from the difficulty and onto His ability to care for you.

Praise increases your faith. Telling God what you love about Him always involves reciting His past actions of might and power on your behalf. You can look back at the times He sent special provision at just the right moment and thank Him for them. This process results in a heart that expands with joy and security in Him.

Praise gives you a sense of identity. When you praise God, you act as one who belongs to Him. According to 1 Peter 2:9, you are a member of "A PEOPLE FOR *God's* OWN POSSESSION, so that you may proclaim the excellencies of Him who has called you out of darkness into His marvelous light" (NASB). That is reason enough to praise Him forever.

Lord, on difficult days—when I don't feel like it—I still want to praise You. Thank You for delivering me from darkness into light. That is reason enough to praise You forever.

(ON HOLY GROUND)

Inconsistency

SCRIPTURE READING: PSALM 119:1–12
KEY VERSE: PSALM 119:10

With my whole heart I have sought You; oh, let me not wander from Your commandments!

An artesian well sits in a pasture along a picturesque rural road. Flowing from a small pipe, the water has provided cool refreshment for man and beast for decades. Its stream, issuing from deep within the earth, has never diminished or varied—even in times of severe drought.

Most believers long for such consistency since we are so often governed by our circumstances or emotions. A good day at home or work is spiritually fortifying. A flat tire or flat speech can be debilitating, leaving us spiritually deflated. That type of elevator Christianity takes its toll spiritually and leaves nonbelievers wondering about the reliability of our faith.

Like the artesian well, the source is the key. When the love and spirit of Christ control us through the indwelling Holy Spirit, we can live consistently. Christ is our life, flowing through our wills, emotions, and personalities with His purity and power, enabling, steadying us in turmoil and disappointment.

Christ never changes; He is always the same. We experience His unchanging life when we steadfastly count on His refreshing presence in every circumstance. Tough times come, but they can never separate us from the constant, steadfast love of God. He is our Source.

Father, I am often governed by circumstances and emotions. Free me from elevator Christianity. Make me consistent. Steady me in the face of turmoil and disappointment.

(ON HOLY GROUND)

Treasure in Heaven

SCRIPTURE READING: COLOSSIANS 1:12–17
KEY VERSES: 1 PETER 1:3–4

Blessed be the God and Father of our Lord Jesus Christ, who according to His abundant mercy has begotten us again to a living hope through the resurrection of Jesus Christ from the dead, to an inheritance incorruptible and undefiled and that does not fade away, reserved in heaven for you.

In his book *The Weight of Glory*, C. S. Lewis noted how believers often underestimate the full riches that God has for His children:

If we consider . . . the staggering nature of the rewards promised in the Gospels, it would seem that our Lord finds our desires, not too strong, but too weak. We are half-hearted creatures . . . like an ignorant child who wants to go on making mud pies in a slum because he cannot imagine what is meant by the offer of a holiday at the sea. We are far too easily pleased.

When you understand the vast riches God has promised you as His child, you are motivated to take hold of all He has available. When you trusted Jesus as your Savior and Lord, you received a priceless inheritance, prepared especially for you, that will never fade or lose its value (1 Peter 1:3–4).

In His tremendous love, Jesus has equipped and fitted you to enjoy many of these treasures right now. Salvation, an abundance of grace, and the gift of righteousness are special blessings for you today.

God also gives you the privilege of laying up treasure in heaven. The more you are faithful with the talents, skills, and opportunities He affords you today, the more rewards He bestows in heaven to enjoy with Him forever.

Father, help me to use my talents, skills, and opportunities to the greatest extent possible. Show me how to lay up treasure in heaven.

(INTO HIS PRESENCE)

Training to Win

The LORD God is a sun and shield;
The LORD will give grace and glory;
No good thing will He withhold
From those who walk uprightly.

Many people make a tremendous mistake by assuming that trial and difficulty are results of something they have done wrong. They have forgotten Paul's analogy of the athlete who must prepare himself mentally and physically to compete and win the prize. Even in Paul's day, an athletic competition was a big event. The only way an athlete became stronger was through training, and that meant having his strength tested.

Training to win is not a light and easy task. It requires hard work, discipline, and the ability to withstand all kinds of pressure. Paul asked, "Do you not know that those who run in a race all run, but only one receives the prize? Run in such a way that you may win. Everyone who competes in the games exercises self-control in all things. They then do it to receive a perishable wreath, but we an imperishable. Therefore I run in such a way, as not without aim" (1 Cor. 9:24–26 NASB).

Trials are God's tools to test your faith in His ability. When you fail to learn a certain spiritual principle, don't be surprised if He allows another trial to arise. He is teaching you how to trust in His strength and not your own. Learning how to handle the valley times of life readies you for the many blessings God has prepared for you.

Lord, thank You that every trial I experience leads to a blessing. Use the
valleys of my life to prepare me for the blessings You have planned for me.

(SEEKING HIS FACE)

The Message of Freedom

SCRIPTURE READING: PSALM 107:1–9
KEY VERSE: PSALM 119:25

My soul clings to the dust; revive me according to Your word.

We receive all kinds of messages in life. Messages tell us how to live, where to vacation, what to eat, how to cook it, and then how to exercise it all away.

God's first concern is always toward the spiritual part of a person's life, not the physical. Because of the relentless spotlight placed on the need to look and act a certain way, depression, eating disorders, and anxiety top the list of problems people are most likely to struggle with.

However, these are only symptoms of a more serious dilemma. When we seek to become something apart from Jesus Christ, we end up chasing a very elusive shadow. Even if we do achieve a certain status, there is always something else on the horizon demanding more from us. Someone is always ahead of us, causing us to think we need something other than what we have in order to be happy.

The person who finds his identity in Jesus Christ has freedom and peace. If you are struggling with thoughts of inadequacy, ask God to make His love for you very clear. He will never place unhealthy expectations on you. Nor does He say you have to reach a certain status before He can love you.

The moment you accept His Son as your Savior, He comes into your heart with perfect love and acceptance. He created you and is bound in love to you forever.

Heavenly Father, I want to find my true identity in You. Free me from the bondage of my limiting inadequacies.

(ON HOLY GROUND)

Good Things in Life

SCRIPTURE READING: PSALM 63
KEY VERSE: PSALM 63:1

O God, You are my God;
Early will I seek You;
My soul thirsts for You;
My flesh longs for You
In a dry and thirsty land
Where there is no water.

To earnestly seek the Lord, to long in your innermost being to know more about Jesus Christ, you must set your mind to do so. It is not an experiential moment in which you are waiting for a feeling or an emotion to affirm that the Lord has spoken to you.

Rather, it is an intentional, deliberate, daily effort at humbly and sincerely trying to find out more about God. If you're going to seek the Lord, you simply must purpose to do it and trust Him to answer your heart's cry.

The primary ways to learn more about God are to read His Word and communicate with Him in prayer. Perhaps you sometimes feel inundated with admonitions to read the Bible and pray. There is a reason. These vital pursuits must be accomplished in earnest before your understanding of Christ is deepened.

The Holy Bible is a product of the mind and heart of God. It is the principal tool He uses to reveal Himself to us. He communicates to us through His Word and His Holy Spirit, and we communicate to Him through prayer.

Yet you also should consciously determine that in your conversations, Scripture study, church attendance, reading, and service, you will be tenacious in longing to discover His will and His ways. These are all methods in which we learn more about God. These are also the ways in which we are richly rewarded with the truly good things in life.

Lord, just as I set my clocks, tune my instruments, and program my computer,
let me also set my mind to seek after You through study, prayer, and
contemplation.

(PATHWAYS TO HIS PRESENCE)

Communion with God

SCRIPTURE READING: JOHN 1:1–14
KEY VERSE: REVELATION 21:3

I heard a loud voice from heaven saying, "Behold, the tabernacle of God is with men, and He will dwell with them, and they shall be His people. God Himself will be with them and be their God."

God's compelling desire since the creation of the world is to live in communion with man. Think of the grandeur and majesty of a God who yearns to befriend man in such a way that man's entire life is lived out in the presence of the awesome, loving God.

So great is His desire to fellowship with man that He has made every provision possible for that intimacy. When sin severed man's union with God and brought spiritual and physical death, God provided a tabernacle. The tabernacle was a place where man could still relate to Him under a divinely imposed order.

When John wrote that "the Word [Christ] became flesh and dwelt among us" (John 1:14), he was referring to the incarnation of Christ. It represents the most passionate means by which God could restore fellowship with man through Jesus' life, death, and resurrection.

The zenith of God's desire to live and dwell among man is found in Revelation 21:3: "Behold, the tabernacle of God is with men, and He will dwell with them, and they shall be His people. God Himself will be with them and be their God."

Salvation does much more than bring you out of darkness and death; it ushers you into the presence of God to experience divine communion in prayer, praise, and worship.

Thank You, Lord, that You made every provision possible for me to experience intimacy with You. I praise You that You dwell in me, I am Yours, and You are my God.

(INTO HIS PRESENCE)

Actions Speak Louder Than Words

Scripture Reading: Psalm 19
Key Verse: Psalm 19:14

Let the words of my mouth and the meditation of my heart
Be acceptable in Your sight,
O Lord, my strength and my Redeemer.

If you could not speak a word, what would your life say to others? Would anyone know something is different about you, that you are a Christian?

We are constantly communicating something. The way we walk into a room tells a great deal about how we feel about ourselves. The way we listen to others communicates whether we are interested or bored.

Nonverbal communication is powerful. Jesus was and is an excellent nonverbal communicator, not just because He understood the heart of man, but because He took time to listen to the hurts and needs of those around Him. He touched people with His hands as well as His heart. He encouraged them with an eternal message of hope. Actions do speak louder than words.

Communicating God's forgiveness and love was the cornerstone of Christ's ministry on earth, and it is yours as well. The Great Commission has been given to each and every one of us.

You are called to be His messenger, encourager, and proclaimer. Maybe not all at once and maybe not to a foreign country, but certainly when the need arises, you are to share His love and forgiveness to a hurting and dying world. Therefore, pray that God's love will be the first and last thing others see in you.

Lord, may Your love be the first and last thing others see in me.

(Seeking His Face)

Fear

SCRIPTURE READING: PSALM 56:1–11
KEY VERSE: 2 TIMOTHY 1:7

God has not given us a spirit of fear, but of power and of love and of a sound mind.

Paul Tournier, the eminent Swiss doctor, made a profound assessment of the Christian life: "Life is an adventure directed by God."

The seed of life-changing faith is contained in such a view. It can be the difference between a confident, rewarding life or a timid, fretful one. When you are confronted with perplexity, it can be the hinge upon which swings the response of either fear or faith.

Fear comes when you are overwhelmed by the magnitude or implications of a situation. It swells to paralyzing proportions when you think of the possibility of disastrous consequences. It can submerge you in waves of anxiety and insecurity.

But once you understand and embrace the truth that God is indeed in charge of your circumstances and has equipped you for every challenge, it is amazing how faith in Christ can change your outlook. Life isn't risk free. God has set a divine course for every believer that He oversees and directs with perfect wisdom and love.

Your faith is in His faithfulness to you, in His power that works on your behalf, in His grace that provides all your needs. God is in charge. Life is an exciting journey in trusting Him as your Guide and Companion.

Begin the adventure today, and drop your fears at His feet. He won't let you down.

Heavenly Father, here I am with all my fears—giving them to You. You have equipped me for every challenge. I know life isn't risk free, but whatever path I travel, You determine my destiny.

(ON HOLY GROUND)

In His Timing

SCRIPTURE READING: 1 JOHN 5:14–16
KEY VERSE: 1 JOHN 4:16

*We have known and believed the love that God has for us. God is love,
and he who abides in love abides in God, and God in him.*

The mother knew her son was not doing well at college. His grades were
fine, and he had even made the football team. But between studying and
practicing, he had not made time for church or personal Bible study as he
had in high school. How could she help him get back on track spiritually?

The apostle Paul faced the same challenge. In a Roman prison cell,
Paul heard discouraging news from Epaphras, the pastor of the new and
growing church in Colossae. The Colossian believers were falling into
the trap of false teaching and losing their focus on Jesus Christ. Yet Paul
knew that even from prison he could directly minister God's truth to the
struggling Christians, through continuous and specific prayer.

The greatest privilege and blessing you have as God's child is to talk
with Him in prayer. You can praise Him and bring Him your needs,
your hurts, your desires. He promises to hear you in whatever you ask
(1 John 5:14–15).

When you ask Him to work His truth into the lives of those you
love, you will see the results. And be prepared! God may call you to long-
term intercession. The Lord will give you His patience and strength as He
answers in His good timing.

*Dear Father, thank You for Your promise that You will hear me in
whatever I ask. Give me patience and strength to wait for the timing of Your
answers.*

(SEEKING HIS FACE)

Magnificent Grace

SCRIPTURE READING: LUKE 15:11–24
KEY VERSES: ROMANS 6:1–2

What shall we say then? Shall we continue in sin that grace may abound? Certainly not! How shall we who died to sin live any longer in it?

Family-oriented movies often end by showing a reunion of loved ones. We see family members with arms around each other in an expression of love and support. Through the parable of the prodigal son, Jesus gave us this same picture of our heavenly Father's attitude toward us (Luke 15:20–24). There, Jesus revealed the magnificence of grace. We see that the one sinned against runs out to eagerly welcome back the one who sinned. The one who was wronged takes the initiative, because of love, to restore the broken relationship; the one mistreated shows compassion to the one at fault.

And there is even more. The prodigal did not know his full rights as a son would be restored. As believers, however, we know in advance what awaits us when we humbly return. Because of grace, we can count on acceptance no matter how long we have been absent from the Father or how far we have wandered. Grace guarantees that the Lord will greet us with compassion and forgiveness and lovingly restore us to full rights as His children.

It is not our performance—not good deeds or even the correct apology—that matters; it is our position in Christ. When God sees that we belong to His Son, He forgives us. The parable of the prodigal son points us to the truth that, because of Jesus Christ, we are forgiven even before we return. While this does not give us license to sin (Rom. 6:1–2), it does give us reason to celebrate. Our Father waits to welcome us home.

You wait to welcome me home, Father. I am assured of Your magnificent grace. Thank You!

(PATHWAYS TO HIS PRESENCE)

Fervent Intercession

SCRIPTURE READING: COLOSSIANS 1:7–13
KEY VERSE: COLOSSIANS 4:12

Epaphras, who is one of you, a bondservant of Christ, greets you, always laboring fervently for you in prayers, that you may stand perfect and complete in all the will of God.

Epaphras, an associate of Paul, was instrumental in founding the church at Colossae. His report to Paul on the condition of the Colossian church prompted Paul's letter to the fledgling believers. At the conclusion of his epistle, Paul used Epaphras's example to give us a grip on a few of the basics of intercessory prayer.

Epaphras was "one of [their] number" (Col. 4:12a NASB). When we are involved in the lives of others through friendship, service, or other means of contact, intercession is much more natural. We can pray for others because we are aware of their concerns.

Epaphras was a "bondslave of Jesus Christ" (Col. 4:12b NASB). God's agenda needs to be ours. When we seek His will first, intercession for the needs of others will be woven into our lives. When our focus drifts from Christ, it is hard to pray for ourselves, much less another.

Epaphras was "always laboring earnestly for [the Colossians] in his prayers" (Col. 4:12c NASB). Intercession is hard work. Intercession is spiritual warfare. It doesn't come easily because Satan does not want you to pray for others.

The end result of fervent intercession is that others may be "fully assured in all the will of God" (Col. 4:12d NASB). That goal fits every need.

Teach me to pray, Lord; to intercede with fervency for the needs of others.

(SEEKING HIS FACE)

Sharing God's Love

SCRIPTURE READING: 2 TIMOTHY 2
KEY VERSE: 2 TIMOTHY 2:15

Be diligent to present yourself approved to God, a worker who does not need to be ashamed, rightly dividing the word of truth.

"Never choose to be a worker for God," advises Oswald Chambers, "but when once God has put His call on you, woe be to you if you turn to the right hand or to the left. We are not here to work for God because we have chosen to do so, but because God has apprehended us."

What has God apprehended you to do? Perhaps you are a schoolteacher, a construction worker, a builder, or a professional working for a large corporation. No one else can do what He has given you to do.

His call to you is the same call He gave the early church: share the love and forgiveness of Jesus Christ with a lost and dying world. This is the truth you received, and it is the same truth that countless individuals are longing to hear.

Ask Him to make you sensitive to the needs of others. Many times people do not know how to share the hurts hidden deep within their hearts. Only God's love can draw these hurts to the surface where healing can take place.

Jesus met people at the point of their greatest need, and He wants you to do the same. Be willing to go to those who are friendless, lonely, hurting, and in need of compassion and a listening heart. This is His call to each of us: "Share My love, My forgiveness, and My grace so that others will know the love of My Father."

Father, help me to share Your love, Your forgiveness, and Your grace so that others will come to know Your love.

(SEEKING HIS FACE)

The Real Thing

SCRIPTURE READING: JOHN 14:1–17
KEY VERSE: PSALM 25:5

Lead me in Your truth and teach me,
For You are the God of my salvation;
On You I wait all the day.

The most potent hearing aid known to man is the Holy Bible. It is the standard of truth against which you can test every message that comes your way.

Making a decision on an issue important to you can be extremely difficult. Sometimes it may seem as if you are hearing two or more voices, all of which make seemingly good points but also tug you in different directions. In these times you must learn to discern the voice of God.

You can apply several principles to what you're hearing to gauge whether it is of God, but the most basic is whether the message conflicts with Scripture. God won't tell you to do something that counters what He already has recorded for all mankind.

Therefore, the best way to know God's voice is to get to know Him. Spend time in His Word and soak in His truths. You must know God's Word before you can differentiate God's instructions from the messages that Satan or your flesh is sending you.

Do you know how investigators are trained to recognize counterfeit money? They don't spend all of their time trying to keep up with the latest technological advances in creating false money. Instead, they first and foremost diligently study the original, the real thing. Then, held against the standard, the imitation stands out.

I want to know You better, Lord—and in so doing, learn to walk in Your will and Your ways.

(INTO HIS PRESENCE)

Distraction

SCRIPTURE READING: 2 CORINTHIANS 2:14–16
KEY VERSE: PHILIPPIANS 3:8

I also count all things loss for the excellence of the knowledge of Christ Jesus my Lord, for whom I have suffered the loss of all things, and count them as rubbish, that I may gain Christ.

After winning a gold medal in the 1988 Olympics, the muscular wrestler was asked if he had any secrets of preparation. "My only secret is that I didn't let anything hinder my goal of winning," he related. "I refused to be distracted by any other competition."

That same zealous pursuit of our relationship with Christ is the highest goal for the believer. Paul termed it "undistracted devotion to the Lord" (1 Cor. 7:35 NASB).

That is true for every Christian—married or unmarried, rich or poor, small or great. God will not tolerate competition (Matt. 6:24).

The relevant question then is, Is there anything or anyone in your life who is in competition with Christ's claim on your life? Does money, marriage, your job, recreation, or your hobby vie for your allegiance to Christ? Do you seek Him first by daily acknowledging His lordship and obeying His will?

When other objects or people distract us from this primary focus to serve and worship the Lord, our spiritual growth is short-circuited. Having undistracted devotion to Christ means putting Christ first in all of our activities, submitting them to His will and guidance. When we do, we always win (2 Cor. 2:14).

Precious Lord, I am easily distracted from the paths of my spiritual journey. Free me from all that competes with Your claims in my life. I want to put You first in all things.

(ON HOLY GROUND)

A Zeal for God

Scripture Reading: John 17:1–5
Key Verse: John 17:3

This is eternal life, that they may know You, the only true God, and Jesus Christ whom You have sent.

Jesus defined eternal life in John 17:3, our key verse today. Thus, while eternal life is certainly the possession of unending fellowship with Christ, the principal context is the quality of relationship with your Savior.

There is no substitute for a personal hunger to know Christ experientially. The God who sought you and saved you jealously desires to reveal Himself to you. But you must pursue Him.

"Everything is made to center upon the initial act of 'accepting' Christ (a term, incidentally, which is not found in the Bible) and we are not expected thereafter to crave any further revelation of God to our souls," A. W. Tozer wrote in *The Pursuit of God.*

> We have been snared in the coils of a spurious logic which insists that if we found Him we need no more seek Him.
>
> I want deliberately to encourage a mighty longing after God. The lack of it has brought us to our present low estate. The stiff and wooden quality about our religious lives is a result of our lack of holy desire. Complacency is a deadly foe of all spiritual growth. Acute desire must be present or there will be no manifestation of Christ to His people.

If your heart for God has dimmed, seek Him today. As Tozer announced, "He waits to be wanted."

Dear Lord, don't let my zeal for You grow dim. Don't let complacency hamper my spiritual growth. Manifest Yourself to me today in a new and deeper dimension.

(Into His Presence)

Learning to Listen

SCRIPTURE READING: MATTHEW 13:10–17
KEY VERSE: MATTHEW 13:16

Blessed are your eyes for they see, and your ears for they hear.

One of the qualities that drew people to Jesus was His ability to listen. He listened with His entire being. That is why we see Him mingling with crowds of people and healing the ones who are sick. Jesus was the greatest communicator the world has ever known. He wasn't worried about getting equal time in conversations or impressing others. He was interested in building relationships. So He listened.

Jesus could sense the hurts and the frustrations on the faces of the people He met. He gave them freedom to express their deepest needs. Two of man's basic needs are love and acceptance. That's how the Savior listens to us, with eyes of love and acceptance.

How do you listen to Him? Do you long to be near Him, to study His Word, and to hear His heart about certain situations? Or do you rush through prayer, afraid of what He might say and require of you?

Until we learn to truly listen, first to God and then to others, we will never know the deeper side of Christ's love. Only in listening for His voice can we truly experience the intimacy of His presence.

Ask Him to help you become the kind of listener that He is to you. If you will listen, you will hear His voice.

Almighty God, I long to be near You, to study Your Word, to hear Your heart about the situations in my life. Forgive me for rushing through my time with You. Help me learn to listen so that I can experience the intimacy of Your presence.

(ON HOLY GROUND)

His Power Will Triumph

SCRIPTURE READING: JUDGES 7:1–11
KEY VERSE: JUDGES 7:2

The LORD said to Gideon, "The people who are with you are too many for Me to give the Midianites into their hands, lest Israel claim glory for itself against Me, saying, 'My own hand has saved me.'"

Gideon understood fear and hopelessness. Imagine his circumstances: Gideon, with a very small army, was called by God to defeat a large army of Midianites. It seemed as though the odds were against him. But he trusted God and obeyed the Lord's commands.

Then the Lord gave Gideon the news: "The people who are with you are too many for Me to give the Midianites into their hands, lest Israel claim glory for itself against Me, saying, 'My own hand has saved me'" (Judges 7:2). Gideon's small, insignificant army was to be reduced even further. Why? To bring God more glory when the tiny army found victory over the legions of Midianites.

Have you ever encountered such a challenge, where your meager resources are cut even smaller and your only recourse is to trust God? Perhaps you find yourself in that situation right now and feel intimidated by the task.

A. B. Simpson offers a word of encouragement: "When God wants to bring more power into your life, He brings more pressure." The more impossible your circumstance seems, the more glory God will receive when your situation is rectified.

As your circumstances become more impossible and the odds seem against you, do not be discouraged. God faithfully brought the victory to Gideon, and He will give you victory too. Trust Him, and watch His power triumph.

Lord, when the tools I have seem inadequate for the job, help me to recognize that the miraculous is where You dwell.

(PATHWAYS TO HIS PRESENCE)

Healthy Faith

SCRIPTURE READING: PSALM 100:1–5
KEY VERSES: PSALM 100:3–4

Know that the LORD, He is God;
It is He who has made us, and not we ourselves;
We are His people and the sheep of His pasture.
Enter into His gates with thanksgiving,
And into His courts with praise.
Be thankful to Him, and bless His name.

In Psalm 100:3–4, words of praise flowed from David's heart like a river pulsing down a mountain. David truly adored God. We know this because Matthew 12:34 teaches, "The mouth speaks out of that which fills the heart" (NASB). If David's heart were not filled with immense love for God, he would not have been able to express himself so eloquently.

Even when David faced immense pressures, he was able to place his hope in God. It was through small steps of worshiping God in the difficulties that his adoration of the Lord grew to overflowing.

When you speak about the Lord, do you praise Him with all your heart? What flows from your mouth may be an indication as to the health of your faith. Are you able to proclaim gladly that the Lord is God?

Is there a flaw in your faith? Then praise Him. Once you allow the spring of praise to course in your heart, it will continue to grow until it overflows through you. Enter His gates with thanksgiving and His courts with praise, and watch Him bring something truly beautiful from your faith.

Lord, I often forget that the words from my mouth are the first evidence of
You that some people hear. Let my words be a receptacle of praise for You.

(PATHWAYS TO HIS PRESENCE)

Salt of the World

SCRIPTURE READING: MATTHEW 5:13–16
KEY VERSE: MATTHEW 5:13

You are the salt of the earth; but if the salt loses its flavor, how shall it be seasoned? It is then good for nothing but to be thrown out and trampled underfoot by men.

Many people on special diets need to limit or even eliminate their intake of salt. To compensate, they search for other ways to spice up their food, from sauces to herb mixes, because some things just taste too bland without it. Salt is used for flavor and is an excellent preservative; no wonder salt remains an important ingredient even today.

It is no surprise, then, that Jesus compared those who belong to Him with salt: "You are the salt of the earth; but if the salt has become tasteless, how can it be made salty again? It is no longer good for anything, except to be thrown out and trampled under foot by men" (Matt. 5:13 NASB).

You are to be the good, Christlike "flavor" in your world. Just as salt without any taste would be useless in its intended functions, so is a believer who refuses to yield his or her life to Christ. He does not lose his salvation, of course, but he does not keep his ability to flavor his world for the Lord.

Salt is also used as a healing agent. Have you ever exposed an open wound to saltwater, in the ocean, for example? It hurts badly, but it usually feels and looks much better afterward. Very often when a believer demonstrates love to a nonbeliever, that love rubs into the open heart wound of the hurting person, causing initial pain. Over time, though, that exposure may bring healing in Jesus.

Dear heavenly Father, make me like salt in this world—a healing agent to those who are hurting.

(SEEKING HIS FACE)

Applying Truth for Victory

SCRIPTURE READING: PHILIPPIANS 4:10–13

KEY VERSE: PHILIPPIANS 4:13

I can do all things through Christ who strengthens me.

In grasping a clear picture of how we can weather the dangers that come with both victory and defeat, we must not forget to apply what we know. Understanding that God is our strength in weakness is one thing, but applying that truth in an effective way is another.

The apostle Paul said he had learned the secret of contentment in any situation—Christ, the source of strength (Phil. 4:11–13). We must do more than just acknowledge God's awesome power—we need to get it into our lives. We must submit our will to His will. Asking God to give us strength to accomplish our will results in burnout. God never promises us strength for our own plans, only for His. That's why submitting to His will is the first step to seeing His power begin to permeate our lives.

We must also trust Him to control our circumstances for His purposes. Once we realize that God's plans and purposes are greater than we could imagine, we also have to realize that the path He is leading us down will result in His glory.

The result of relying on God's strength is that we cease to struggle against that which we cannot control. And victory is found in trusting in the Lord's strength.

Heavenly Father, I trust Your strength as I face the challenges of life today. I praise You because I will walk in victory!

(PATHWAYS TO HIS PRESENCE)

Friendship with Jesus

SCRIPTURE READING: PSALM 67:1–7
KEY VERSE: ISAIAH 61:1

The Spirit of the Lord GOD is upon Me,
Because the LORD has anointed Me
To preach good tidings to the poor;
He has sent Me to heal the brokenhearted,
To proclaim liberty to the captives,
And the opening of the prison to those who are bound.

What is God like to you? Do you see Him as Someone who listens to your prayers with an open heart? Or do you imagine that He has His mind made up about your circumstance even before you come to Him?

Jesus had a reason for calling us His friends. He wanted to convey truth to us in such a way that we would accept and not reject the closeness of His love. A friend is someone you can call on any time of the day or night.

Friends listen patiently without judging the context of your words. You can vent your frustration without worrying about being judged. Friends weather the storms of life together. When life becomes rough and lonely, they hang tough.

Always give the Lord your adoration and devotion, but also be willing to give Him your love through fellowship. Make Him your very best Friend. It's okay to seek the counsel of other godly friends, but make a habit of going to Him first with your heartaches, troubles, and requests. Let Him speak the words of encouragement you so desperately need.

The God who listens as you pray wants you to know that He loves you completely. When you step into His presence, you enter into an inexhaustible pool of possibilities. It is His holy chamber, but it is also a place of loving friendship.

Take me into the holy chamber with You, Father. Let me rest in Your
presence and have my vision renewed with limitless possibilities.

(INTO HIS PRESENCE)

The Mind-Set of Faith

SCRIPTURE READING: EXODUS 3:1–14
KEY VERSE: EXODUS 3:14

God said to Moses, "I AM WHO I AM." And He said, "Thus you shall say to the children of Israel, 'I AM has sent me to you.'"

We often think faith begins when we step out and trust God for something He has promised, but actually faith begins even before this point. Faith is an attitude, a mind-set that has the power to chart our course through life.

Those who bypass faith in God experience discouragement because they are left to trust in their own abilities. What is human capability in light of God's omniscience?

Moses faced several critical points in his walk of faith. One came very early in his relationship with the Lord. The first time God spoke to Moses, He challenged Moses' ability to trust Him: "Come now, and I will send you to Pharaoh, so that you may bring My people, the sons of Israel, out of Egypt" (Ex. 3:10 NASB).

The situation appeared overwhelming to Moses. How could he possibly go to Pharaoh and tell him to let God's people go? He couldn't! At least, he couldn't in his own strength.

Are you facing a situation in which you know God wants you to trust Him, but the way seems dark and unsure?

Moses felt totally inadequate to do what God wanted him to do. God understood. This is what is so endearing about our Savior; He understands our frailties. All He asks is for you to be willing. Trust His love and care, and be strengthened by His power.

Precious heavenly Father, thank You for understanding my frailties. Even when my pathway seems dark and unsure, I know You will strengthen me. I rest in Your love and care.

(ON HOLY GROUND)

Demonstrating Peace

SCRIPTURE READING: 2 CORINTHIANS 13:5–11
KEY VERSE: 2 CORINTHIANS 13:11

*Finally, brethren, farewell. Become complete. Be of good comfort, be of
one mind, live in peace; and the God of love and peace will be with you.*

Here is a scene that you could witness on almost any playground in the
world. Two boys are playing together in a sandbox or at the base of a slide.
Suddenly, a fight breaks out and the two young children are embroiled
in a heated exchange with fists flying. Their peaceful playtime has come
to a violent end.

Where did these children learn to act like this? Apparently, human
beings are not programmed for peace. Too often, a person's initial response
to displeasure or stress is to strike out violently against the source of his
frustration. The base nature of sinful man is to protect oneself first and
foremost. However, one's disposition toward anarchy is certainly no excuse
for failing to strive toward peaceful living.

The New Testament contains no fewer than eight direct commands
for peace among believers. This clearly reveals that God's will is for men
and women to live in peace with one another. Knowing that God demands
His people to live in peace may seem too much to ask when countered
by mankind's sinful, selfish desires. Yet, if peace is God's will—and it
is—then He must have made it possible to achieve. Sometimes peace may
not be one's natural reaction, but according to God's Word, it is possible.

Pray today for the Holy Spirit to reveal ways in which you can demonstrate the peace of God.

*Dear heavenly Father, reveal ways in which I can demonstrate Your peace
to those with whom I come in contact today.*

(PATHWAYS TO HIS PRESENCE)

The Quilt

SCRIPTURE READING: 1 PETER 4:7–10
KEY VERSE: ROMANS 12:6

Having then gifts differing according to the grace that is given to us, let us use them.

Not only do you possess spiritual gifts, but you also have innate abilities that God transforms for use according to His purposes when you let Him do so. No matter who you are—old, young, rich, poor, or somewhere in between—God wants to use you to bless the lives of others.

In his book *The Quilt*, T. Davis Bunn tells the fictional story of an elderly grandmother named Mary, who invests her life and energies into enriching those around her for the Lord. Now she is very old, with hands twisted by arthritis. Even though she is ready to be with the Lord anytime He calls her, she cannot shake the burning feeling that God wants her to do one more thing.

When she shares with her family and friends that she feels this last big work should be the making of a giant quilt, they are incredulous. How can a woman her age, with useless hands, do such a thing? Then Mary unfolds her real plan. She would oversee the making of the quilt and provide the pattern and materials. Any lady who wanted to help could come to her home and quietly assist, but everyone had to promise one thing: with every stitch she had to say a prayer of thanksgiving.

There was no way to measure the spiritual transformations in the lives of these women. The quilt became a living testimony of God at work.

Dear Lord, use me to bless the lives of others through my spiritual gifts and abilities.

(SEEKING HIS FACE)

The Power of Solitude

SCRIPTURE READING: PSALM 4:1–8
KEY VERSE: PSALM 4:7

You have put gladness in my heart,
More than in the season that their grain and wine increased.

The phrase "quiet time" has become widely used in Christian circles over the past several years. Preachers preach it, teachers teach it, and prayer warriors rely on it. However, when we say "quiet time," what are we really thinking?

Most likely, as you read this very passage, you are in the midst of your own quiet time. Perhaps you have soft Christian music in the background, a Bible on the table, and a soothing cup of coffee at your side. Maybe you have a cat nestled at your feet, and a lovely green yard outside the window. What warm and comfortable images!

All of these things are conducive to a refreshing prayer experience, a lengthy discussion with the Lord, or a moment of individual worship. However, even this peaceful scene is full of distractions.

Right now, you are actively reading; in a moment, you will spend a minute or two in prayer. However, this is not true "quiet time." Your mind is full of thoughts, words, and quiet conversation. Although this time is vital, it is not solitude.

Richard Foster wrote, "Without silence, there is no solitude." A true moment of silence does not involve formulating your next thought or action, but instead is a moment of complete silence. Calm your mind, and even stop praying for a moment. Sit back and listen for a while. You may be surprised by what you hear.

Lord, I am unaccustomed to solitude—the deep silence in which You dwell.
Teach me how to quiet the noise around me to hear Your voice.

(PATHWAYS TO HIS PRESENCE)

Walking Away from God

SCRIPTURE READING: PSALM 73
KEY VERSE: PSALM 73:25

Whom have I in heaven but You? And there is none upon earth that I desire besides You.

His family could have been in upheaval. Maybe he had just witnessed the promotion of a man he knew to be a fraud and a thief. Whatever the causes were, Asaph was discouraged to the point of questioning his faith or, rather, the point of his faith.

If trusting God was such a good thing, why were evil men getting away with murder? Why were the arrogant only getting richer and more powerful by the day, while humble and good people were suffering? These questions could just as easily be asked today. And maybe you have asked them.

What finally turned Asaph's heart around and put fresh wind in his spiritual sails? He realized once more these powerful truths: "Nevertheless, I am continually with You; You hold me by my right hand. You will guide me with Your counsel and afterward receive me to glory. Whom have I in heaven but You? And there is none upon earth that I desire besides You. My flesh and my heart may fail, but God is the strength of my heart and my portion forever" (Ps. 73:23–26).

The glory of the wicked, when viewed from an eternal perspective, was shown to be fleeting, shallow, and temporary. Asaph had to take a journey through doubt and anger and questioning before he could feel secure in God again. Never be afraid to take this journey.

Dear heavenly Father, when I look at others and question why, help me remember to view things from an eternal perspective. Let my journey through doubt and anger be swift so that I can feel secure in You again.

(ON HOLY GROUND)

Lord, Make Me!

SCRIPTURE READING: EPHESIANS 3:14–21
KEY VERSE: EPHESIANS 3:16

[I pray] that He would grant you, according to the riches of His glory, to be strengthened with might through His Spirit in the inner man.

In his book *Walking with Christ in the Details of Life*, Patrick Morley explains the growth of the prayer life:

> We are needy people. When God found us, we were consumed with needs: relational, emotional, financial, moral, psychological, and spiritual needs. . . . It seems quite natural, then, that until our temporal lives begin to straighten out, temporal needs would preoccupy our early prayers. The distinctive of our prayers in this first phase of our spiritual life is that they are prayers of petition. . . . When once we see the faithfulness of God to care for us, we want to learn how to follow Him. We come to that point where we want to surrender the silliness of our own ideas to the way of the Lord. Instead of praying, "Lord, give me," we start praying, "Lord, make me." Surrendering to the will of God becomes pre-eminent in our thinking.

This maturity in attitude is implied in what the apostle Paul prayed for the Ephesian church. The day-to-day concerns of the believers were essentially no different from yours today, but notice what Paul requested for them: "That He would grant you, according to the riches of His glory, to be strengthened with power through His Spirit in the inner man" (Eph. 3:16 NASB).

The Lord wants you to come to Him for even the smallest detail. But He wants you to feel free to pray for deeper spiritual riches as well.

Precious Lord, I surrender to Your will. Strengthen my inner man with power through Your Spirit according to the riches of Your glory.

(ON HOLY GROUND)

Discovering Your Life Message

SCRIPTURE READING: PSALM 119:1–8
KEY VERSE: PSALM 119:57

You are my portion, O LORD;
I have said that I would keep Your words.

God builds a life message in a variety of ways. Never seek to have the same message that another believer has. Though you may gain many insightful lessons from those who are strong in their faith, your life is unique and special before God. He has a message for you that no one else can share.

That is why it is imperative to ask Him to give you a love for His Word. Studying His Word and committing yourself to prayer are sure ways to learn more about Him and develop spiritually. In times of meditation and worship, He reveals His desire and will in a mighty way. Nothing can so train you for life like the time you spend alone with Jesus.

This is where He can motivate you toward certain goals and aspirations. Many people long to know God's will for their lives. They feel as though they do not have a life message, but God has one for them. The heavenly Father doesn't overlook anyone.

The key to discovering your life message is spending time alone with Him. Doing this takes real discipline and determination. Realize there remains a battle for your thoughts, and the enemy to your soul is continually seeking to throw you off and discourage you. Stay on course, and you will soon have an effective life message to share with others.

Father, keep me on course with Your will and Your Word. Give me a life message that will touch the lives of others.

(SEEKING HIS FACE)

The Good Things in Life

SCRIPTURE READING: PSALM 34:1–10
KEY VERSE: MATTHEW 5:6

Blessed are those who hunger and thirst for righteousness, for they shall be filled.

Everyone wants the good things in life. But God's idea of the good things is much different from most people's. Where some may pursue material gain or satisfaction in relationships, God knows real contentment comes from elsewhere. In His eyes, sometimes even trial, heartache, and suffering are good things in our lives.

The best things in life are the things that fit within the purpose and plan God has for your life. They may include wealth or prestige. But they may also include tribulation that God uses to mold you into the servant He has long envisioned.

"Those who seek the LORD shall not lack any good thing" (Ps. 34:10). What does it mean to seek the Lord? Believers already have His Spirit living within us, right? Yes, but Jesus said in Matthew 5:6, "Blessed are those who hunger and thirst for righteousness, for they shall be filled." Seeking the Lord means longing and thirsting for Him, for a daily intimate relationship with Him.

This process is fascinating. In seeking worldly gain, many people find that the more they get, the more they want. The same is true with Jesus Christ. The more you understand your wonderful Savior and Lord, the more you long to know Him better still. The good things in life come when you seek Him and know you shall be filled.

My heart cries out for You, dear Lord. I hunger and thirst for your righteousness. I long for an intimate relationship with You.

(INTO HIS PRESENCE)

A Marvelous Creation of God

SCRIPTURE READING: PSALM 71
KEY VERSE: PSALM 71:5

You are my hope, O Lord GOD; You are my trust from my youth.

Most of us know hope when it appears. We start our day with the anticipation that something good is just around the corner, but then it happens—disappointment steals our hope, and we wonder if the excitement and joy we felt were from God or our imagination.

Hope stealers are at work twenty-four hours a day. They include the criticism of others, difficult circumstances, trials, feelings of rejection and self-doubt, and more. What can you do to safeguard yourself against such thought patterns?

First, tell yourself the truth about your situation. Don't beat yourself down. God never does (Rom. 8:1).

Second, remember that God is the God of possibilities. In *The Attributes of God*, A. W. Tozer maintained,

> God is kindhearted, gracious, good-natured and benevolent in intention. . . . We only think we believe, really. We are believers in a sense, and I trust that we believe sufficiently to be saved and justified before His grace. But we don't believe as intensely and as intimately as we should. If we did, we would believe that God is . . . gracious and that His intentions are kind and benevolent. We would believe that God never thinks any bad thoughts about anybody, and He never had any bad thoughts about anybody.

What does God think about you? Marvelous. Wonderful. His creation. You are His child, and He is proud of you.

Father, as I face criticism, difficult circumstances, trials, and rejection today, help me remember Your declaration concerning me: I am marvelous, wonderful, Your creation. I accept Your evaluation and reject the negative opinions of others.

(ON HOLY GROUND)

The Riches of God's Grace

SCRIPTURE READING: EPHESIANS 1:3–6
KEY VERSES: EPHESIANS 1:3, 5–6

*Blessed be the God and Father of our Lord Jesus Christ . . . having
predestined us to adoption as sons by Jesus Christ to Himself, according
to the good pleasure of His will, to the praise of the glory of His grace,
by which He made us accepted in the Beloved.*

Have you ever questioned your acceptability? Have you ever wondered
if you are truly lovable? When God holds out His salvation to you, He
is not extending a membership to an obscure club. He is inviting you to
a profound, wonderful relationship that was made possible through His
death on the cross.

Ephesians 1:5–6 teaches us that God's will was to adopt you as His
own through the work of Christ. It was His will that your bond to Him
be the strongest it could be, so He did it through the most precious relationship He has ever created: He is accepting you as His child. William E.
Brown of *Baker's Evangelical Dictionary* has written, "God is a father who
graciously adopts believers in Christ into his spiritual family and grants
them all the privileges of heirship. Salvation is much more than forgiveness of sins and deliverance from condemnation; it is also a position of
great blessing. Believers are children of God."

The riches of God's grace provide a wonderful family for you. God
does not want a detached relationship. His desire is for deep communion,
because He loves you with an overwhelming love. You are accepted by
God and special to Him. Enjoy your position as His child.

*Lord, thank You for the riches of Your grace. Thank You that I have been
adopted into Your family and that I am loved and accepted by You.*

(PATHWAYS TO HIS PRESENCE)

Your True Identity

SCRIPTURE READING: ROMANS 8:14–17
KEY VERSE: ROMANS 8:16

The Spirit Himself bears witness with our spirit that we are children of God.

Determining identity is a lifelong struggle for many people.

Teenagers look to peers and parents trying to discover their unique identity. Possessions and status are the criteria for the majority of their conclusions.

Adults tend to define their identity by their vocation, financial bracket, or social strata. Determining our identity greatly affects our behavior. We act like who we think we are.

One of the greatest assets of the Christian is that his identity is rooted in the person of Jesus Christ. Because he is a child of God—an heir of God, a citizen of heaven as well as earth, a saint, and God's workmanship—he can act accordingly.

Do you know who you are in Christ?

Your marriage, career, relationships, and ambitions all hinge upon your new relationship with God's Son, Christ Jesus.

Your values, priorities, and perspectives are determined by this new relationship with Jesus. You are secure in Him. You are complete in Him. Your past, present, and future are bound up in the person of Jesus Christ.

Father, I am thankful that I am complete in Your Son, Jesus Christ. My past, present, and future are bound up in Him. Let my values, priorities, and perspectives always reflect this divine relationship.

(ON HOLY GROUND)

God's Immeasurable Riches

SCRIPTURE READING: COLOSSIANS 2:1–10
KEY VERSE: HEBREWS 1:2

[God] has in these last days spoken to us by His Son, whom He has appointed heir of all things, through whom also He made the worlds.

The word *heir* evokes thoughts of money or property handed down from generation to generation, with some special person receiving a legacy from a parent or relative. The heir is granted full benefits and ownership privileges and has the gratifying knowledge that he is unique, blessed, chosen for honor in some way.

Not many of us will inherit a vast estate or get a surprise phone call from a wealthy relative. But with Jesus as your Savior, you are already an heir with Him of all God's immeasurable riches. God the Father gave everything to Jesus, "whom He has appointed heir of all things, through whom also He made the worlds" (Heb. 1:2). He is your fullness and abundant supply for every part of your being.

Do you need strength? God has all power and gives energy for every task. Do you lack wisdom? He provides discernment and insight that cut through even the densest fog of confusion. Are you searching for contentment? Jesus gives you peace beyond human understanding.

A bank account can be depleted; a fortune can dwindle away; houses and property can be taken. But the inheritance you have in Christ is untouchable, unchanging, and inexhaustible.

Thank You, dear Lord, that my inheritance in You is untouchable, unchanging, and inexhaustible. You are all I need!

(INTO HIS PRESENCE)

Abundant Life

SCRIPTURE READING: ISAIAH 43
KEY VERSES: ISAIAH 43:18–19

Do not remember the former things, nor consider the things of old. Behold, I will do a new thing, now it shall spring forth; shall you not know it? I will even make a road in the wilderness and rivers in the desert.

In *The Root of the Righteous*, A. W. Tozer urged readers, "Keep your feet on the ground, but let your heart soar as high as it will. Refuse to be average or to surrender to the chill of your spiritual environment."

As believers, we must live out the truth given to us in Hebrews 11. Our citizenship is registered in heaven, where we have an eternal destiny. When we view life with this perspective, our outlook is positive and hope filled.

We are fully alive through Jesus Christ, who lives in us by the power of His Spirit. In fact, we are much more alive now that we have received God's Son as our Savior than when we walked this earth in physical form only. We are alive eternally to spiritual things that were once beyond our ability to understand.

The Old Testament saints could only imagine what was to come. They lived and died in their faith. However, they were not disappointed. Their devotion to God—and His to them—was sufficient for all their needs.

Are you living as Tozer suggested, keeping your feet firmly planted in the truth of God's Word, all the while dreaming and thinking of what God has for you in the not-so-distant future? This is the faith that draws you even closer to the reality of God's precious love. Jesus came so that we might have abundant life now—a tiny foretaste of what is yet to be.

Almighty God, I want to keep my feet on the ground while my heart soars to heights unlimited. Help me not to surrender to the chill of my spiritual environment. Plant my feet firmly in Your Word as I dream of the unlimited future You have planned for me.

(ON HOLY GROUND)

Transforming Thoughts

SCRIPTURE READING: EPHESIANS 4:17–24
KEY VERSES: EPHESIANS 4:23–24

Be renewed in the spirit of your mind, and . . . put on the new man
which was created according to God, in true righteousness and holiness.

In 1758, when Robert Robinson was a vibrant and energetic twenty-three-year-old pastor, he penned the words to the beloved hymn "Come, Thou Fount of Every Blessing."

Many years later, on a stagecoach trip, he sat next to a woman singing his hymn. When she asked him if he was familiar with the song, he began to cry and replied, "Madam, I am the poor unhappy man who wrote that hymn many years ago, and I would give a thousand worlds to enjoy the feelings I had then."

The man who wrote the words "Prone to wander, Lord, I feel it" experienced the same discouragement in his walk with the Lord that we often feel. But God does not want us to ride an emotional roller coaster; He wants us to abide in the security of His truth.

God's desire is "that you be renewed in the spirit of your mind, and put on the new self, which in the likeness of God has been created in righteousness and holiness of the truth" (Eph. 4:23–24 NASB).

The Lord renews your mind when you acknowledge your position in Christ that was secured at the cross and choose to set your mind on this truth. Read and study God's Word each day, and let Him transform your thoughts with His perspective.

Father, please renew my mind. I want to put on the new me that is in Your
likeness, created in righteousness and holiness.

(SEEKING HIS FACE)

Ready to Receive

SCRIPTURE READING: 1 PETER 5:5–9
KEY VERSES: 1 PETER 5:6–7

Humble yourselves under the mighty hand of God, that He may exalt you in due time, casting all your care upon Him, for He cares for you.

Your morning begins with a problem. You turn on the shower but no water comes out. In frustration, you pick up the phone to call the repairman. However, when you dial the number, no one answers the phone. Now you have reached your breaking point. But your anger is justified, isn't it? After all, you need a solution to your problem, and you need it right now.

In our fast-paced world, we have become accustomed to receiving messages, money, packages, and answers almost instantaneously. This may be why it is difficult for so many Christians to wait upon the Lord. When we lift our prayers to Him, we oftentimes treat God like the faucet repairman—He should be ready and waiting to fix our problems in a moment's notice.

Though God is always with us through the presence of the Holy Spirit (John 14:16), He answers our prayers in a time frame determined by His divine will and plan for our lives (1 Peter 5:6–7).

Why does He do this? It is not to make our lives more difficult. Instead, it is to encourage us to trust Him and to rely upon Him completely. God is faithful to answer our prayers, but His answers come when we are truly ready to receive them.

When you feel anxious about an unanswered prayer, don't give up or get angry. Rather, seek God with a patient heart, and trust His timing.

Lord, I am finite and impatient. I am used to instant responses. Help me to wait on You, and in the waiting, understand that You operate outside our time frame.

(PATHWAYS TO HIS PRESENCE)

God's Dependent

SCRIPTURE READING: LUKE 15:11–32
KEY VERSE: LUKE 15:18

I will arise and go to my father, and will say to him, "Father, I have sinned against heaven and before you."

As we grow up, we long for more autonomy, the freedom to make our own choices and function as adults. Can you remember waiting for certain "milestone" ages? The day you could go to school, the day you could drive a car—these are important steps in becoming mature.

If parents are wise, they help their children learn how to make the right choices for themselves. In fact, from a social perspective, a person is often not looked upon as being a complete adult until he is able to support himself and be responsible for his decisions. That is why it is difficult for many to understand the principle of dependence when it comes to abiding in Christ.

The prodigal son in Jesus' parable, in one way, represents all believers when we choose to go in our own direction with complete disregard for our Father. God does not want you to live as a child in the sense of being irresponsible as you function in daily life. However, He does want you to live as a spiritual child, humbly acknowledging your complete dependence upon Him and His Word.

When you order your life on the principles of God's Word, you can relax in His care, rest in His love, and know beyond doubt that He is leading you in a good direction. He is the perfect Father, and He longs for you to return home again to Him if you are wandering in your own selfish ways. It's never too late to be God's dependent.

Make me Your dependent, Father. I want to relax in Your care, rest in Your love, and follow the path You have ordained for me.

(INTO HIS PRESENCE)

Complete in Christ

SCRIPTURE READING: COLOSSIANS 2:6–10

KEY VERSE: COLOSSIANS 2:10

You are complete in Him, who is the head of all principality and power.

On a scale of one to ten, how complete would you say your life is? What person, job, object, or achievement would make your life more fulfilling? Most of us would have probably scored moderately high on the first question and added a few names or items to the second.

Did you know, though, that the apostle Paul insisted that once we place our trust in Christ as Savior, at that instant we become "complete in Him"? The word *complete* in the original Greek meant "full." When a person is full, he has no room for anything more. Think about this: if Christ is in you, your life is a "ten." In Jesus Christ is "all the fullness of Deity" (Col. 2:9 NASB). That is, Christ is the sum of all perfection—without blemish or want.

That same Christ resides in you and supplies all your needs. Therefore, when you have Christ, you have it all. You lack nothing. You possess eternal and abundant life. In Him are all of the wisdom, love, patience, kindness, and comfort you will ever need. No demand is unmet through the limitless resources of the indwelling Christ. Since you are complete in Him, your search for meaning is over. Christ is your life, and that is enough.

Almighty Lord, thank You that I am complete in You. My life is a "ten." All my needs are supplied. I have it all. I lack nothing!

(ON HOLY GROUND)

The Infusion of God's Grace

SCRIPTURE READING: EPHESIANS 2:8–10
KEY VERSE: ROMANS 6:4

We were buried with Him through baptism into death, that just as Christ was raised from the dead by the glory of the Father, even so we also should walk in newness of life.

You cannot come to Jesus apart from the grace of God. If you could save yourself, then there would be no need for a Savior. But God's pattern for salvation includes the infusion of His grace in the lives of those who come to Him.

Grace is all-important to the believer. It is God's personal touch, His handprint of intimacy in your life. It is the evidence of His advent and the one thing that keeps you grounded in His abiding love. His grace breathes potential into all that you do and say.

The apostle Paul told us that we have been saved by grace and have been raised up with Christ "so that in the ages to come He might show the surpassing riches of His grace in kindness toward us in Christ Jesus" (Eph. 2:5–7 NASB).

He reminded us that we have been buried with Jesus through baptism into death, so that as Christ was raised from the dead through the glory of the Father, we, too, might walk in newness of life (Rom. 6:4). The mission of grace did not end at the cross. It overflows into every area of our lives, filling us with hope and the blessed assurance that we are loved with an eternal love. Thus, God has called us to be distributors of His grace to others. It has been freely offered to you; let grace motivate you to share it with someone today.

God, thank You for Your grace that fills me. Help me to share it with someone today.

(SEEKING HIS FACE)

An Inseparable Relationship

SCRIPTURE READING: JOHN 21

KEY VERSE: JOHN 21:6

*He said to them, "Cast the net on the right side of the boat, and you
will find some." So they cast, and now they were not able to draw it in
because of the multitude of fish.*

All the disciples knew to do was to go on about their business. Now that
Jesus wasn't with them physically, they had to make many adjustments.
What would life be like now that they were not traveling around the region
with Him every day? What did it mean to be fishers of men? Was it all over?

The mood was probably quiet that night on the boat as they fished.
Peter must have mused silently as he tugged at the nets, hoping for a
catch. The light seemed to have gone out of his life. His heart was sore,
for the last thing his Lord had heard him do was betray Him and deny
he ever knew Him. Discouragement weighed him down with doubts and
fears about the future.

Dawn came. As the light grew stronger, the disciples could make out
a figure on the beach. The man called to them, "Cast the net on the right-
hand side of the boat and you will find a catch." When John said, "It is
the Lord," Peter dived into the water to swim to shore.

Peter would never forget the conversation they had that day by the
breakfast fire. He knew Jesus still loved him, and he had the chance to
tell Him the same. Jesus knew exactly how to comfort Peter, reassure him
of His eternal love, give him hope, and reignite his vision for the future.
Jesus can do the same for you.

If you've shut Him out for any reason, He is still waiting for you on
the shore.

*Father, forgive me for the times I have shut You out of my life. Reassure me
of Your love, give me renewed hope, rekindle my vision for the future.*

(ON HOLY GROUND)

Fellowship with Jesus

SCRIPTURE READING: JOHN 1:9–14
KEY VERSE: JOHN 1:14

The Word became flesh and dwelt among us, and we beheld His glory, the glory as of the only begotten of the Father, full of grace and truth.

Before sin entered the world, man enjoyed unbroken fellowship with the Lord. In Genesis, we read that God would come to Adam, walking in the cool of the day. There was a natural flow of fellowship between God and man. No hint of discontentment or pressure emerged—just loving fellowship. However, that came to an abrupt end when man disobeyed God by eating of the tree of knowledge.

God loves you with an everlasting love. He does not have evil in mind for your life but is constantly seeking to bring blessing and hope to encourage you along the way. Man's sin struck the first hurtful blow to the heart of God. For that, man suffered a grave consequence—separation from the abiding presence of God.

The eternal love of God did not burn dim, and God was motivated to send His Son as an atonement for our sins. The birth of Jesus Christ brought restoration to a lost world. God in His grace once again reached out to mankind.

Now we can enjoy what the Old Testament patriarchs could only envision—continual fellowship with almighty God. Just as God walked in the Garden with Adam and Eve, He walks with you. No detail in life is too small for Him, and nothing is too difficult for Him to handle. When you come to Him, He listens and brings hope to whatever you face.

Father, I thank You that there is no detail in my life that is too small for You to handle. There is no problem too large for You.

(INTO HIS PRESENCE)

Poor Self-Image

SCRIPTURE READING: EPHESIANS 2:1–10

KEY VERSE: EPHESIANS 2:10

We are His workmanship, created in Christ Jesus for good works, which God prepared beforehand that we should walk in them.

Christian psychologist Dr. James Dobson once took a poll of women who, by their own admission, were basically cheerful and secure individuals.

Dobson listed ten sources of depression. Included in the list were such topics as fatigue, boredom, in-law conflicts, and financial problems. The women were asked to identify which factor contributed most heavily to periods of depression.

The overwhelming reply was lack of self-esteem. Were the same poll taken by Christians at large, the results would probably be similar.

Proper and healthy self-esteem is possible when we receive God's evaluation of ourselves, relying on His estimation of our worth, not the faulty opinion of others or our fluctuating personal performance.

A Stradivarius is valuable because of its maker. We are worthy because God is our Maker. God not only created us; He treasured us enough to make us in His image.

The apostle Paul said, "I can do all things through Him who strengthens me" (Phil. 4:13 NASB). We have His adequacy, His power, His competency. Should we ever feel inferior again?

Dear God, thank You that my worth is not based on the faulty opinion of others or my own fluctuating performance. I am worthy because You are my Maker.

(ON HOLY GROUND)

Truth in Action

SCRIPTURE READING: I SAMUEL 17:34–51
KEY VERSE: I SAMUEL 17:45

David said to the Philistine, "You come to me with a sword, with a spear, and with a javelin. But I come to you in the name of the LORD of hosts, the God of the armies of Israel, whom you have defied."

At some point during our relationship with Christ, we have to plunge into the unknown with some measure of faith. The circumstances could vary—a new job, a new relationship, a battle with an illness—and we have no idea what the outcome will be.

Yet we put our faith to the test, trusting that God will bring about the best for our lives. As He works, transforming us into the image of Christ, our faith builds. Faith isn't merely a concept anymore. It is truth in action.

Conquering faith develops from faith that has been tested and has seen the faithfulness of God. And conquering faith never forgets past victories won by the Lord. When David approached King Saul about fighting Goliath, he went with great confidence. While Goliath was large and intimidating, David remembered from where he derived his strength: God. During his days as a shepherd, David battled a lion and a bear, defeating them both through the strength of the Lord. He knew that it had nothing to do with his own strength, just his faith. He believed God would deliver him again in a battle against Goliath.

In our desire to have a conquering faith, we must never forget where we have been with the Lord. It is necessary to get where we are going.

Lord, give me conquering faith. Help me remember where I have been with You in the past so that I may arrive at my future destiny.

(PATHWAYS TO HIS PRESENCE)

Focus on Jesus

SCRIPTURE READING: ACTS 16:22–32
KEY VERSE: ACTS 16:25

At midnight Paul and Silas were praying and singing hymns to God, and the prisoners were listening to them.

If we are not careful, we can become guilty of allowing emotions to govern our lives. God instructs us to keep our focus on Jesus in order to grow spiritually. When we do this, the emotional ups and downs of this life will not shake or change our world.

In *Telling Yourself the Truth*, William Backus wrote about joy:

Joy comes from your relationship to God and His unchanging faithfulness. You don't need to live in perfect circumstances to be happy. It's pleasant to be loved and appreciated, but not vital to your happiness.

The Bible tells how two men of God, Paul and Silas, were brought before Roman authorities at Philippi and beaten with rods and then thrown into jail. . . . But did Paul and Silas moan and complain, "If it weren't for the cruelty of the unbelievers, we wouldn't be wounded and bleeding. We'd be happy!" No.

Paul and Silas had a strong belief that transcended circumstances, events, people, feelings; it even transcended pain. That belief was in the person, power, and presence of Jesus Christ. They believed their suffering wasn't as important as the message they carried. . . .

They sang so loudly their voices were heard throughout the prison! And not only that, God . . . opened the prison doors for them. Their happiness came from the belief in Jesus Christ within them and not from circumstances around them.

Keep my focus on You, Jesus, instead of the circumstances of my life.

(SEEKING HIS FACE)

The Throne Room of God

SCRIPTURE READING: PSALM 55:1–3
KEY VERSE: PSALM 57:7

My heart is steadfast, O God, my heart is steadfast;
I will sing and give praise.

Our first course of action when facing a problem should be to take our burden to God in prayer and praise Him for the answer. Believers in Jesus Christ can avail ourselves of the wisdom, power, and counsel of God Himself through the supernatural gift of prayer. Unbelievers have no such resource. They must deal with crises in their limited strength and wisdom.

As a follower of Christ, you have the immeasurable, fathomless power of prayer at your disposal. When you were saved by faith in Christ through the riches of His grace, you were given access to God: "Therefore, brethren, having boldness to enter the Holiest by the blood of Jesus . . . draw near with a true heart in full assurance of faith" (Heb. 10:19, 22). You are reconciled to Christ forever.

You are His friend. You are forgiven of all your sins—past, present, and future. The moment you placed your faith in Christ, the doors of heaven were opened for you to approach the heavenly Father with complete assurance.

You can bring anything to Him. He will not reject you. As you turn to Him with your problems in prayer, the Lord Jesus Christ providentially works to supply your needs and help you.

Turn it all over to Him in prayer. Praise Him for the answer. The red carpet of Christ's blood has paved your way into the throne room of God.

Dear Lord, thank You for access into Your throne room. Christ's blood has paved the way for me.

(INTO HIS PRESENCE)

Heir to an Immeasurable Fortune

SCRIPTURE READING: PSALM 19
KEY VERSE: ACTS 20:32

So now, brethren, I commend you to God and to the word of His grace, which is able to build you up and give you an inheritance among all those who are sanctified.

"If only I were a Rockefeller or a Vanderbilt, my future would be secure." Most of us have probably dreamed what our lives would be like if we were heirs to such massive fortunes.

How would your thinking and living change if today you understood that you are the heir of treasures beside which even the wealthiest earthly estates pale?

The amazing truth is that God has named you an heir of His holdings: "And now I commend you to God and to the word of His grace, which is able . . . to give you the inheritance among all those who are sanctified" (Acts 20:32 NASB).

What does He own? He owns it all. As Creator of heaven and earth and all that is in them, God is the sole proprietor of the universe. It is in His hands to bestow His unspeakable wealth upon you.

God is your Father. You are His son or daughter. All that is His belongs to you. You have an inheritance that will never fade or tarnish because you are an heir of the Father's immeasurable fortune.

O God, You are my Father. I am Your child. All You have belongs to me. Thank You for an inheritance that will never fade.

(ON HOLY GROUND)

The Supreme Moment in History

SCRIPTURE READING: COLOSSIANS 2:11–15
KEY VERSES: COLOSSIANS 2:12–13

[You were] buried with Him in baptism, in which you also were raised with Him through faith in the working of God, who raised Him from the dead. And you, being dead in your trespasses and the uncircumcision of your flesh, He has made alive together with Him, having forgiven you all trespasses.

In our lives, there are defining moments determining what path we will take. There are events that forever change us. The moment we see the truth brought to light, we run for it, realizing that all we have ever known pales in comparison.

For the world, that moment was when Jesus died on the cross. His death at Calvary closed the chapter on mankind's separation from God, making a way for all to know Him—and know Him intimately. As the perfect sacrifice for the entire world, Jesus served as the atoning death necessary for us to come into relationship with our heavenly Father.

Jesus' death on the cross changed the way we live and interact with Him today. God judged sin. With the world's sin on Jesus' shoulders, God showed us how much He abhors sin, letting His Son die. God defeated Satan. Our heavenly Father triumphed over the enemy, stripped him of his powers, and exposed him as a liar and a destroyer.

Paul wrote that God made us alive, forgiving us, and paying the price for our sin (Col. 2:13–14). Through Christ's death, the barrier between God and us has been removed.

Lord, there is no place for me to take my burden, other than the cross. Thank You for triumphing over sin and setting me free.

(PATHWAYS TO HIS PRESENCE)

God's Plan for the Resurrection

SCRIPTURE READING: 1 CORINTHIANS 15:12–28
KEY VERSE: 1 CORINTHIANS 15:20

Now Christ is risen from the dead, and has become the firstfruits of those who have fallen asleep.

The foundation of Christianity is the resurrection of Jesus Christ. The apostle Paul told the Corinthian church that without belief in this primary tenet of our faith, then our faith is in vain (1 Cor. 15:14).

Since we believe in Jesus' bodily resurrection from the grave after His crucifixion, then we also believe in the promise of *our* bodily resurrection into eternity. The alternative is to believe in nothing that is real, nothing that is hopeful or redeeming.

We cannot separate these truths. Jesus is the firstfruits of those raised from the dead. When Paul said this in 1 Corinthians 15:20, he used a verb tense in the Greek that means Jesus not only was raised but is still alive. He lives forevermore.

George Sweeting has written:

In Glendale, California, at Forest Lawn Cemetery, hundreds of people each year stand before two huge paintings. One pictures the crucifixion of Christ. The other depicts His resurrection. In the second painting the artist has pictured an empty tomb with an angel near the entrance. In the foreground stands the figure of the risen Christ. But the striking feature of that huge canvas is a vast throng of people, back in the misty background, stretching into the distance and out of sight, suggesting the multitude who will be raised from the dead because Jesus first died and rose for them.

Lord, thank You for Your death on the cross and Your resurrection. I rejoice in this hope. I praise You!

(PATHWAYS TO HIS PRESENCE)

A Living Savior

SCRIPTURE READING: MARK 15–16
KEY VERSE: LUKE 24:6

He is not here, but is risen! Remember how He spoke to you when He was still in Galilee.

One cannot diminish the torture or agony of the cross. Christ suffered and died for our sin, willingly laying down His life for the transgressions of men. Yet there can likewise be no diluting the supernatural power of the resurrection.

None of the benefits of the cross—forgiveness of sin, justification of sinners—could be ours today without a living Savior. The resurrection of Christ attested more than any other event to His full and absolute deity. Jesus met and conquered death, Satan, and sin, proclaiming His divine nature and displaying His divine power.

Today, the believer can enjoy the exquisite delight of union with the resurrected Christ. At work, in the store, in the house, or on the road, you have Jesus Christ in you, and God has placed Him in you.

The resurrected Christ lives in you so that you may partake of His life and sup with Him. He helps you, comforts you, guides you, loves you, and pours His life out through you. Jesus does more than just live. He lives in you, makes His abode in your heart, and infuses your ordinary life with supernatural meaning, strength, and hope. He arose just as He said He would, and He lives to give you the abundant life He promised.

Jesus, You live in me! I am a partaker of Your life. I can fellowship with You. Come and comfort, guide, and pour Your life through me. Infuse my ordinary life with supernatural meaning.

(ON HOLY GROUND)

The Miracle of the Resurrection

SCRIPTURE READING: MARK 16:1–21
KEY VERSES: MARK 16:9–10

When He rose early on the first day of the week, He appeared first to Mary Magdalene, out of whom He had cast seven demons. She went and told those who had been with Him, as they mourned and wept.

When you read the account of Jesus' death and resurrection in the Bible, do you ever stop to wonder why He appeared to His disciples and friends after the resurrection? They already knew that the stone had been rolled away and that His body was not there. He had already promised them that He would rise again on the third day.

It is common belief that Jesus' multiple appearances were to answer the questions that existed among them and to cast out disbelief. He appeared to Mary Magdalene to rule out the possibility of His body being stolen and to expound upon the scriptural prophecies that were now fulfilled. He appeared to Thomas to prove that His broken, punctured body had indeed risen from the grave. He also appeared to Peter to reestablish His love, even after being denied.

These important visitations equipped the new messengers of the gospel with further knowledge and evidence of Jesus' true identity as the Son of God. If any had held the slightest doubts in their hearts before, they could not doubt now. Jesus suffered the death of a criminal to rise as a King. He is alive, and His love is great enough to conquer doubt.

Meditate on the miracle of His resurrection as you lift your prayers to Him today.

Lord, just as You appeared to Your followers to equip them for ministry, so, too, help my finite mind grasp the wonder of Your death as a criminal and resurrection as a King.

(PATHWAYS TO HIS PRESENCE)

God's Forgiveness

SCRIPTURE READING: JOHN 8:1–11
KEY VERSE: JOHN 8:11

Jesus said to her, "Neither do I condemn you; go and sin no more."

Although scholars debate whether or not the woman caught in adultery was a setup by the Pharisees in order to trap Jesus going against the Law of Moses, the overarching theme is forgiveness. God's love, mercy, and grace were all present and active. He did not condemn the woman but instead challenged her accusers to throw the first stone if one among them could be found without sin.

After the Pharisees departed, Jesus looked at the woman lying at His feet. It was likely not the first time she had committed such an act, but it was the first time she had appeared before Jesus. There was no doubt in her mind that He was a man of God. How exposed and embarrassed she must have felt—that is, until the Savior revealed His word of forgiveness and hope to her heart.

Perhaps there is something in your life you wish you could erase. Just the thought of it brings feelings of condemnation and sorrow. Adultery was an act that was punishable by stoning according to the law, yet Jesus set the woman free.

He gave her a second chance, and this is what He gives each of us. If there is something you have done, know that when you bring it to God in prayer seeking His forgiveness, it is forgiven. God will never bring up the matter again. His Son's death at Calvary was sufficient payment for all your sins. Only almighty God can love us this much.

O Lord, I thank You that Calvary paid for all my sins. Only You could love me this much.

(SEEKING HIS FACE)

The Cry of the Cross

SCRIPTURE READING: I CORINTHIANS 2
KEY VERSE: I CORINTHIANS 2:2

I determined not to know anything among you except Jesus Christ and Him crucified.

To some, a cross might seem an odd symbol for a religious faith. It does, after all, carry the same meaning as an electric chair or a hangman's noose—death.

Yet this gruesome form of Roman torture stands at the heart of Christianity. An emblem such as the sign of the fish is a legitimate New Testament expression, but the cross of Jesus Christ is the authentic badge of Christianity.

You see, God so loved you that Christ died for you. There was no way around it. Sin—the state and condition into which all men are born—had carved an abyss between God and man that nothing but the cross could traverse. The message of the cross is love—God's immeasurable, amazing love for man. The holy love of God sent His Son to earth in human form and placed Him on two pieces of timber.

When you contemplate the cross and the pain that accompanied it—from nails, thorns, and whips to ridicule—think of the overwhelming love of God. Because the Father loves you, Christ died for you and rose again. He saves all who trust Him for forgiveness of sin and reserves a place in eternity for every believer. That is the love of God displayed through the cross.

Lord, thank You for Your overwhelming love demonstrated at Calvary. You died for me. You were raised for me. You saved me and have reserved eternity in my name. Thank You that I have heard the cry of the cross.

(ON HOLY GROUND)

God Never Gives Up

SCRIPTURE READING: COLOSSIANS 3:1–17
KEY VERSE: COLOSSIANS 1:13

He has delivered us from the power of darkness and conveyed us into the kingdom of the Son of His love.

When Christ told Peter of his coming denial, Peter stiffened and protested, "Even though all may fall away because of You, I will never fall away" (Matt. 26:33 NASB). But Jesus knew the truth. Peter would deny Him, not once but three times.

Peter vowed passionately that he would never forsake Jesus. But within a matter of hours he was reduced to fear and hiding from Jewish and Roman officials. But Jesus didn't give up on Peter, and He doesn't give up on us.

Among Christ's last words to Peter before His death were words of restoration: "I have prayed for you, Simon, that your faith may not fail. And when you have turned back, strengthen your brothers" (Luke 22:32 NIV). Jesus knew Peter would fall, and He loved him anyway. He gave His zealous disciple hope of future service when He said, "Strengthen your brothers."

God takes our weaknesses and turns them into points of strength and honor for Himself. Jesus was totally committed to Peter. He knew Peter would suffer a bitter defeat, but there was an event coming that would revolutionize his thinking—the resurrection.

Imagine Peter's amazement as Jesus stepped into the Upper Room the night of His resurrection. Christ extended love and acceptance to Peter despite his failure. This same love is yours today.

Dear heavenly Father, let the message of the resurrection revolutionize my life, as it did Peter's. Through the power of the resurrection, take my weaknesses and turn them into strengths that will bring glory and honor to You.

(ON HOLY GROUND)

A New Level of Love

SCRIPTURE READING: MATTHEW 16:21–26
KEY VERSE: ROMANS 5:8

God demonstrates His own love toward us, in that while we were still sinners, Christ died for us.

Peter was privy to the greatest spiritual teaching. He also was the first disciple to proclaim Jesus as Messiah. The spiritual insight he gained helped to build his faith and self-esteem. Therefore, when Jesus began to talk of His death, Peter did not hesitate to say, "God forbid it, Lord! This shall never happen to You" (Matt. 16:22 NASB).

However, Peter miscalculated his own spiritual maturity. He thought he understood the ways of God, but in actuality he understood only what made him feel good on the inside. He liked being close to Jesus.

There is something very rewarding in finding our self-worth in Christ. Yet we must be sensitive to the complete will of God. The life of Christ was given as a gift to demonstrate God's great love. It is only through Jesus that we have eternal salvation. He paid the price for our sins. Peter missed the bigger picture that Christ had to die so that we could live for eternity with the Father. Often God takes a different route from the one we think is necessary. Acceptance of His will positions us for spiritual maturity and blessing.

Are you trusting your feelings and wishing that God would work a certain way? Let Him have the entirety of your life and the lives of your loved ones. When you do this, you will find that you have grown to a new level of loving a holy, infinite God.

Lord, I give You the entirety of my life and the lives of my loved ones. Move me to a new level of loving You.

(SEEKING HIS FACE)

Communion with the Father

SCRIPTURE READING: 1 CORINTHIANS 11:23–28
KEY VERSE: 1 CORINTHIANS 11:26

As often as you eat this bread and drink this cup, you proclaim the Lord's death till He comes.

Whenever we celebrate the Lord's Supper, we must remember its sacred significance. It is a holy remembrance of Christ's shed blood and its inauguration of a new covenant based on the forgiveness of sin through Christ's death.

When you drink of the cup, realize that your fellowship with the Father is grounded on the blood of Christ. You may talk with Him and receive His friendly guidance and eternal embrace all because God chose to crucify His Son on your behalf.

The barrier of sin could not be removed except by the death, burial, and resurrection of Jesus. The stain of sin could not be taken away apart from His blood. The blood of Christ covers your sin and clothes you in God's righteousness.

As you eat of the bread, think upon the fathomless love of God that divinely initiated the blood-soaked beams of Calvary. God's love sent Jesus to the cross for you, and God's love forgives and restores you to communion with the Father.

Because Jesus was broken and bloodied for you, you can enjoy the wholeness, joy, and peace of a personal, living relationship with Christ. Christ's blood is God's love demonstrated.

Father, Your love was demonstrated through Christ's blood. Thank You for the provision of peace that Your gift brought to me.

(SEEKING HIS FACE)

The Name of Jesus

SCRIPTURE READING: LUKE 10:1–17

KEY VERSE: PHILIPPIANS 4:13

I can do all things through Christ who strengthens me.

There is power in the name of Jesus. We can see it in the lives of the seventy disciples mentioned in Luke 10:1–17. The evidence of their ministry was dramatic, but they did not have success because of their own abilities. "Even the demons are subject to us in Your name" was their testimony to Jesus.

It is keenly important for you to understand the significance of Christ's name. Just saying the name of Jesus does not make a significant difference in and of itself. A powerful change takes place when you acknowledge His lordship and sovereignty.

The seventy disciples were sold out for Christ. And because of their dedication, they experienced something that was miraculous in nature. This moving of God's Spirit is available to you as well.

The apostle Paul proclaimed, "I can do all things through Him who strengthens me" (Phil. 4:13 NASB). Paul made a conscious decision to lay aside his personal desires and rights in order to follow Jesus Christ. The life of Christ within him gave him the ability to meet all demands, reach all goals, and accomplish all things.

Are you aware of who is in control of your life? Or are you still clinging to the reins and hoping that somehow your human ability will make a difference? Nothing but Jesus will ever satisfy your longing, and only the name of Jesus will bring true peace and forgiveness.

Take control of my life, Lord. I want to experience true peace and forgiveness.

(SEEKING HIS FACE)

The Great All

SCRIPTURE READING: HEBREWS 11:1–6
KEY VERSE: HEBREWS 11:6

Without faith it is impossible to please Him, for he who comes to God must believe that He is, and that He is a rewarder of those who diligently seek Him.

A. W. Tozer underscored the vital necessity of reckoning with the unseen reality of God and His power:

> The spiritual is real. . . . We must shift our interest from the seen to the unseen. For the great unseen reality is God. "He that cometh to God must believe that he is, and that he is a rewarder of them that diligently seek him" (Heb. 11:6 KJV). This is basic in the life of faith.
>
> Every man must choose his world. . . . As we begin to focus on God, the things of the Spirit will take shape before our inner eyes.
>
> Obedience to the Word of Christ will bring an inward revelation of the Godhead (John 14:21–23).
>
> A new God-consciousness will seize upon us, and we shall begin to taste and hear and inwardly feel the God Who is our life and our all.
>
> More and more, as our faculties grow sharper and more sure, God will become to us the great All and His Presence the glory and wonder of our lives.

Tozer concluded with this prayer. Lift it as your own today:

Dear Lord, open my eyes that I may see; give me acute spiritual perception; enable me to taste Thee and know that Thou art good. Make heaven more real to me than any earthly thing has ever been.

(ON HOLY GROUND)

The Focus of Your Life

SCRIPTURE READING: PSALM 26
KEY VERSES: PSALM 26:2–3

Examine me, O LORD, and prove me;
Try my mind and my heart.
For Your lovingkindness is before my eyes,
And I have walked in Your truth.

In Psalm 27, David was in the process of rousing his faith back to the point where he could say without a doubt that "the LORD is my light and my salvation; whom shall I fear?" (Ps. 27:1).

However, in Psalm 26, things did not appear so bright, and David pleaded his case before the Lord. When you face doubts and fears, what do you think of? Are God's hope and intervention realities you believe? They should be.

God answers the heartfelt cries of His people. He wants you to know and believe that He will deliver you from all trouble. And even if the trouble remains for a season, He will provide and care for you.

Your responsibility is simply this: be willing to love and worship God. Sound too simplistic? Try it for a week. Let go of arguing your point of view. Put aside resentment, self-righteousness, and any pride that have placed enmity between you and others. Then set the focus of your life and heart on Jesus Christ. Doing this may be one of the toughest things you have ever done.

But over time, you will notice small irritations have vanished. The need for recognition disappears, and there is an inner peace like nothing you have felt before. Instead of nervously worrying about tomorrow, you realize that God is the Captain of your soul. You can wait for God's blessing just as David did because you have tasted His goodness.

Thank You for the inner peace that comes in Your presence, Lord. Help me to keep my focus on You instead of worrying about the future.

(INTO HIS PRESENCE)

The Importance of Relationship

SCRIPTURE READING: LUKE 19:1–10
KEY VERSE: LUKE 19:8

Behold, Lord, half of my possessions I will give to the poor, and if I have defrauded anyone of anything, I will give back four times as much.
(NASB)

The story of Zaccheus is usually taught with an emphasis on his complete enthusiasm to see Jesus. The picture of this short man climbing a tree just to get a glimpse of the Messiah is an example of how eager we should be to meet with the Savior.

It can be easy to overlook the life change that Zaccheus experienced after Jesus called him down from the tree and asked if He could come to his house. Zaccheus's heart flooded with joy when Jesus loved and accepted him.

As they were on their way to his house, Zaccheus said, "Behold, Lord, half of my possessions I will give to the poor, and if I have defrauded anyone of anything, I will give back four times as much" (Luke 19:8 NASB). Zaccheus knew in his heart that his account of sin had been wiped clean because he placed his faith in Jesus. In that first moment of exultant freedom, he wanted to set accounts right with his fellow men.

Notice that Zaccheus changed his viewpoint only after he experienced the unconditional love of Christ. Before that day, Zaccheus could not possibly have understood God's priorities. Even if someone had explained the truth to him logically and carefully, he could not comprehend it until he had a one-on-one heart encounter with Jesus.

Only on the foundation of a relationship with the Lord can you grasp the application of His truth and the power of the cross in your life.

Father, deepen my relationship with You. Let me grasp the application of Your truth in my life.

(SEEKING HIS FACE)

Answered Prayer

SCRIPTURE READING: JOHN 14:12–14

KEY VERSE: JOHN 14:14

If you ask anything in My name, I will do it.

We can be assured that God will answer our prayers in Jesus' name because of our:

- *Association.* After salvation, we have a new relationship with God through His Son Jesus. Our association with Christ makes it possible to have intimacy with God the Father.
- *Access.* We can come to God's throne of grace with boldness and confidence. The reason is that Jesus' death and resurrection blotted out our sin problem and cleared the way for us to have unhindered access to God the Father.
- *Authority.* Because of the shed blood of Jesus, believers are coheirs with Him (Rom. 8:17), identified eternally with God's holy Son. As such, we are delegated His authority and have the right to pray in Christ's name. Jesus, who sits at the right hand of the Father, gives us this privilege.
- *Agreement.* To pray in Christ's name, we not only must have His authority but also be in agreement with Him. If we ask for something outside of God's will, we can be assured that it will not be granted. Our request must be in keeping with the character of God and the content of His Word. Essentially, when we ask something in Jesus' name, we are saying that we believe Jesus Himself would make the same petition, were He in our situation.
- *Assurance.* Asking "in Jesus' name" means praying in confidence. Jesus meant it when He said He would give us what we ask—as long as we are in association and agreement with Him.

Lord, thank You for answered prayer! I claim the access, authority, agreement, and assurance that makes this knowledge a reality.

(PATHWAYS TO HIS PRESENCE)

Never Give Up!

SCRIPTURE READING: REVELATION 3:20–22
KEY VERSE: MATTHEW 16:18

I also say to you that you are Peter, and on this rock I will build My church, and the gates of Hades shall not prevail against it.

The title of today's devotion—"Never Give Up!"—brings to mind a stirring memory of the people who fought in World War II. On the brink of destruction, Churchill's call to arms rallied his troops. The result was a shift in the way England fought the rest of the war.

Setting its focus on one thing—victory—England refused to be dominated by any outside force. It rose from the charred ruins of wartime to become once again a great and mighty nation. Looking back to that defining moment in history brings a sense of pride. Here is a group of people who said, "No, we will not go down in defeat. We believe there is a future for us, and we will step forward through the darkness to find a candle of hope."

When you are tempted to give up, think back to this point in history. What would have happened if England had given in to the evil of Hitler's rule? Oppression and a sense of loss would have swept through the nation with such vengeance that recovery would have been hard, if not impossible.

England had made its choice even before the Allies joined the war. The inner strength of the nation was the motivating factor. Are you facing what appears to be a sure defeat? Are air-raid sirens sounding all around you? Stand firm in your faith in God. Cling to Him, and declare that with His help, you will never give up. The victory you long to receive is yours.

Dear heavenly Father, I declare it: I won't ever give up! As I travel the rough pathways of this world—in the face of danger or defeat—I will stand firm in You. The victory is mine!

(ON HOLY GROUND)

Eternal Life

SCRIPTURE READING: PSALM 103
KEY VERSE: PSALM 103:4

Who redeems your life from destruction, who crowns you with lovingkindness and tender mercies.

Whether on the deserted streets of Bombay or in a plush oceanfront home, whether clothed in tattered jeans or a fine suit, you can enjoy the good life that Jesus Christ imparts to all who believe and abide in Him. The good life is eternal life received as a gift through faith in Christ's sacrifice for our sins.

Eternal life is as good as it gets. It is the everlasting, unending, unceasing presence of the eternal God, lavishing all of His goodness upon you in His limitless mercy and grace. It is a permanent possession, unaffected by the rise and fall of money, men, or nations. It is guaranteed by Christ's death, burial, and resurrection.

But you can experience the reality of eternal life here and now. A new quality of life is available to all who have become one with the Savior. It is the abundant sufficiency of Christ for every circumstance.

Each day is an opportunity to draw from the divine well of peace, joy, love, faithfulness, gentleness, goodness, patience, and self-control without diminishing the supply by one ounce. Do not ever be deceived. Real life is in Jesus, and Jesus is in you. Inexhaustible, boundless life for you forever.

Precious heavenly Father, thank You for the inexhaustible, boundless life that is in Your Son, Jesus. Let me continually draw from Your divine resources.

(ON HOLY GROUND)

Rejoicing in Salvation

SCRIPTURE READING: 1 TIMOTHY 1:12–15
KEY VERSE: PSALM 55:9

Destroy, O Lord, and divide their tongues,
For I have seen violence and strife in the city.

The person who used the word *joy* more than any other writer of Scripture was the apostle Paul. That appears incredible. Wasn't Paul beaten, stoned, ridiculed, and mocked wherever he preached? Wasn't Paul the fellow who knew the inside of a prison cell better than the average criminal?

How could he even think of rejoicing, much less use it so liberally in his epistles? Paul's delight came from an overwhelming gratitude for God's work of salvation: "The grace of our Lord was exceedingly abundant. . . . This is a faithful saying and worthy of all acceptance, that Christ Jesus came into the world to save sinners, of whom I am chief" (1 Tim. 1:14–15).

If you have placed your faith in Christ as Savior, think of the supernatural transformation that transpired. You were brought from the domain of Satan into the kingdom of God; you were delivered from unending punishment and gifted with everlasting life.

You became God's friend, His child. He became your heavenly Father because through the agency of His Spirit, you were born again. Consider the greatness of your salvation; then rejoice in it today.

God, You are my Friend and my heavenly Father. I rejoice in You and my salvation.

(INTO HIS PRESENCE)

The Fullness of Blessing

SCRIPTURE READING: PROVERBS 12:1–5
KEY VERSE: PROVERBS 12:2

A good man obtains favor from the LORD,
But a man of wicked intentions He will condemn.

While the phrase "walking with the Lord" may sound like a trite, overly used phrase within the Christian world, its imagery is perfect in describing what a life with God should be like.

Our relationship with God should not wear us out; rather, it should be refreshing. That does not mean that we will not be challenged from time to time and stretched in our faith. However, God isn't trying to leave us behind. A steady, thriving relationship with God is one in which we grow in our understanding of who He is and what He wants to do with our lives. And in the process of nurturing this relationship, we find His favorable hand resting upon us.

Proverbs 12:2 describes a good man. We become "good" men and women when we walk with God. Our desire for righteousness increases as we walk in the light of His glory. We recognize sin in our lives and long for Him to transform us completely.

In order to stay step for step with God, we must maintain our pace with Him, seeking to honor and glorify Him in all that we do. It is there that we find His favor and experience the fullness of His blessing upon our lives.

Lord, I want to walk in Your presence, side by side with You. Take my hand and keep me on pace when I am apt to wander or fall behind.

(PATHWAYS TO HIS PRESENCE)

Butterfly Living

SCRIPTURE READING: 2 CORINTHIANS 5:17–21
KEY VERSE: 2 CORINTHIANS 5:17

If anyone is in Christ, he is a new creation; old things have passed away; behold, all things have become new.

To get a grasp of this verse, imagine the old you as a caterpillar and the new you in Christ as a matured butterfly. What you may find in your life experience, however, is that even though you are a butterfly, you are still drawn to the caterpillar way of life. How can you end this tension?

In his letter to the Romans, Paul wrote to exhort them to consistent "butterfly living." The temptations in their society to relapse into "caterpillar living" were strong, much as they are today. He wrote, "Do not be conformed to this world, but be transformed by the renewing of your mind, so that you may prove what the will of God is, that which is good and acceptable and perfect" (Rom. 12:2 NASB).

This principle is so dynamic, you cannot afford to miss it. "Transformed" is a translation of the Greek *metamorphosis*, the process by which a caterpillar becomes a butterfly.

Renewing your mind is in essence taking on the mind of Christ; it means changing your thinking in accordance with the truth of God's Word. What you believe about God defines the quality of that relationship. Remember, you are not a caterpillar with wings glued on—you are truly a butterfly.

Dear Lord, thank You for changing my "caterpillar" mentality, so I can experience "butterfly" living. This month, as I reflect on the wonders of spiritual change, continue Your divine miracle of transformation.

(ON HOLY GROUND)

Close to the Father's Heart

SCRIPTURE READING: JOHN 17:1–8
KEY VERSE: PSALM 145:18

The LORD is near to all who call upon Him,
To all who call upon Him in truth.

The believer who lives close to the Father's heart is free to express his feelings to Him. You do not have to be uptight with God. He knew every detail of your life the moment He created you. When you were saved, the Lord Jesus Christ understood all of your past failures and hang-ups and your future struggles.

Because you are now His child for all eternity, you can be completely honest with Him. You can pour out your hurts, your anger, your disappointments, your secrets, and your dreams to the Lord. He will never reject you (Heb. 13:5). You can never turn away His steadfast love.

There will be times when you do not understand what God is up to in your life. God's presence may seem distant. Because you have God's assurance of His presence and because of His unceasing activity on your behalf, you can still cling to Him and worship Him in the knowledge of His love for you. Refuse the advances of competing lovers—money, fame, power—and deny doubt and unbelief.

Have you the kind of intimacy with God so that the Father is your most adored Friend? Does your unswerving allegiance belong to Him? If not, confess your need for such a relationship, let Him gather you into His waiting arms, and worship Him.

Father, let me learn to worship You even when Your presence seems distant.
Help me deny doubt and unbelief and refuse the advances of money, fame,
and power.

(INTO HIS PRESENCE)

Ability and Capability

SCRIPTURE READING: 2 CORINTHIANS 12:7–10
KEY VERSE: 2 CORINTHIANS 12:10

I take pleasure in infirmities, in reproaches, in needs, in persecutions, in distresses, for Christ's sake. For when I am weak, then I am strong.

You don't notice God's ability as much in your areas of capability. For example, let's say you are gifted with your speech and are able to strike up a conversation with anyone and set him at ease. It's not a challenge for you to enter a social setting in which you do not know many people. You have several new friends before you leave the room.

As a result, you often do not think of asking God to give you His strength and wisdom when you interact with people. He is the One who gifted you in that way, of course, but you are not as conscious of His involvement. But let's also imagine that you are not a good cook. No matter how closely you follow a recipe, something always goes wrong. People politely don't say much when they taste your dishes.

When you are asked to deliver a meal to a person with a long-term illness, a shiver of dread runs down your spine. You want to help, but you also know that this is not your area of expertise. In this situation, you would not hesitate to run to the Lord to ask for help.

That is the purpose of our weaknesses, whether they are physical, emotional, spiritual, or vocational. God wants you to run to Him; He desires your dependence because it reminds you of His loving care and sufficiency. The truth is, He wants you always to rely on His ability, and He lets you have weaknesses so you'll be sure to ask.

Father, help me learn to thank You for my weaknesses. They make me rely more on You.

(SEEKING HIS FACE)

April Showers

SCRIPTURE READING: 1 CORINTHIANS 13
KEY VERSE: ROMANS 8:35

Who shall separate us from the love of Christ? Shall tribulation, or distress, or persecution, or famine, or nakedness, or peril, or sword?

It has been said that April showers bring May flowers. If you've had April showers, don't be surprised if God awaits with a gorgeous bouquet of May flowers. It could come tomorrow. Perhaps it won't come until sometime later. But don't be discouraged.

Jesus Christ will bring His elegant bouquet, everything perfectly arranged. He may resolve your turmoil just as you prayed. He may resolve it in a different, much better way. Or He may choose not to resolve it at all. Still, you can be assured His thoughts are higher than your thoughts and His plan is perfection. He knows what is best for you.

Someday He will knock, holding your bouquet of May flowers. They will be your favorite color, beautiful and bright and wonderfully scented, a sweet savor unto the Lord.

Your April showers could be anything: trouble, sickness, sin. Perhaps they have left you feeling unworthy of God's attention and love. Understand that His is an unconditional love, and you have done nothing for which He won't forgive or restore you.

God's May flowers are a symbol of His eternal love that was demonstrated at the cross. He is able to cultivate them in season and out of season. They will have been planted, fertilized, and grown with the greatest of care by the ultimate Gardener. Jesus will bring the flowers after using your April showers to water them perfectly.

Lord, I thank You for the April showers that bring May flowers in my life.

(SEEKING HIS FACE)

Passing Along the Praise

SCRIPTURE READING: PSALM 92:1–5
KEY VERSE: PROVERBS 27:2

Let another man praise you, and not your own mouth;
A stranger, and not your own lips.

Praise sometimes can seem intoxicating. Although we all want to feel accepted and loved, our focus occasionally can be misdirected.

It is wise to worry less about what men think and to keep our hearts set on Jesus. The best praise we could ever hear is, "Well done, good and faithful servant," and there is nothing wrong with making that a motivating goal.

God loves you so much, so unconditionally, that no praise on earth can compare to the approval and acceptance His love brings. His Holy Spirit will warm you when you have done well and will convict you when you need improvement. Waiting for man's nod is waiting for second best.

The proper response to earthly praise is to take it for what it is: a momentary acknowledgment from someone to whom you ultimately do not have to answer. Say something like, "Thank you very much. You're very kind," or "Thank you. That is an encouragement to me." That is all you need to say. Meanwhile, inside your heart make it a practice to funnel the praise directly to God.

Even as the person is complimenting you, simply think, *Thank You, Father. You are so good to me.* You will pass along the praise to whom it really belongs instead of letting it settle in and ferment.

Thank You, Father. You are so good to me. I am passing along the praise.

(SEEKING HIS FACE)

The Lover of Your Soul

SCRIPTURE READING: HOSEA 11:1−9
KEY VERSES: LAMENTATIONS 3:22−23

Through the LORD's mercies we are not consumed,
Because His compassions fail not.
They are new every morning;
Great is Your faithfulness.

The nation of Israel grieved God's heart continually by chasing after other gods and withholding their devotion and adoration from Him. To provide the errant nation with a living illustration of His righteous grief and anger, God gave the prophet Hosea an unusual command.

He told him to wed a harlot and begin a family with her. Without questioning, Hosea obeyed and took the prostitute Gomer to be his wife. Though she wandered and continued in an unfaithful lifestyle, Hosea obeyed the Lord and did not cast her away. The book of Hosea contains God's words to the people of Israel as revealed through Hosea's dramatic example of steadfast love.

The moving poetry of this book also reveals the longing of God for uninterrupted intimacy with His people. Can you feel the agony of separation in these words?

How can I give you up, Ephraim?
How can I hand you over, Israel? . . .
My heart churns within Me,
My sympathy is stirred.
I will not execute the fierceness of My anger. (Hos. 11:8–9)

God longs for the same intimate relationship with you. He would do anything to get your love—and He did. In the most radical display of all time, He provided His Son, Jesus Christ, as the means to make such fellowship possible. God is the passionate and faithful Lover of your soul.

Dear God, thank You for displaying Your love by giving Your Son, Jesus Christ, to restore my fellowship with You.

(INTO HIS PRESENCE)

Bearing Burdens

SCRIPTURE READING: GALATIANS 6:1–5
KEY VERSE: GALATIANS 6:2

Bear one another's burdens, and so fulfill the law of Christ.

The casual chat over the fence turns serious. The routine conversation about teenage dilemmas leads into an emotional admission by your neighbor.

"My son is about to be suspended from school for something he said to his teacher. I am going to talk with the principal today and would appreciate your prayers. I'm pretty upset about the possible consequences."

You wince. You are not sure what to say. Since you both attend the same church, you assure him that you will pray for his son. He is grateful.

The next weekend you notice your neighbor working in his yard. You would like to walk over and inquire about his son's status, but you are apprehensive about how to approach the subject.

Bearing the burdens of a fellow Christian is a ticklish issue. We do not want to appear nosy and certainly don't desire to say something that could be misconstrued. For the most part, we keep at arm's length, opting for our basic generic prayer. This approach is far removed from the biblical notion of bearing one another's burdens, which entails a significant sharing of the spiritual and emotional weight.

Have you entered into this kind of burden bearing? Aren't there episodes when you desperately need this kind of assistance? God has a way to make it happen.

Dear Lord, make me sensitive to the needs of others. I want to be a burden bearer.

(INTO HIS PRESENCE)

Life at Its Best

SCRIPTURE READING: 2 SAMUEL 7
KEY VERSE: 2 SAMUEL 7:18

*King David went in and sat before the LORD; and he said: "Who am I,
O Lord GOD? And what is my house, that You have brought me this far?"*

David was stunned by Nathan's announcement. God was crafting a divine
covenant with the former shepherd that exceeded David's fondest hopes.
His household and the people of Israel would reap of God's extraordinary
beneficence.

The king and warrior was overcome with gratitude: "Who am I, O
Lord GOD, and what is my house, that You have brought me this far?" (2
Sam. 7:18 NASB).

In a different sense but of far grander import, God has formed a covenant with each believer in Christ. It is the new covenant of forgiveness of
sin and the gift of God's righteousness. The incredible blessings of life in
Christ, eternal and abundant, are inextricably bound up in this profound
new relationship with deity.

This new life in Christ—a new beginning, a new perspective, a new
destiny, a new power—is the only context to define life at its best. It does
not get any better than intimate fellowship with our Guide and Sustainer,
Jesus Christ.

Our response, when we ponder the immense weight of "every spiritual blessing in the heavenly places in Christ" (Eph. 1:3 NASB), should
mimic the awe and wonder of David. Who are we that God has chosen
us to know and enjoy Him?

Don't gauge your level of success or satisfaction by materialistic criteria. You live in a covenant relationship with the Savior and King.

*Father, who am I that You have chosen me to know and enjoy fellowship with
You? I am overwhelmed by the privilege of my covenant relationship with You.*

(ON HOLY GROUND)

Building Bridges to Others

SCRIPTURE READING: MATTHEW 25:31–46
KEY VERSE: MATTHEW 25:45

He will answer them, saying, "Assuredly, I say to you, inasmuch as you did not do it to one of the least of these, you did not do it to Me."

He invited a coworker to go backpacking with his church group. He knew the man wasn't saved, but that didn't matter. He was building a bridge of friendship. He knew once the relationship was established, God would provide an opportunity to share the gospel message.

She waited for God's timing before asking her neighbor to visit her church. For months the women had exchanged recipes and stories about their children. Even though the neighbor did not attend church regularly, she began to show interest in spiritual things. A year later she prayed to receive Christ as her Savior.

Many times God will allow you to tell of His saving grace immediately. Other times He may want you to wait before leading another down salvation's path. It's important to remember that God is in control of each situation. Waiting offers great opportunities for the construction of relational bridges by which His love and acceptance can travel.

Think of Jesus and the many ways He related to people. At one point the Pharisees tried to insult Him by calling Him a friend of tax collectors, but it didn't work. Matthew was a former tax collector and could testify to Jesus' love and acceptance of all.

Lord, help me to build bridges to others. Make me sensitive to Your timing.

(SEEKING·HIS FACE)

Experiencing God's Presence

SCRIPTURE READING: PHILIPPIANS 1:1–30
KEY VERSE: PHILIPPIANS 2:13

It is God who works in you both to will and to do for His good pleasure.

Eric Liddell, the athlete whose life inspired the movie *Chariots of Fire*, once remarked that he felt God's pleasure when he ran. Enjoying our relationship with Christ, or feeling His pleasure while we work and live, is not simple, but certainly possible.

You can enjoy God as you watch Him work through your circumstances (Phil. 1:12; 2:13). Troubling situations can overwhelm us for short or extended seasons. Handling them with an optimistic perspective that God is somehow at work for good is the way to live above difficulties. Trust Him to use your situations for eventual good, as foreboding as they may appear.

Enjoy God as you live under His grace, not law. You don't have to perform to please God. You already are pleasing to Him. Living under grace severs the legalistic mesh of "I must do this" or "I should do that" to gain God's acceptance. You are accepted by grace, and His favor is extended to you freely. God has forgiven you. Forgive yourself.

Enjoy God by learning to live one day at a time. Worrying about the future is a great thief and one that Scripture urges you to avoid by trusting God for your daily needs. Don't get ahead of Him. Accept His provision and daily challenges. Living under a load of anxiety rapidly depletes your joy and peace.

Christ came to give not only eternal life but abundant life as well. That is life to the fullest, and you can experience it!

Father, help me learn to live one day at a time, enjoy You, and experience Your pleasure.

(INTO HIS PRESENCE)

A Fresh Encounter with God

SCRIPTURE READING: ISAIAH 6:1–9
KEY VERSE: PSALM 139:3

You comprehend my path and my lying down, and are acquainted with all my ways.

Have you ever approached your devotional time with the idea of actually meeting with God? It is easy to reduce a quiet time to little more than a perfunctory Bible reading or study and a quick prayer if you forget the real purpose of setting aside that time.

God wants you to have a real and fresh encounter with Him each day. You don't generate this meeting through any formula or particular method; you simply come before Him with a humble, repentant heart and a genuine desire to know Him more.

You gain a sense of His presence. Isaiah knew immediately that he was in the presence of the living God. When the meeting ended, Isaiah walked away a changed man. You cannot experience God's presence and be the same; God's holiness is life changing, and through the Holy Spirit, He lives inside you forever.

You are never without His presence. You sense your unworthiness. As you come face-to-face with God's holiness, you realize your needy state. His awesome brightness eclipses even the angels in heaven.

The standard of His righteousness illuminates the sin in your life. You need to understand His forgiveness. The purpose of recognizing sin is not for condemnation and guilt, but for repentance. Christ forgives all your sins, but He wants you to confess them in order to experience His wondrous grace.

Precious Lord, I want to have a fresh encounter with You today. I want to know You better. Meet with me, and when our meeting ends, let me walk away changed.

(ON HOLY GROUND)

End of Construction

SCRIPTURE READING: EPHESIANS 4:1–3
KEY VERSE: EPHESIANS 4:1

I, therefore, the prisoner of the Lord, beseech you to walk worthy of the calling with which you were called.

In her book *Footprints of a Pilgrim*, Ruth Bell Graham provided a suggested epitaph for herself: "End of construction. Thank you for your patience."

Though humorous, her expression is based in truth. In Philippians 1:6, Paul placed his confidence in the fact that God will continue perfecting the good work He began in us until the day of Christ Jesus. This process of perfection began with sanctification—being set apart—and continues until the end of our lives. It is the period of progression between these two events that requires our full attention.

Once we have been born again, we should begin a life of progressive growth toward Christlikeness. We should seek to be conformed to the likeness of Christ in character, conversation, and conduct (Rom. 12:1–2). We should also progress by allowing Christ to live out His life through us (Eph. 4:1).

Of course, as Christians, we will all stumble and fall at times. However, as we understand more truth and apply it to our lives, we will be better equipped to avert the enemy's fiery darts.

Examine your life in terms of spiritual growth and progress. Have you increased in biblical knowledge since your conversion? Are you experiencing new levels of intimacy with God? If not, begin moving forward today—away from complacency and toward perfection in Christ.

I know, Lord, that I am under construction and that I will only be completed when I go to be with You. Help me to be a willing participant in this process of sanctification.

(PATHWAYS TO HIS PRESENCE)

God in Your Boat

SCRIPTURE READING: ROMANS 5:1–5
KEY VERSE: ISAIAH 51:12

I, even I, am He who comforts you.
Who are you that you should be afraid
Of a man who will die,
And of the son of a man who will be made like grass?

There is no escaping it. Trouble comes at some point to everyone, but there also is a victory in suffering that cannot be overlooked. Joni Eareckson Tada explains, "I believe those who suffer the greatest on earth have the greatest confidence of sharing in His highest glory. This is a wonderful inspiration to those who are hurting. Amy Carmichael wrote something I will never forget: 'We will have all of eternity to celebrate the victories, but only a few hours before sunset in which to win them.'"

Some of our greatest triumphs come as a result of being willing to weather the storms of life. When we commit ourselves to trusting Jesus regardless of the outcome, God's power is released in mighty ways. The disciples did not forget what it was like to face the gale-force winds of the Sea of Galilee. Neither did they forget the power of the hush that came as a result of Christ's command to the wind and the sea.

The faith they gained in troubled times could not be imitated or duplicated. It became a part of their personal testimony to a great and wondrous God. Jesus saves those who place their trust in Him.

Are you facing something much greater than your ability to handle? Turn your fear and sorrow over to Jesus. Allow Him to take your hurt and disappointment. When He is in your boat, there is no need to worry.

Father, I turn every fear and sorrow over to You today. Take my hurt and disappointment. I know there is no need to worry because You are in my boat!

(INTO HIS PRESENCE)

A Living Message

SCRIPTURE READING: PHILIPPIANS 1:1–6
KEY VERSE: PHILIPPIANS 1:6

Being confident of this very thing, that He who has begun a good work in you will complete it until the day of Jesus Christ.

As the saying goes, "There is only one you." You are a living message for Christ in a one-of-a-kind way that no one else can duplicate. Message building is a lifelong process, and the Lord wants you to participate actively in developing His purpose for you in many ways:

Read and study the Scriptures. Time in God's Word is essential for growth. As you learn who God is and what He has done, He unfolds His truth in a personal way through the Holy Spirit and gives you wisdom and understanding for everyday life.

Realize God's ultimate goal. While His specific plans for you are custom made, His goal for every believer is the same—to conform us to the likeness of His Son—so your words and actions are reflections of Jesus' character.

Review God's pattern of operation. Ask, "How has He gotten my attention before? What is He teaching me in this present situation?" Read and study the many character portraits in the Scriptures.

Reach out to serve others. Meeting the needs of others and becoming involved in their lives challenge you to trust the Lord to provide the resources. Your faith will grow as He uses you to bless others.

Dear Lord Jesus, make me a living message of Your love.

(SEEKING HIS FACE)

The Growth Process

SCRIPTURE READING: PHILIPPIANS 3:7–16
KEY VERSES: PHILIPPIANS 3:13–14

Brethren, I do not count myself to have apprehended; but one thing I do, forgetting those things which are behind and reaching forward to those things which are ahead, I press toward the goal for the prize of the upward call of God in Christ Jesus.

Penelope Stokes acknowledges in *Grace Under Pressure*:

Just as physical growth takes many years and much struggle, spiritual maturity comes hard as well. It takes time to grow—time to learn and mature—and the process isn't as simple in reality as it looks on paper. When we strive against the time necessary for our development, we live in frustration. But when we can relax in God's timetable for our growth, depending upon His grace for the work His Spirit wants to do in our lives, we can experience the joy and wonder of growth, change, and fruitfulness.

Do you remember as a child being anxious to grow up? It seemed forever until that certain birthday when you would be able to do more things and be treated like a grown-up. Of course, by the time you got there, that age did not seem so old.

Such longings are typical in the Christian life as well, especially when you look at the example of a mature believer whom you admire. It's okay to look forward to where God is taking your life, as long as you understand that there are no shortcuts.

Paul expressed his balanced desire for maturity this way: "Brethren, I do not regard myself as having laid hold of it yet; but one thing I do: forgetting what lies behind and reaching forward to what lies ahead, I press on toward the goal" (Phil. 3:13–14 NASB).

Lord Jesus, the growth process often seems long. Spiritual maturity isn't simple. Help me forget the past and press toward the goal You have set for me.

(ON HOLY GROUND)

Discovering Your True Identity

SCRIPTURE READING: EPHESIANS 2:8–10
KEY VERSE: PSALM 139:14

I will praise You, for I am fearfully and wonderfully made;
Marvelous are Your works,
And that my soul knows very well.

The alarm clock rings. Another day awaits. The early morning news brings word of the newest economic summit, the nominees for this year's Nobel Peace Prize, and a report on the national gathering of governors.

Meanwhile, the only financial summit you have is a monthly talk with your spouse to reconcile the checkbook. The only peace you are interested in is stopping the constant bickering between your teenagers. And the only gathering of important people you attended was the recent family reunion.

You can feel small and insignificant in a world of billions of people, millions of worthwhile developments, and thousands of news clips of notable happenings that make your contribution seem almost meaningless.

Although God cares about financial stability, world peace, and social justice, He has one great thing on His mind today—you. You are His workmanship, His masterpiece. There is no one else like you, and God cares for you with infinite watchfulness. He knows exactly how many hairs came out in your brush this morning. Your checkbook matters as much as the federal budget, harmony in your home as much as harmony among nations.

I am Your workmanship! I am Your masterpiece. There is no one else like
me, Lord, and You care for me with infinite watchfulness.

(INTO HIS PRESENCE)

Nothing Is Impossible with God

SCRIPTURE READING: MATTHEW 28:16–20
KEY VERSE: MATTHEW 28:19

Go therefore and make disciples of all the nations, baptizing them in the name of the Father and of the Son and of the Holy Spirit.

The idea that nothing is impossible for God is very comforting. Just think about the parting of the Red Sea, the tearing down of the walls of Jericho, and the resurrection—great overtures that God has accomplished.

However, when it comes to God doing something miraculous through you, you may have doubts. You wonder if God is interested in using you for a great work. Yet when God formed you, He did so with a very special design in mind. And Jesus spoke about His plans in Matthew 28:19 when He told His disciples to make disciples of the whole world. To Jesus, no nation or tribe is excluded from the gospel. God's desire is for everyone to enter the kingdom of heaven through the blood of His precious Son.

Henry Ford said, "I'm looking for a lot of men with an infinite capacity for not knowing what can't be done." That's what God is looking for too. He seeks believers who know that nothing is impossible with God. He wants disciples who willingly follow with full trust in the Savior. There are no boundaries for what God wants us to do and what He wants us to accomplish.

Lord, give me vision without boundaries. Work in and through me to accomplish Your will.

(PATHWAYS TO HIS PRESENCE)

The Light of Life

SCRIPTURE READING: JOHN 1:1–13
KEY VERSE: EPHESIANS 5:8

For you were once darkness, but now you are light in the Lord. Walk as children of light.

Lamps were among the most valued possessions in Israelite homes. Light was a symbol of life, and a good lamp provided light for every household function. In fact, an Israelite woman checked her lamp all through the night, adding more oil or fixing the wick, to make sure the light stayed strong and sent the message "all is well."

Jesus wants our lives to be like a good lamp, sending out the daily signal that all is well in our relationship with Him. When people see you, they should see the light of Christ and give glory to God.

Can those around you see Jesus in the way you behave and the way you talk? Does your life communicate His positive truth, or do you send negative statements of criticism or discouragement? Do your actions make someone want to know more about your Lord?

Perhaps the statement your life is making right now is not what it should be. Maybe you are discouraged by inconsistency or feelings of inadequacy. Remember that Jesus gives you the strength and wisdom you need because He is the Light of life. God promises to continue building His truth into your life day by day so that your character and conduct reflect His distinguishing presence.

Lord, let others see Your light in me and give glory to You. Let my character and conduct reflect Your presence.

(SEEKING HIS FACE)

Don't Believe a Lie

SCRIPTURE READING: COLOSSIANS 3:1–5
KEY VERSE: MATTHEW 16:23

He turned and said to Peter, "Get behind Me, Satan! You are an offense to Me, for you are not mindful of the things of God, but the things of men."

Paul reminded the Corinthians of their position in Christ—holy, righteous, and blameless—because he knew their thinking must change before their behavior could be altered.

Here is where many fail to overcome unwanted habits. We try to change our actions without conforming our thinking to God's truth.

We inevitably act the way we perceive ourselves. If we feel like unworthy sinners, then we will usually act like them—guilt-ridden, erratic, and unhappy. Satan points his dirty finger at our actions and accuses us as vile sinners until we finally believe him.

Don't believe a lie! Don't yield to the father of lies and the accuser of the brethren, who has no truth in him.

This is the truth: you are a saint who occasionally sins. However, nothing you did yesterday, today, or tomorrow can change your position in Christ. When you do sin, even habitually, you are not acting according to your true desires or identity as God's holy one. You are acting inconsistently with your new nature in Christ.

God says you are a saint now that you have received Christ. That is why you can experience victory over all sin. Christ is in you. He will make you more than a conqueror as you know the truth that sets you free.

Dear Lord, help me to walk in the victory that is mine. Make me more than a conqueror over sin.

(INTO HIS PRESENCE)

An Eternal Perspective

SCRIPTURE READING: MATTHEW 21:18–22
KEY VERSE: MATTHEW 21:21

Jesus answered and said to them, "Assuredly, I say to you, if you have faith and do not doubt, you will not only do what was done to the fig tree, but also if you say to this mountain, 'Be removed and be cast into the sea,' it will be done."

Some of the most noble and valiant events in history were born out of hearts that had an eternal perspective.

George Washington, renowned Revolutionary War general and first president of the United States, demonstrated such a heart. From his earliest days, he was taught by his mother to put God first in his life. When he accepted a position of leadership in the war, he had no idea how much his faith would be put to the test.

One of the most precious documents Washington ever produced as a young man was a small prayer diary that he titled "Daily Sacrifice." Peter Marshall and David Manuel recount Washington's prayer in *The Light and the Glory*:

O most glorious God . . . I acknowledge and confess my faults; in the weak and imperfect performance of the duties of this day. . . . O God, who art rich in mercy and plenteous in redemption, mark not, I beseech Thee, what I have done amiss. . . . Cover my sins with the absolute obedience of Thy dear Son . . . the sacrifice of Jesus Christ offered upon the cross for me.

Washington made a habit of private prayer, and his faith inspired his men in the most brutal conditions. He is remembered for his great deeds, certainly, but it is his faith that made his impact lasting. Only when your focus is on the eternal will your work have eternal merit.

Father, like George Washington, I confess that I am often weak and imperfect. I praise You for Your mercy in covering my sinfulness with the blood of Jesus.

(PATHWAYS TO HIS PRESENCE)

Fruit Producing

SCRIPTURE READING: JOHN 15:1–8
KEY VERSE: JOHN 15:5

I am the vine, you are the branches. He who abides in Me, and I in him, bears much fruit; for without Me you can do nothing.

What kinds of sounds do you hear in a grape arbor or other fruit orchard? You can probably hear birds chirping, the wind rustling through leaves, and many other usual outdoor sounds.

You do not hear the sounds of the vines or trees groaning and straining. The plants are not laboring to produce their fruit; the fruit just comes out of the branches naturally as a part of the growing process. The vine does not have to concentrate on producing grapes. When the vine is healthy and has all the water and nutrients it needs, the grapes come forth.

Jesus compared your life to the branches on a grapevine. He said, "I am the vine, you are the branches; he who abides in Me and I in him, he bears much fruit, for apart from Me you can do nothing" (John 15:5 NASB).

The secret to fruit producing is as basic for you as it is for a real grapevine: stay attached to the Vine and focus all of your energy and attention to simply being there, or abiding, in Christ. Worship Him, praise Him, meditate on His words, seek solitude in Him, and let yourself be absorbed into His purposes.

Through the power of the Holy Spirit, who bears testimony that you are attached to the Vine, your "grapes" will grow. Your fruit is a direct reflection of the quality of your relationship with Christ.

Precious Lord, help me give up groaning and straining and simply learn to abide. I'm tired of trying to do it in myself. Produce Your fruit in me.

(ON HOLY GROUND)

Avenues of Hope

SCRIPTURE READING: PSALM 103:1–22
KEY VERSE: PSALM 103:6

The LORD executes righteousness
And justice for all who are oppressed.

After Peter Marshall's death, three well-meaning friends approached his wife, Catherine, with the news that she had very little money to live on. She listened to their advice but felt something was missing from their counsel. In *The Best of Catherine Marshall* she recalls the experience:

> Alone in my room later, I stared out the window into the moonlight shining on swaying treetops. . . . Suddenly, standing there at the window, I knew what the missing factor was.
>
> My three friends who saw my many inadequacies, who had meant to be so kind, had reckoned without God. I remember how often Peter had faced this same attitude with his church officers. He would come home from a trustees' meeting sad and grim. "Catherine, no matter what's presented for their approval, their litany is always the same: 'But Dr. Marshall, where is the money coming from?' Where's their faith in God?"
>
> Either God was with me—"I am that I am," a fact more real than any figures or graphs—or He was not. If He was there, then reckoning without Him was certainly not being "realistic." In fact, it could be the most hazardous miscalculation of all.

Catherine Marshall discovered one of the purest truths of the Christian life: God is in control of all things. He holds our futures within His omniscient hand. Impossibilities are grand avenues of hope to Him.

Father, help me realize that my impossibilities are avenues of hope. I am assured that You hold my future in Your omniscient hand.

(PATHWAYS TO HIS PRESENCE)

Unshakable Peace

SCRIPTURE READING: PHILIPPIANS 4:5–7
KEY VERSE: JOHN 14:27

*Peace I leave with you, My peace I give to you; not as the world gives do
I give to you. Let not your heart be troubled, neither let it be afraid.*

Charles Spurgeon. Martin Luther. John Wesley. Prominent names of
Christendom, yet not without great personal struggles.

Spurgeon, known for his compelling sermons at the Metropolitan
Tabernacle, battled recurring seasons of depression throughout his splen-
did ministry.

Luther, whose emphasis on justification by faith alone shattered cen-
turies of false ideology, struggled with numerous physical afflictions.

Wesley, whose preaching filled the towns and villages of colonial
America, endured a difficult marriage that created an unstable family life
at best.

Their legacies, however, are noble and their achievements memorable.
Despite their problems, the peace of God was rooted deeply in their spirits, serving as both rudder and stabilizer for their ministry and lives.

It is perfectly normal to have your cage rattled by strained relationships, financial tremors, or emotional surges. Jesus told us to expect such
predicaments. But because you have Christ, you have unshakable peace in
your innermost being. You can wade through dilemmas without yielding
to irrational fears or anxiety. Keep Him at the center of your life, and you
will reflect the peace of Christ.

*Thank You, Lord, that Your unshakable peace will sustain me throughout
the challenges of this day.*

(INTO HIS PRESENCE)

A Vessel of Love

SCRIPTURE READING: 1 TIMOTHY 2:1–8
KEY VERSE: 2 TIMOTHY 4:2

*Preach the word! Be ready in season and out of season. Convince, rebuke,
exhort, with all longsuffering and teaching.*

Paul's foremost desire was that all men and women would come to know
Jesus Christ as Savior and Lord. From the first day he taught the truth of
the gospel until his death in Rome, Paul was driven by one message: the
salvation of the cross. He was consumed by God's love, and he wanted
others to experience it in a personal and abiding way.

Paul had a tremendous ability to communicate clearly across social,
philosophical, and economic lines. He met people on their own turf and
presented the gospel shamelessly. He was fearless in his approach to the
gospel message because his own life had been radically changed. Once a
persecutor of Christians, he became a missionary for Jesus Christ.

He wasn't repulsed by sinful men; he was drawn to them out of compassion, as Christ was to the people of His day. For Paul, each encounter
was an opportunity to tell someone about Jesus Christ and the forgiveness
that was his if only the person would believe in God's Son.

We live in a world besieged by sin and darkness where people lack
identity and hope. Ask God to help you understand the desperate needs
of our society and its people and to use you as a vessel of His love.

*Dear God, please give me an understanding of the desperate needs of society,
and then use me as a vessel of Your love.*

(SEEKING HIS FACE)

God's Best for Your Life

SCRIPTURE READING: EPHESIANS 1:3–6
KEY VERSE: EPHESIANS 1:3

*Blessed be the God and Father of our Lord Jesus Christ, who has
blessed us with every spiritual blessing in the heavenly places in Christ.*

The discovery of King Tut's tomb is considered one of the richest in history. However, archaeologists had no idea what waited for them beyond the first chamber; robbers had earlier plundered it. Yet a closer examination revealed an undisturbed sepulchral chamber and treasure room.

Excavators found priceless gold and silver items along with precious stones. There was also an abundance of rings and bracelets so ingenious and perfect in design that even a magnifying glass could not reveal the soldered joints.

With gold, silver, and priceless jewelry surrounding them, archaeologists could not help wondering why earlier intruders had stopped at the outer chamber. Did they not realize they had entered the burial chamber of a king?

As puzzling as this may seem, many of us do the same thing in our Christian walk. We plunder the outer chamber of God's blessings, never realizing there is an entire throne room waiting for us if only we would seek Him above all else.

Don't allow yourself to be robbed of God's best for your life. Ask Him to make you aware of the blessings He has for you. As you seek His will, submit all that you are to all that He is; and His wealth of eternal blessings will be yours.

*I don't want to be robbed of Your best, God. Make me aware of the blessings
You have for me. I submit all that I am to all that You are.*

(INTO HIS PRESENCE)

The Worth of Weakness

SCRIPTURE READING: 2 CORINTHIANS 12:1–10
KEY VERSES: 2 CORINTHIANS 12:9–10

He said to me, "My grace is sufficient for you, for My strength is made perfect in weakness." Therefore most gladly I will rather boast in my infirmities, that the power of Christ may rest upon me. Therefore I take pleasure in infirmities, in reproaches, in needs, in persecutions, in distresses, for Christ's sake. For when I am weak, then I am strong.

In our society, physical strength is a hallmark of success and power. It doesn't take long to figure out the messages behind countless advertisements for fitness centers, health clubs, and exercise equipment.

Of course, staying in shape and taking good care of your body are worthy, healthful goals with the right perspective (1 Tim. 4:8). But the underlying assumption of people who value physical training as an ideal in itself is that weakness is shameful. For them, physical weakness represents who you are as a person, pathetic and helpless and unattractive.

In spiritual terms, weakness carries a far different message. It says, "I have a problem, and I need a Savior who can fix it." Weakness becomes an opportunity for God to demonstrate His power on your behalf: "'My [God's] grace is sufficient for you, for power is perfected in weakness.' Most gladly, therefore, I [Paul] will rather boast about my weaknesses, that the power of Christ may dwell in me. Therefore I am well content with weaknesses, with insults, with distresses, with persecutions, with difficulties, for Christ's sake; for when I am weak, then I am strong" (2 Cor. 12:9–10 NASB).

Do weaknesses prompt you to hide or attempt to make the changes by yourself? They should be your signal to ask the Lord for the help that only He can give.

Precious Lord, there is intrinsic value in weakness. Help me embrace it, realizing that therein lie dormant strength and unlimited potential for greatness.

(ON HOLY GROUND)

The True Light

SCRIPTURE READING: JOHN 14:21–23

KEY VERSE: JOHN 1:9

That was the true Light which gives light to every man who comes into the world.

Too many people go to church and come home without discovering the personal love of Jesus Christ. Some may even be baptized and still not know the intimate love of the Savior. They never develop a one-on-one relationship with the Lover of their souls. God has called us to worship Him, but even before this He calls us to intimate fellowship with Him. In the garden of Eden He walked in the cool of the day with Adam and Eve. Throughout history, He has continued to reach out to mankind.

His greatest display of love and devotion comes to us through the life of Jesus Christ. However, as A. W. Tozer wrote in *The Pursuit of God,* "To most . . . God is an inference, not a reality. He is a deduction from evidence which they consider adequate, but He remains personally unknown to the individual."

The responsibility of relationship is not all God's. We must have a desire to know Him, walk with Him, and enjoy His company. He habitually reveals Himself to us, but are we seeking His presence?

"God formed us for His pleasure," wrote Tozer, "and so formed us so that we . . . can, in divine communion, enjoy the sweet and mysterious mingling of kindred personalities. He meant us to see Him and live with Him and draw our life from His smile." If we will cultivate our relationship with Him, we can know "the true Light which gives light to every man" (John 1:9).

Lord, give me the desire to know You better, walk with You, and enjoy Your company. Reveal Yourself to me as I wait in Your presence.

(SEEKING HIS FACE)

A Personal Invitation

SCRIPTURE READING: MATTHEW 11:28–30
KEY VERSE: PSALM 116:7

Return to your rest, O my soul,
For the LORD has dealt bountifully with you.

It marked a turning point in Jesus' ministry. He preached to great crowds, His words convicting and startling. He healed many, to their wonder and amazement. Yet up to that point, only the disciples had experienced personal intimacy with the Savior. Following a stinging rebuke to those who refused His message, Jesus issued a compassionate invitation: "Come to Me, all you who labor and are heavy laden, and I will give you rest" (Matt. 11:28).

"I'm here," Jesus in essence said to His listeners, "to lift the burdens of life from your shoulders. I'll take them on Me if you will let Me."

If you are oppressed and bent under the accumulation of too many demands and concerns, Jesus stands ready to lighten your load. If you are exhausted from juggling bills, kids, work, and other pressing problems, Jesus can restore your weary spirit.

He invites you to come to Him. There are no strings attached, no restrictions, no fine print. He won't condemn you for past failures. His arms are open wide to take you as you are and give you the help you need.

What a relief! What a Savior! Accept His personal invitation, and get out of the pressure cooker and into His rest. In the shadow of His wings you will find unconditional love and acceptance. Whatever you are facing, let the Savior face it with you.

I accept Your invitation, Lord. I enter into Your rest and hide myself in the shadow of Your wings.

(INTO HIS PRESENCE)

Things Not Shaken

SCRIPTURE READING: HEBREWS 12:25–29
KEY VERSE: JOHN 14:8

Philip said to Him, "Lord, show us the Father, and it is sufficient for us."

The *Titanic* was deemed unsinkable, invincible. Yet today it lies at the bottom of the ocean. Its tragic demise is a reminder that no matter how invincible we perceive things to be, nothing on this earth is beyond destruction. Only God and His Word are indestructible.

Jesus told His disciples that He would not leave them as orphans (John 14:18). However, after His arrest they began to doubt His Word to them. By the time He was crucified, their doubts had turned to fear. When Jesus was alive, it was easy to believe that He was the Messiah. However, two days after His death, with their prayers seemingly unanswered, they began to doubt, and their faith sank.

We do the same thing. We place our faith in Christ and then, through a turn of events or sorrows, we find ourselves crying out to God. We also doubt His promises to us and wonder why He allows adversity to touch our hearts. But be assured—even when we feel shaken, God is not. He is our firm, immovable anchor of hope.

Have you placed your faith in something that is unshakable? Or have you given your hopes and dreams to something that will sink whenever the slightest adversity strikes? Only God is unshakable. When your heart is anchored to His, no storm or adversity can harm you.

Lord, when doubt smolders, do not let me fan it into flames of fear. I choose to believe in the indestructible nature of Your person and Your word.

(PATHWAYS TO HIS PRESENCE)

The Peace of God

SCRIPTURE READING: EPHESIANS 2:14–16
KEY VERSE: I PETER 5:7

[Cast] all your care upon Him, for He cares for you.

When we lose our perspective of God's overriding, unceasing care of us, we usually lose our sense of God's peace as well.

Writing to a church under intense strain, Peter closed his first letter by telling them to give their troubles to God because "He cares for you."

What a relief of pressure! What troubles me and upsets my spiritual well-being, even the slightest irritant, matters to God. He is so concerned that He invites me to give Him every care.

Cast your burdens on Him in prayer. Tell God what bothers you, what robs your joy and peace, and then really believe that He has heard you and will answer. If you truly trust Him to handle the problem, then experiencing His peace is a supernatural result. The situation is in God's hands. He is in control despite appearances. He is able to bring about a solution, whenever and however He chooses.

When you reach that point, the peace of God is yours. The storms may brew, but God is very concerned about you and has taken your cares upon Himself. When the pressure mounts, cast every burden on Him. All is in His care, and that will settle your soul as no other thought.

Father, when the pressures mount today, help me remember that You have taken all my cares upon Yourself. I cast my burdens on You, knowing that everything is in Your care.

(INTO HIS PRESENCE)

Be Still and Listen

SCRIPTURE READING: GALATIANS 5:16–23
KEY VERSE: GALATIANS 5:16

*I say then: Walk in the Spirit, and you shall not fulfill the lust of
the flesh.*

Paul told us that if we walk by the Spirit, we will not carry out the deeds
of the flesh (Gal. 5:16). Many times this is not an easy task. The only way
you can walk in the Spirit is to be conscious of God's indwelling presence
and your lack of ability.

The moment you try to live like Christ is usually the time you face
difficulty. This happens because you set your focus on becoming something instead of allowing Christ to live His life through you. There will be
times of failure in your life. These times are the very moments God uses
to instruct you in great ways.

However, this can happen only if you are open to listening to the
Spirit's voice. There can be no distraction inside you—no desire to get it
right or work things out on your own. Let Jesus show you the way.

Submitting yourself to God's will opens the way for spiritual discernment. So many people try this or that in an effort to grow spiritually when
all they really need to do is to learn how to sit before the Lord and be still in
their spirits. Today when irritating thoughts come or something goes awry,
allow the new you—the part of you that is controlled by God's Spirit—to
take control of the situation.

Be still, if only for a moment, and listen for His voice. He will provide
the wisdom, patience, guidance, and love you need to carry on in this life.

Master, because You live inside me, I have new and glorious freedom.
Remove the distractions. Still my restless heart. Let the new me emerge.

(ON HOLY GROUND)

Trusting God

SCRIPTURE READING: ROMANS 4:16–21
KEY VERSE: HEBREWS 11:3

By faith we understand that the worlds were framed by the word of God, so that the things which are seen were not made of things which are visible.

A young woman was babysitting her four-year-old niece. When the pair stepped outside to look at a backyard playset, they managed to lock themselves out of the house. There were no spare keys hidden on the property, and the little girl's parents wouldn't be home for quite some time.

After trying all the doors one more time and looking in vain for an open window, the young adult finally remembered to ask her heavenly Father for help.

This story is simple and childlike. Did God answer? Yes, and while He did not send a miracle key to mysteriously open the door, He provided a lesson of faith. He showed the young woman and her niece that His provision sometimes comes in unexpected packages. How? God gave her peace about breaking a window to get inside.

"Well," you say, "that wasn't much of a provision." But it was! God provided something much more comforting than the material evidence of His power. He provided peace and the assurance that He was in control. We need a God like this, Someone who brings hope and calm to our storm-driven lives. Prayer may not always be the first thing we think of in times of emergency, but it is our strongest source of hope. Simply put, God hears when we call to Him.

Trust Him and you will be amazed at the peace He brings to your heart and life.

Help me to trust You, Lord. Give me faith in the face of difficult circumstances.

(INTO HIS PRESENCE)

Free to Rejoice

Scripture Reading: John 15:13–15
Key Verse: Psalm 139:13

For You formed my inward parts; You covered me in my mother's womb.

How often do you stop to thank God for your freedom? Whether or not you live in a free country—even if you are reading this message from inside a jail cell—if you have trusted Jesus Christ as your Savior, you are the recipient of the greatest kind of freedom. It is freedom from eternal suffering and death.

The Bible tells us that no one is worthy of this gift. We have all sinned and fallen short of God's likeness (Rom. 3:23). But Jesus' death on the cross removed our collective death penalty once and for all. Therefore, you are now secure in Him.

Why did God give you this great gift? It is because He has something wonderful in mind for your life (Jer. 29:11). He wants you to accomplish great things for His kingdom and to share the joy of your faith with others (Matt. 28:18–20). God designed you for a purpose when He formed you in your mother's womb (Ps. 139:13).

If you are struggling with feelings of doubt, regret, or depression surrounding something in your past, receive this message of hope today: God sent His Son to die for you so that you may have freedom from the bonds of sin. You are forgiven because of His great love.

Before you end your quiet time today, read John 15:13–15. In it, Jesus explains that He made so great a sacrifice because He loves us so much. No longer are we slaves to sin, but we are instead free to rejoice in the love of our Savior and Friend, Jesus Christ.

Lord, I have been created by design to walk in the way of freedom. I praise You for forgiving me and setting my feet free to follow You.

(PATHWAYS TO HIS PRESENCE)

A Heart of True Praise

SCRIPTURE READING: JOHN 12:1–8
KEY VERSE: PSALM 68:4

Sing to God, sing praises to His name;
Extol Him who rides on the clouds,
By His name YAH,
And rejoice before Him.

Pouring perfume on Jesus' feet may seem an awkward or overly emotional act to some of us today, but it was a pure expression of the love and worship in Mary's heart. Cultures and traditions may change through the years, but God always wants you to pour out your heart to Him in praise and adoration.

True praise longs to give something of value. Have you ever had a close and intimate relationship with another person? It was the natural inclination of your emotions to want to give something of great personal worth to that individual. It didn't have to be something that cost a lot either. In the same way, God wants you to give yourself to Him.

True praise is not inhibited by the attitudes of others. Mary wasn't concerned about how many people were watching or what they thought. And some around her certainly had strongly negative opinions. Jesus recognized the purity of her gesture. If you're concerned about possible condemnation from others, ask God to help you focus on Him alone.

True praise moves you to love God for who He is. The book of Psalms is filled with descriptions of God's eternal character and unchanging righteousness as the basis for praise. When you praise Him for His attributes, you put your attention on His worthiness, and that's the very purpose of your worship.

God, I worship You for who You are. You are worthy of my praise.

(SEEKING HIS FACE)

How to Live Your Life

SCRIPTURE READING: 2 CORINTHIANS 5:14–17
KEY VERSE: 2 CORINTHIANS 5:17

If anyone is in Christ, he is a new creation; old things have passed away; behold, all things have become new.

The woman explained how she had witnessed her love for Christ to another friend over a period of several years: "I tried not to preach to my friend. Instead, I sought to 'live out' God's love by loving this person unconditionally. I wondered if what I had said and lived made a difference. Then one day, my friend came to me and thanked me for loving her and telling her that Jesus loves her too."

The unconditional love of God changes hearts and people, though we may not see the immediate results. Jesus was serious about sin, but His first concern always was the sinner. He wanted those who came to Him to understand one thing: God loves them.

If we live for ourselves, the fruit of our labor will be obvious: a need to be noticed first, receive credit for what we do, and a continual striving for a material reward. We could summarize the self-centered life with four words: convenience, comfort, covetousness, and compromise.

Servanthood, personal sacrifice, and a genuine love for others mark the Christ-centered life. Instead of asking what you can get out of this situation, job, or friendship, ask, "Lord, how can You use me to bring glory to You in this particular situation? Whom can You love through me?" Pray that you will live your life in such a way that men and women will see your good deeds and glorify your Father in heaven.

Lord, I know that the Christ-centered life is the only effective life. Use me. Love through me. Let my life bring You glory today and in the days to come.

(PATHWAYS TO HIS PRESENCE)

When the Odds Are Against You

SCRIPTURE READING: ISAIAH 61:1–7
KEY VERSE: ISAIAH 61:3

*To console those who mourn in Zion, to give them beauty for ashes, the
oil of joy for mourning, the garment of praise for the spirit of heaviness;
that they may be called trees of righteousness, the planting of the LORD,
that He may be glorified.*

For years God had given him a dream to start a school where men and
women could be trained for Christian service. In 1907, he invested the
culmination of his prayers and life savings into what had been a rambling
old hotel overlooking a spring-fed lake in northeast Georgia.

With enrollment increasing, plans for expansion were underway.
Then it happened—the test of faith. Cinders in one of the stone fire-
places found their way through the mortar and onto the aging wood.
Within moments the two-story structure was ablaze, and within an hour
the dream reduced to rubble.

The next day as he poked through the smoldering ashes, Dr. R. A.
Forrest came upon what was left of his books. He later wrote, "I broke
down and wept like a baby. Had I misunderstood God?" Suddenly God's
Word broke through: "I will give you beauty for ashes" (Isa. 61:3). And He
did. Today, Toccoa Falls College remains a testimony to God's promises.

When the odds are against you and everything around you shouts:
"Give up! Quit! It'll never work!" remember, God is sovereign. He has a
plan for your life, and He has promised to bring it to completion.

*Lord, when the odds are against me, help me to remember that You have a
plan for my life.*

(SEEKING HIS FACE)

Life Is an Adventure

SCRIPTURE READING: ACTS 8:26–40
KEY VERSE: PSALM 37:23

The steps of a good man are ordered by the LORD, and He delights in his way.

Philip had no way of knowing what was about to happen. All he knew was that God told him to go down the road from Jerusalem to Gaza, and he obeyed without a single question. Imagine his amazement when he found an Ethiopian eunuch, riding in his chariot and reading a passage from the book of Isaiah. In the forefront of the Ethiopian's mind was an unanswered question—who was the Lamb of whom the prophet spoke?

God put the two men on that path together for a special reason. Philip knew the gospel, and the Ethiopian was ready to receive it. Then the two experienced the wonders of God's perfect plan.

It has been said that there is no such thing as coincidence, just God's plan unfolding in unexpected ways. Certainly that is true in the lives of believers. Have you been a part of a miracle of God's timing? Maybe you ran out of gas by the side of the road and someone came along with a gas can before you had to seek help. Maybe it was an unanticipated meeting with an old friend, who really needed your encouragement in the Lord.

When you understand that God's ways are perfect and that He is continually working, you will begin to see your life as the adventure that it is. You may not know exactly what's ahead or when change will occur, but you can know that every experience is from Him.

Dear Lord, Your way is perfect. Thank You for being continually at work in me. I may not know what is ahead or what changes will come, but I rejoice in the confidence that each experience is from You.

(ON HOLY GROUND)

He Never Slumbers

SCRIPTURE READING: ACTS 17:22–31
KEY VERSE: PSALM 121:3

He will not allow your foot to be moved;
He who keeps you will not slumber.

At no time are you outside the presence of God. The apostle Paul made that clear while speaking to the philosophers on Mars Hill. Near there they had erected an altar to the "unknown god" (Acts 17:23).

The Athenians were zealous in their pagan worship and wanted to make sure no god was overlooked. Thus, they made a place of worship to the God who remained unknown. Realizing they would not understand the basis of Christianity, Paul shifted his delivery of the gospel to include this peculiarity of their pagan beliefs. He explained that the true God, the one they deemed as "unknown," was really the Creator of all things.

The Lord is a personal God, not limited by time or space, One who inhabits the hearts of all who believe in Him. Therefore, no temple or building can contain His presence because He is eternally present throughout the universe.

Have you ever thought that God is with you in all you do and say throughout the day? He is not just present in the morning when you awake. He is with you in the grocery store, in the doctor's office, at work, even at play. No matter where you go, God goes with you. Praise Him for His care over your life, for His devotion that never slumbers.

Father, thank You for Your constant care over me. Your devotion never slumbers. You are with me every moment of each day.

(INTO HIS PRESENCE)

The Victory Is Near

SCRIPTURE READING: PSALM 23
KEY VERSE: PSALM 23:4

*Yea, though I walk through the valley of the shadow of death, I will fear
no evil; for You are with me; Your rod and Your staff, they comfort me.*

The above Scripture reading is a favorite. It also is one that children can
easily learn. Many who memorize Psalm 23 early in life find themselves
repeating it later, especially when trouble arises. The most outstanding
feature of this psalm is the sense of trust and safety it brings.

David spent much of his young life as a shepherd in his father's field.
There he encountered all kinds of dangers. His love and devotion to God
stabilized his heart. When the temptation to become fearful arose, David
focused on God's sovereign ability to protect and keep him.

Are you facing a particularly difficult situation? Maybe there has
been a change in your home or work environment. Perhaps someone has
attacked your personal reputation, and it seems that no amount of words
or explanation can change his opinion.

What do you do when things go wrong or turn out badly? How do
you cope when your loved one dies or leaves home? How do you handle
the teenager whose course in life seems set on destruction?

There is only one way. It may sound simple or trite, but it works
each and every time. Lay down your expectations. Be still in your heart
and quiet in your spirit, and listen for God's word to you. Trust Him as
David did to lead you through the valley and back out into the light of
His eternal hope. The victory is near.

*Precious Lord, I lay my expectations at the foot of the cross. Quiet my heart
and spirit so that I can hear Your word to me. Lead me through the valley
and back into the light of Your eternal hope. I rejoice because victory is near!*

(ON HOLY GROUND)

Your Eternal Future

SCRIPTURE READING: REVELATION 22:1–5
KEY VERSE: REVELATION 21:27

There shall by no means enter it anything that defiles, or causes an abomination or a lie, but only those who are written in the Lamb's Book of Life.

Do you ever wonder what heaven will be like? John Newton said, "If I ever reach heaven I expect to find three wonders there: first, to meet some I had not thought to see there; second, to miss some I had expected to see there; and third, the greatest wonder of all, to find myself there."

The Bible tells us that heaven is a very definite place. Jesus said, "In My Father's house are many mansions; if it were not so, I would have told you. I go to prepare a place for you" (John 14:2).

Do you know if you will be in heaven? Do you know how to get there? It is not something you can work to make happen. You cannot earn your way. There is only one way to receive eternal life—accept what Jesus Christ did at the cross.

The crucifixion is God's way of making it possible for every single person who believes in Jesus Christ to spend eternity in heaven. The Bible tells us that when you are saved by the grace of God, you become a citizen of heaven. Your name is in the Lamb's Book of Life (Rev. 21:27).

As His child, God wants you to have a personal relationship with Him now and for eternity. As you anticipate with great joy your eternal future, hunger and thirst to know God more each day.

Lord Jesus, I am speechless at the thought of You preparing a place in heaven for me. I am unworthy. Thank You for dying for me so I could spend eternity with You.

(PATHWAYS TO HIS PRESENCE)

Seeking God First

SCRIPTURE READING: MATTHEW 14:14–21
KEY VERSE: JOHN 6:26

Jesus answered them and said, "Most assuredly, I say to you, you seek Me, not because you saw the signs, but because you ate of the loaves and were filled."

How many times have you thought: *I wish God would bless me?* Maybe those words came to you when you were asking God to answer a specific prayer or when you sensed some type of adversity approaching. There are many different ways to receive God's blessings, but most often we think of it from a material sense. The people who followed Jesus did the same thing.

After feeding the five thousand, Jesus exposed this materialistic attitude: "Most assuredly, I say to you, you seek Me, not because you saw the signs, but because you ate of the loaves and were filled" (John 6:26). Many followed the Lord in order to receive something. Their eyes were set on seeing miracles and material provisions. But Jesus wanted them to see Him as the Bread of Life in whom all their needs would be met.

The greatest of all God's blessings has nothing to do with material wealth and social position, and everything to do with the closeness of His presence. That was why He instructed His disciples by saying, "Seek Me first, and all these things will be added to you."

Are your eyes set on the Savior because of what He provides or because you love Him? The test of true love is this: abiding with the One you love regardless of anything else. Learn to love Him and Him alone; then all your cares will be satisfied.

Dear Lord, I am not seeking things. I am not pursuing blessings. I am seeking You and You alone.

(INTO HIS PRESENCE)

The Greatest Goal

SCRIPTURE READING: ROMANS 4:13–22
KEY VERSES: ROMANS 4:20–21

He did not waver at the promise of God through unbelief, but was strengthened in faith, giving glory to God, and being fully convinced that what He had promised He was also able to perform.

When Abraham was about to die, his descendants did not number the stars in the sky or the grains of sand on the seashore. However, that did not stop him from believing that God would do just as He had promised.

Abraham saw his reward from afar and didn't waver, and ultimately his relationship with God was strengthened. The true gift for Abraham was that he was able to know God intimately. The promise of many descendants was an additional benefit of that relationship.

In your own life, God has given you promises that He is faithful to fulfill. Yet it is not just the promises that you pursue; it is the Promise Giver. In Colossians 4:12, we learn that Epaphras's prayer was for believers to stand assured of God's will.

It is God's will that you know Him and help others receive Him. Even if you are only able to see His promises fulfilled from afar, you are still gaining the far greater gift of knowing God more. Jesus is the greatest goal of all your pursuits. Do not waver in your faith, but grow strong. Life with Christ is a blessing above and beyond all you could ask or imagine.

Lord, in trusting You to see beyond what I am able, I come to know You and rely on You more completely. I give You my future so You can shape my today.

(PATHWAYS TO HIS PRESENCE)

Approaching God

Scripture Reading: Hebrews 10:19–22
Key Verse: Hebrews 4:16

Let us therefore come boldly to the throne of grace, that we may obtain mercy and find grace to help in time of need.

Orel Hershiser was the confident catalyst who led the Los Angeles Dodgers to a World Series victory in 1988. He was so aggressive that his teammates nicknamed him "Bulldog." Hershiser displayed the boldness and tenacity that should characterize the Christian's relationship with God.

Your prayer life should not be weak and indecisive, but bold and confident. You can present your needs, desires, and petitions to God with reverent assurance. If your sins have been washed away by the blood of Christ, you have unhindered access to the Creator of the universe. Before the advent of Christ, God's presence was reserved for the privileged few who came to Him in fear and trembling. Today, believers can approach Him freely—calling Him *Abba*, Father (Gal. 4:6).

You can be confident in approaching God to worship because Christ is now your sympathetic, understanding High Priest. You come to a throne of grace, which floods you with His tender mercy.

The Lord Jesus Christ is for you, not against you. He understands your frailties, your mood swings, your habits. He does not ever condemn you, for He was condemned in your stead (Rom. 8:1–4). Your confidence is also in the sure promises of God. He will do what He says in His Word. Praise Him for that today!

Lord, I praise You that I can come into Your presence to worship and commune with confidence, knowing You will do all You have promised.

(Into His Presence)

Unworthiness

SCRIPTURE READING: ISAIAH 43
KEY VERSE: ISAIAH 43:25

I, even I, am He who blots out your transgressions for My own sake; and I will not remember your sins.

God never ridicules us or makes us feel unworthy. Instead, we read these words of Jesus:

"Just as the Father has loved Me, I have also loved you; abide in My love." (John 15:9 NASB)

"If you continue in My word, then you are truly disciples of Mine; and you will know the truth, and the truth will make you free." (John 8:31–32 NASB)

"I have called you friends, for all things that I have heard from My Father I have made known to you." (John 15:15 NASB)

Love and truth. God is love and the source of all truth. The love He has for you is the same love He has for His Son, the Lord Jesus Christ. He gives you this love through His grace and mercy. It is a pure love, not tainted by guilt or obligation.

Regardless of how deep your past transgression may be, God is near to free you with the truth of His Word. Nothing is stronger than His love. When He forgives, He forgets (Ps. 103:12; Isa. 43:25). Once you have confessed sin, there is no need to beg or plead for His forgiveness. It is a done deal!

You can walk freely in the light of His love because He calls you His child. Your life is inscribed within the palm of His hand.

You are the apple of His eye; all of heaven rejoices at the sight of your name written in the Lamb's blood.

Dear God, thank You that I am worthy! I walk freely in the light of Your love. I am Your child, the apple of Your eye. My name is written in the Lamb's blood. I belong.

(ON HOLY GROUND)

Hope for the Future

SCRIPTURE READING: TITUS 2:11–15
KEY VERSES: TITUS 2:12–13

We should live soberly, righteously, and godly in the present age,
looking for the blessed hope and glorious appearing of our great God
and Savior Jesus Christ.

No matter how shaky things in this world are, we find assurance in the fact that God remains the same as He changes us and those around us. God doesn't expect us to change into perfect human beings overnight, but He does desire to begin a process that changes our lives forever.

Once we enter into a relationship with God by receiving His forgiveness and grace and then inviting Him to be Lord over our lives, He begins to transform us in ways we never imagined possible.

When we accept Christ as our Lord and Savior, God calls us His own, His sons and daughters, joint heirs with Jesus. No longer does He view us as sinners—He sees us as saints. However, there is still much work to be done in our hearts.

We can rest in the assurance that there is no time limit to the process of renewing our hearts and minds. God touches our hearts in calling us His children, but the work of transforming us into His image is a long-term plan.

When looking at our own hearts, we could despair when we realize just how much we need to be transformed. But we don't have to despair, because we receive hope in Him, hope that His Holy Spirit will indeed complete the work that He has begun in the lives of each man and woman who would be willing to live for Him.

Lord, thank You for the work of transformation that You are doing in my
life, and that You have a master plan for me.

(PATHWAYS TO HIS PRESENCE)

Praying for the Lost

SCRIPTURE READING: ACTS 24:10–27
KEY VERSE: ACTS 24:25

As he [Paul] reasoned about righteousness, self-control, and the judgment to come, Felix was afraid and answered, "Go away for now; when I have a convenient time I will call for you."

In Acts 24, Paul stood before Felix with a clear conscience. He had professed the gospel message without violating the moral and judicial laws of his day. Yet he was arrested and accused of stirring up dissension and being "a ringleader of the sect of the Nazarenes" (v. 5). Knowing Paul's citizenship rights, the governor had little recourse except to be lenient in his judgment of the apostle.

God is creative in His approach to mankind's need for salvation. Paul did not compromise his convictions; he preached the gospel of Christ openly in the temple and later under house arrest to the guards who were chained to his side. Sensitivity to the leading of the Holy Spirit achieves far more in the area of witnessing than we ever could accomplish in our own strength.

As a result of Paul's obedience to Christ and then to the authorities over him, Felix began visiting Paul and inquiring about the Way (terminology used by early Christians to describe their life in Christ). Although it appears that Felix never accepted Jesus as his Savior, he was given a divine opportunity to do so through the testimony of the apostle Paul. What a privilege it is to witness to and pray for our government officials. Even though they have tremendous authority, they are not above God in their decisions; they need your prayers.

Father, I thank You for the opportunity to witness to and pray for government officials.

(SEEKING HIS FACE)

New Levels of Praise

SCRIPTURE READING: EXODUS 3:1–6
KEY VERSE: HEBREWS 3:15

Today, if you will hear His voice,
Do not harden your hearts as in the rebellion.

A river that runs through one U.S. city is extraordinarily clean and clear. Its pristine quality can be attributed to a large watershed area in which rainfall gradually seeps through a thick layer of forest and rock before trickling into the river's ecosystem.

This is illustrative of the biblical practice of meditation. It is the absorption and retention of truth that distills the essence of Scripture, making it clear, relevant, and applicable to personal needs.

Meditating—thinking through what God has said, why He said it, and what it means to us today—is the means by which we weave the power and life of God's Word into our spiritual and emotional fabric. God's Word is alive, so full of spiritual truth and wisdom that even a single passage can be digested for a lifetime.

God has something to say to you personally, but you must have ears to hear. You can behold wonderful things from God's Word if you are willing to quietly and thoroughly examine its content through biblical meditation.

Put God's Word to work in your innermost being—your mind, will, and emotions. Allow it to seep into your spirit, receiving its full richness, and you will be inspired to new levels of praise.

Father, as I meditate on Your Word today, quicken it to my innermost being
so that I can receive its richness. Lift me to new levels of praise and worship.

(INTO HIS PRESENCE)

Faith Defined

SCRIPTURE READING: HEBREWS 11
KEY VERSE: HEBREWS 11:1

Faith is the substance of things hoped for, the evidence of things not seen.

So much is written about faith these days. We think and talk about trusting God, and try, even though we stumble at times, to walk by faith. Many times it is our trying that trips us up. God wants us to learn to live by faith and not by sight (2 Cor. 5:7). This means living with the idea that He is able to do what we cannot do for ourselves. What a victorious thought! It is also a marvelous invitation to experience freedom from doubt, worry, and disbelief.

Before we can trust God fully, we must come to a point of helpless dependence. It is here that we realize we simply cannot do it all, be all that is needed, and have all the answers. If we could, there would be no need for God. We would be in total control and very proud of it. While God gives us the ability to solve many of the problems we face, His greater desire is for us to live our lives dependent on Him. Godly dependence is not a sign of weakness but one of immeasurable strength and confidence. There are problems in life that only God can solve, tasks only He can perform, and solutions that can only be discovered through the wisdom He gives.

The basic foundation to faith is this: trust God more than you trust yourself. When you do this, you gain wisdom and hope for every area of life.

Dear Lord, help me to trust You more. Give me a confident conviction that You keep Your promises.

(PATHWAYS TO HIS PRESENCE)

A Messenger of Victory

SCRIPTURE READING: ACTS 18:9–11
KEY VERSE: ACTS 18:9

The Lord spoke to Paul in the night by a vision, "Do not be afraid,
but speak, and do not keep silent."

Corinth was a difficult place to live, especially for a believer. It was a port city, one that embraced visitors and businessmen from all over the known world. Along with an atmosphere of open commerce was a very liberal view of religion. Paganism and cult worship were common practices.

Warren Wiersbe wrote, "Corinthians' reputation for wickedness was known all over the Roman Empire. . . . Money and vice, along with strange philosophies and new religions, came to Corinth and found a home there."

God is not afraid to send His messengers to places where evil abounds. These are the very places the gospel message is needed. Therefore, God sent Paul to Corinth, but the ministry was under tremendous attack. The conversion of Crispus, a well-known Jewish leader, was the evidence that Paul needed to continue preaching God's message of truth. We must never abandon the post God has given us.

In Acts 18, the Lord spoke to Paul through a dream, encouraging him not to let fear hold him back from speaking (vv. 9–10). This was just the encouragement that Paul needed, and it is the same encouragement He has for you.

God is aware of your situation. Take courage and be full of hope. His truth will be taught or spoken. You are His messenger to those who need it most, and you will be victorious in your labors.

Lord, let me be a light in darkness, bringing the message of the gospel to those
who need it most.

(PATHWAYS TO HIS PRESENCE)

God Is Talking

SCRIPTURE READING: PSALM 138:1–8
KEY VERSE: ISAIAH 49:1

Listen, O coastlands, to Me,
And take heed, you peoples from afar!

If you've ever wondered whether God still talks to people, allow Him to use today's verse to give an answer: God calls for people to listen and take heed (Isa. 49:1). God wants people to listen. Therefore, He must be talking.

Although God was speaking primarily to the nation of Israel in Psalm 138, you can be sure that His voice still guides, confirms, disciplines, and assures His children.

Generally, there are four reasons He speaks. (1) God desires to have fellowship with us, His most precious creation, and loves us just as much as He loved the saints of the Bible; (2) God knows that we need clear direction in a difficult world; (3) God realizes we need comfort and assurance just as much as did Abraham, Moses, Peter, Paul, and others; and, (4) God wants us to get to know Him.

But how do we know when God is speaking to us? Today, He uses four primary ways to share His heart with ours. God speaks (1) through His Word, the foremost tool He uses to impart His truth; (2) through the Holy Spirit, who witnesses to our spirits; (3) through other believers who are walking in His Spirit; and (4) through circumstances He providentially arranges. It may be a still, small voice, but it resounds loudly because of whose voice it is.

Dear Lord, speak to me today through Your Word, Your Spirit, other
believers, and the circumstances of my life.

(INTO HIS PRESENCE)

The Greater Good

SCRIPTURE READING: ISAIAH 50:8–11
KEY VERSES: LAMENTATIONS 3:21–22

This I recall to my mind,
Therefore I have hope.
Through the LORD's mercies we are not consumed,
Because His compassions fail not.

When we are mistreated, our natural tendency is to lash out at those who have hurt us. We might even go so far as to plan how we can get even. But the Scripture says that revenge is God's responsibility. Regardless of how others treat us, we are to trust God and let Him handle those who have wronged us.

Trouble, trial, and injustice can tempt you to be disobedient. When this happens, you can respond one of two ways. You can take matters into your own hands, and as the prophet Isaiah recorded, you will receive no help from God: "All you who light fires and provide yourselves with flaming torches, go, walk in the light of your fires and of the torches you have set ablaze. This is what you shall receive from my hand: You will lie down in torment" (Isa. 50:11 NIV). Or you can experience the greater good by trusting God to save and protect you.

God wants you to depend on Him. Not just for the big things, but for the everyday trials as well. When was the last time you faced a situation that appeared too great for you to handle? Were you determined to go through on your own steam? If you were, you missed the wonder of God's deliverance. There is a tremendous hope to be gained in this life, but you must lay down your rights and allow God to be your very life in order to experience it.

Lord, help me to lay down my rights and allow You to be my life. I seek the greater good!

(SEEKING HIS FACE)

How to Listen to God

SCRIPTURE READING: ISAIAH 30:15–18
KEY VERSE: ISAIAH 50:4

The Lord GOD has given Me the tongue of the learned, that I should know how to speak a word in season to him who is weary. He awakens Me morning by morning, He awakens My ear to hear as the learned.

The center of the Christian life is a relationship with Jesus Christ—personal, unique, and rewarding. At the core of this relationship is communication—expressing ourselves to God in prayer and His speaking to our spirits.

We must admit, though, we are usually far better at the former than the latter. Listening to God is a realm in which we are sometimes uninformed and frequently uncomfortable. *Is that God I am hearing or just the echo of my own thinking?* we wonder.

It helps to demystify the terminology. God usually doesn't speak to us audibly as He did to the Old Testament characters. Today, He speaks through the Scriptures, the sound advice of other Christians, and the presence of the Holy Spirit who lives within each believer. We hear His voice as we meditate on the truth of His Word, listen and sift through the counsel of others, and commit each day to His sovereign control, trusting Him to order our ways and thoughts.

God communicates His will to us so that we might comprehend His truth and be conformed to it. He always takes the initiative to make it happen. Our best move is to quiet our busy souls and allow Him to speak (Isa. 30:15).

There is so much God wants to share with you. He has something to say about everything that touches your life. Who wouldn't want to hear from Him?

Dear heavenly Father, speak to me through Your Word today. Communicate Your will to me so that I can be conformed to the truth. Quiet my busy soul so that I can hear Your voice.

(ON HOLY GROUND)

Sharing Your Story

SCRIPTURE READING: ACTS 22:3–15
KEY VERSE: ACTS 22:10

I said, "What shall I do, Lord?" And the Lord said to me, "Arise and go into Damascus, and there you will be told all things which are appointed for you to do."

Do you remember what your life was like before you asked Jesus to be your Savior? You might have looked "good" on the outside yet struggled with strong urges on the inside. How did you feel when the burden of all the guilt was lifted away? It was wonderful, wasn't it? That is your testimony.

A testimony is not just an overdramatic story told by someone who committed high-profile sins and then came to the Lord. This kind of conversion experience, like Paul's on the road to Damascus, may be the kind with which you are most familiar. You may even feel inferior or insecure about your story, secretly believing that it is not interesting enough.

Once you believe in the inefficacy of your story, you are more hesitant to tell it and could even come to question the validity of your salvation experience. What a sad condition. If only you could grasp that the grace that Jesus gave to you is the same grace He pours on all His people.

As an aid to remembering the tremendous work Christ has done and is continuing to do, make a list of transformations that you noticed in your heart and behavior. Then pause to give Him thanks for each one, and ask the Lord for an opportunity to share with someone who needs to hear exactly your story.

Lord, thank You for the changes You have made in my life. Give me the opportunity to share with someone who needs to hear my story.

(SEEKING HIS FACE)

Called with Confidence

SCRIPTURE READING: MARK 16:14–18
KEY VERSE: MARK 16:15

He said to them, "Go into all the world and preach the gospel to every creature."

After the resurrection, Christ appeared to two of the disciples. However, the news of Jesus' resurrection seemed too good to be true, so the other disciples, in their discouragement, did not believe the reports. When Jesus appeared to them, He rebuked them for their unbelief. He knew they would need great faith to take on the commission God had for them, and that faith had to begin with an understanding of God's power.

Eleven men had the responsibility of spreading the gospel to the whole world. They were eleven simple men with an overwhelming goal, fueled by the power that raised Jesus from the dead. Surely our task is not as daunting as that which the disciples faced, yet Christians often consider evangelism impossible.

Clarence Hall wrote, "The problem is not that we have exhausted our frontiers. The problem is that we fail to recognize them! And as our vision shortens, our pessimism deepens."

Lord, I have been guilty of failing to recognize the frontiers for the gospel. Forgive my shortsightedness and infuse me with a powerful drive to witness for You.

(PATHWAYS TO HIS PRESENCE)

Hearing and Doing

SCRIPTURE READING: JAMES 1:22–25
KEY VERSE: JAMES 1:25

He who looks into the perfect law of liberty and continues in it, and is not a forgetful hearer but a doer of the work, this one will be blessed in what he does.

How you enter church each week will have a great impact on how you exit it. The reference here is to attitude and intention, not to whether you look or act just right.

James told us to be doers and not just hearers of the Word. The only way to be a doer is to be an intense hearer. We must know what to do and how to go about it before we can be doers. It is imperative that we walk into church services having resolved that we will intently, actively listen to the preaching of the Word of God.

Pray for God to prepare your heart for what He wants you to hear from your pastor. Take notes. Pray during the message. Say something like, "Lord, what are You trying to teach me here?" If there is a particular point that God continually is impressing upon your spirit, ask Him, "Father, what am I missing? Reveal what You would have me learn. How can I absorb what I am hearing and apply it to my life?"

Comprehending God's Word will help you become a doer of God's Word. This is the truth behind Romans 8:29, in which God would have us to be conformed to the image of His Son. You must comprehend to be conformed, and you must be conformed to effectively communicate in speech and deed the Word of God.

Make me an intense hearer, Lord, so I can be an obedient doer. Conform me to the image of Your Son, so I can effectively communicate Your Word in speech and deed.

(INTO HIS PRESENCE)

God's Plan for Good

SCRIPTURE READING: NEHEMIAH 1:3–11
KEY VERSE: NEHEMIAH 1:4

So it was, when I heard these words, that I sat down and wept, and mourned for many days; I was fasting and praying before the God of heaven.

Do you sometimes feel that a dark cloud of discouragement is following you no matter what you do? Have your peace and joy been replaced by feelings of hopelessness and frustration?

Certainly the prophet Nehemiah experienced great discouragement as he learned of the distress and destruction in Jerusalem. Nehemiah 1:4 tells us that in response to this news, he grieved and prayed for days.

The interesting part of this passage is the description of what Nehemiah did next. After his period of mourning, he offered God a four-part prayer.

First, Nehemiah offered praise to God for His faithfulness and loving-kindness (v. 5). Next, he confessed the collective sins of his people (v. 7). Then, he acknowledged the appropriateness of God's judgment (v. 8). And finally, he asked God to show him success and compassion (v. 11).

Nehemiah's heartfelt petition contains valuable insight for the discouraged: no matter what happens in the physical world around us, God is in control. He is able to work all things, including our failures, into His plan for our good.

If you are discouraged today, use Nehemiah's words to create your own prayer to God. Give Him praise, confess any sin in your life, acknowledge the authenticity of His Word, and request His favor as you get up and try again.

The Lord is faithful in all things. Don't let discouragement block your view of His awesome love and power.

Dear Lord, thank You for Your faithfulness and lovingkindness. Renew my focus. Help me get up and try again.

(PATHWAYS TO HIS PRESENCE)

Encouraging Others

SCRIPTURE READING: NEHEMIAH 2:17–20
KEY VERSE: NEHEMIAH 2:18

I told them of the hand of my God which had been good upon me, and also of the king's words that he had spoken to me. So they said, "Let us rise up and build." Then they set their hands to this good work.

Yesterday we discovered how the prophet Nehemiah used prayer to overcome discouragement. Today, as we move to the second chapter of Nehemiah, we will see how he used the same situation to encourage others to be successful.

Traveling to Jerusalem to assist with the reconstruction of the destroyed city walls, Nehemiah was immediately confronted with a chance to testify to others concerning God's goodness. He told his people of God's guidance and care. Seeing his confidence in the Lord, the people began to help with his project.

Then, in verse 19, we see that as he worked, Nehemiah was challenged by doubters and mockers. They constantly questioned him, but despite their questions, the prophet remained strong, giving glory to God, in whom his trust lay.

Once again we can learn a valuable lesson from Nehemiah's example. When faced with the daunting task of rebuilding the fallen city walls, he did not fear his enemies, nor did he collapse under pressure from skeptics. The Lord had given him a task, and he was bound to complete it no matter what obstacles stood in his way.

What was the source of this confidence? Nehemiah's foundation of faith was firmly established upon the God of promise. Therefore, not only was he able to move forward with confidence, he was also able to encourage others to trust in the Source of his strength.

Lord, help me to keep You at my core, so that others can be encouraged by the faith they see at work in me.

(PATHWAYS TO HIS PRESENCE)

Transforming Prayer

SCRIPTURE READING: COLOSSIANS 4:2–4
KEY VERSE: ISAIAH 26:3

You will keep him in perfect peace,
Whose mind is stayed on You,
Because he trusts in You.

In the movie version of *Shadowlands*, which portrays the endearing relationship between Christian apologist C. S. Lewis and Joy Gresham, a friend comments to Lewis that God finally answered his prayers. As part of his response, Lewis says, "Prayer doesn't change God; it changes me."

How profound and true that is! Your communication with God is your intimate connection with Him, and He allows you to participate in the work that He is doing and even to see His actions in relationship to your prayers. God hears and answers every prayer, but His purposes in prayer go far beyond giving you a measurable response.

God wants to transform your life through the process of prayer. Your personal relationship with Christ is deepened and enlarged when you spend time talking to Him. As you come into His presence with reverence and a quiet heart, ready to listen, He begins to purify your heart and sift your priorities. You develop a passion for obedience to God, and you begin to see Him as the Provider for all your needs.

Most important, you experience the peace that comes from knowing God is in control (Phil. 4:6–7). Your anxiety melts away as you learn to trust Him. These are just some of the ways God uses prayer to change your heart. The more you pray, the more transformations you'll discover.

Change me, Lord, as I wait in Your presence. Let my anxiety melt away and
help me learn to trust You.

(INTO HIS PRESENCE)

The Key to Listening

SCRIPTURE READING: 2 SAMUEL 7
KEY VERSE: PSALM 46:10

Be still, and know that I am God; I will be exalted among the nations, I will be exalted in the earth!

God had just made a covenant with David. Among many things, God promised to give him a son (Solomon), who would someday build the temple David had dreamed of building. The throne of rulership over Israel would never depart from David's house, though interrupted at times, and would one day find its ultimate fulfillment in Jesus Christ.

What an overwhelming set of promises, and what a mighty demonstration of complete grace! God made this covenant with David *before* he sinned with Bathsheba. God knew what David would soon do, but He in grace chose to love him and establish a never-ending relationship with him. David's response to this promise is a prime example of why David is called "a man after [God's] own heart" (1 Sam. 13:14).

David's heart priority was on worshiping and loving his God. He said, "Now therefore, O LORD God, the word that You have spoken concerning Your servant and his house, confirm it forever, and do as You have spoken" (2 Sam. 7:25 NASB).

You and I are called to worship God wholeheartedly. That is what David did, and that is why his fellowship with God was so sweet. If you seek intimacy with God, falling down before Him in worship is the place of beginning.

Master, I seek a greater intimacy with You. I know it will come through worship, so teach me how to worship in spirit and truth.

(ON HOLY GROUND)

Proverbs of Peace

SCRIPTURE READING: PROVERBS 17:13–15
KEY VERSE: PROVERBS 17:22

A merry heart does good, like medicine,
But a broken spirit dries the bones.

The book of Proverbs is rich in wisdom. It amplifies the truth that we can have peace and be content in all circumstances. Let's examine a few of these proverbs of peace:

- Proverbs 1:7: Fear and reverence of the Lord, which leads to surrender and submission, is the first step in enjoying contentedness.
- Proverbs 1:10–19: There are those who seek happiness through ill-gotten gains and wickedness. Never look at the world in envy, especially when you consider that their methods take away the life of the possessors.
- Proverbs 11:5, 30: Righteousness leads to peace because right thinking and right actions are a joy to the Lord.
- Proverbs 16:32: It is better to have self-control than one's own dynasty.
- Proverbs 17:22: There is no way to put a price tag on good health brought on by joy and peace through a life lived for the Lord.
- Proverbs 18:12; 22:4; 25:6–7; 29:23: Humility is a cornerstone to peace and contentment, because humility never allows you to make yourself more than what God would have you to be.
- Proverbs 21:26; 22:1: Generosity and a good name are the natural results of honoring the Lord with obedience and staying our minds on Him.
- Proverbs 25:27; 27:23–24; 28:19: Living a righteous life produces gains beyond measure.

Father, make me content in every circumstance. Give me peace in every situation. I claim these proverbs of peace to be manifested in my life today.

(PATHWAYS TO HIS PRESENCE)

Well-Equipped for Victory

SCRIPTURE READING: EPHESIANS 6:10–18
KEY VERSES: ROMANS 13:14

Put on the Lord Jesus Christ, and make no provision for the flesh, to fulfill its lusts.

In the lifelong struggle with temptation and natural desire, believers are told to "put on" the Lord Jesus Christ. This becomes a daily activity by which you decide who is going to live your life for you today. Are you going to live in the flesh, or is Jesus going to have the privilege of living His life through you?

People have different terms for the "flesh," but simply put, it is the natural part of each person that desires to operate in opposition to God. It usually manifests itself by challenging the restrictions that the Lord set for mankind's good.

Once we are saved, we fluctuate between two mind-sets—that of the Spirit leading toward God and that of the flesh leading away from Him. While we will always retain old fleshly patterns of thinking, we do not have to succumb to living by them, because we have the Holy Spirit dwelling within us.

But since our two ways of thinking are in opposition to each other, conflict and warfare naturally result. We are in a real battle, which requires real weapons. The Lord has given us the helmet of salvation so that we will not surrender our minds to ungodly thinking. The breastplate of righteousness protects our emotions from giving way to natural desires. We also put on the belt of truth, which enables us to walk in keeping with godly principles rather than according to the flesh. And the Lord has provided a true shield of faith for us because there are actual darts of doubt.

In other words, we are at war, but we are well equipped for it. God always leads us in triumph.

Thank You, Lord, that You always lead me in triumph. Thank You for the weapons of spiritual warfare that assure my victory.

(PATHWAYS TO HIS PRESENCE)

The Presence of God

SCRIPTURE READING: ACTS 17:22–31
KEY VERSE: MATTHEW 28:20

Lo, I am with you always, even to the end of the age.

One of the most debilitating emotions is loneliness. Maybe you've felt that way in a hospital or emergency room, in a new city or job, or even in the midst of friends and family. Feeling as if there is no one to care or share with is a terrifying sensation. It can even be deadly.

That is why one of the most comforting names given to our Savior is Immanuel, "God with us." Because of the indwelling Christ, believers are never separated from His permanent presence. We are in Christ and He is in us. What an encouragement! What a comfort! What an assurance! We always have a shoulder to lean on, the broad shoulders of Immanuel. We always have Someone to listen to our heartache, our constant Companion, Friend Jesus.

The gods of other religions are usually in some far-off, remote corner. Not so with our Creator and Redeemer. Once in us, He will never leave us, abandon us, or forget us.

Don't let our adversary and accuser rob you of the peace and joy that come from experiencing and enjoying the sweet presence of our God. No sin, no deed, no trial can ever diminish the full presence and acceptance of Christ once you have become His child through faith. God is for you. God loves you. Allow His presence to fill any void.

Lord, I am so thankful that I can lean upon You in prayer today. No trial can diminish the sweetness of Your presence in my life.

(INTO HIS PRESENCE)

No Fishing Allowed

SCRIPTURE READING: HEBREWS 10:16–18
KEY VERSE: MARK 11:25

Whenever you stand praying, if you have anything against anyone, forgive him, that your Father in heaven may also forgive you your trespasses.

In the book *Tramp for the Lord*, Corrie Ten Boom addresses the subject of forgiveness: "Forgiveness is the key which unlocks the door of resentment and the handcuffs of hatred. It breaks the chains of bitterness and the shackles of selfishness. The forgiveness of Jesus not only takes away our sins, it makes them as if they had never been." This is the same principle mentioned in Hebrews 10:17: "THEIR SINS AND THEIR LAWLESS DEEDS I WILL REMEMBER NO MORE" (NASB).

Hanging on to past failures and sins distorts God's view of who we are in Christ. He tells us that we are new creatures, saved and redeemed, but guilt and shame keep us from looking up into His wondrous face of love and acceptance. By focusing on the past, we block God's future intent for our lives.

Buying into false guilt leads to feelings of defeat that may end in hopelessness and fear. People who struggle with lingering guilt often have a hard time accepting God's love. They cannot imagine how the Lord could possibly use them for His glory, especially when they think about their past sins.

But think for a moment. If this were true, God would have never chosen Moses, David, and Paul as vessels for His work. Corrie had a saying that many people have come to love: "When God forgives your sin, He buries it in the deepest sea and puts up a 'No Fishing' sign." When Christ forgives, He also forgets!

Dear Lord, please break the shackles of selfishness from my life. Take my sins and cast them into Your sea of forgetfulness.

(SEEKING HIS FACE)

Stewards of His Grace

SCRIPTURE READING: 1 PETER 4:7–10
KEY VERSE: ROMANS 12:13

Share with God's people who are in need. Practice hospitality. (NIV)

One man's Sunday school class began a supper club designed to help members get to know one another and to be a ministry to people outside the church. Hosting one of the dinners was an ideal opportunity for involvement, but he was afraid to offer. *I'm living alone now,* he thought. *I don't cook that well, I don't know much about being a host, and it's been awhile since I've had people over.* With great hesitation, he finally put his name on the list.

As the day approached, he was amazed when several class members called and volunteered to help him get ready. Some made food, some brought chairs, and others even donated festive decorations. The dinner was a success, and everyone felt welcomed and loved.

Hospitality isn't just for certain homemakers with large homes or a special knack for party throwing. The same command is given to all believers: "Be hospitable to one another without complaint. As each one has received a special gift, employ it in serving one another, as good stewards of the manifold grace of God" (1 Peter 4:9–10 NASB).

It doesn't matter how experienced or equipped you are. What counts is offering what the Lord has given you. God uses everything for His glory. Your home and belongings become a blessing many times over when you open them up to someone else.

Father God, use everything I have for Your glory—my home, my finances, my talents and abilities. Whatever I have, it's Yours.

(ON HOLY GROUND)

Everyday Opportunities

SCRIPTURE READING: PSALM 61:1–8
KEY VERSE: EPHESIANS 2:10

*We are His workmanship, created in Christ Jesus for good works, which
God prepared beforehand that we should walk in them.*

The Holy Spirit is always at work in your life, conforming you to the image
of Christ; this is called sanctification. And though you do not enhance this
development through self-effort, God wants you to pay close attention to
what He's doing, even asking Him specifically to show you the aspects of
His activity.

His goals for you are not mysterious; God is not trying to hide His
plans for you. When you ask Him to give you direction, whether it's for
coping with daily activities or for grasping His larger vision, He will give
you the guidance you request (James 1:5).

All of us have sinful habits and negative behaviors that aren't read-
ily apparent to us. God may use the words of friends to point out such
problem areas to you, as painful as that may be. Or He may choose to
quietly convict your heart without outside assistance. Either way, He'll let
you know what He wants to change next.

Did you know that God has already planned spiritual activities for
you (Eph. 2:10)? Ask Him to open your eyes to everyday opportunities
to demonstrate His love to others. He'll even give you creative ideas for
ministry. Remember, all of His riches are yours for the asking.

*Dear Lord, as I wait in Your presence today, show me where I need to
change. Open my eyes to everyday opportunities to demonstrate Your love
to others.*

(INTO HIS PRESENCE)

Come as You Are

SCRIPTURE READING: ROMANS 5:12–21
KEY VERSE: ROMANS 5:17

If by the one man's offense death reigned through the one, much more those who receive abundance of grace and of the gift of righteousness will reign in life through the One, Jesus Christ.

Imagine being approached with this inquiry: "I don't know anything about God. Would you describe Him to me?" How would you explain to that person what God is like? When the conversation was over, how would the person walk away? Would he or she be discouraged about ever having a relationship with the Lord, or confident and assured about being able to have a permanent, personal relationship with God?

There is a lot of confusion, even among believers, about who God is. Some, thinking He's a God of judgment and vengeance, live in fear of Him. That belief can leave us doubting and afraid, wondering exactly what would cause God to stop loving us.

Scripture reveals the truth: He is the God of grace. Grace is God's goodness and kindness that is lavishly shown toward us, and it has two amazing qualities.

First, grace is given to us regardless of whether we deserve it. Our good works or stellar personal qualities cannot bring us God's grace, nor can our failures cause God to withdraw it. We look at grades, scorecards, and performance appraisals in determining who receives what, but God does not look at merit. Amazing, but true.

Second, grace is given freely to us. There is no cost. Our world does not operate this way, but our God does. Not only at the point of salvation but throughout our Christian life, we are invited to come as we are, acknowledge our sinfulness, and receive forgiveness and God's grace.

Lord, I come just as I am with assurance that You will receive me, forgive me, and bestow Your grace upon me.

(PATHWAYS TO HIS PRESENCE)

The Risk of Obeying God

SCRIPTURE READING: LUKE 5:1–11
KEY VERSE: LUKE 5:4

When He had stopped speaking, He said to Simon, "Launch out into the deep and let down your nets for a catch."

Jesus was speaking to the crowds on the shore of the Sea of Galilee. As they listened, they pressed closer. When Jesus saw two boats lying on the edge of the water near where the fishermen were washing their nets, He got in Simon Peter's boat, continuing to teach.

When He was finished teaching, Jesus said to Peter, "Launch out into the deep and let down your nets for a catch" (Luke 5:4). Peter had a choice—either to obey or disobey God. He chose to obey. The result was so many fish that the nets began to break.

Through the simple act of obedience, Peter witnessed a miracle. He realized that Jesus had his best interest at heart, even when he did not understand what Jesus was telling him to do. Peter had toiled all night without catching any fish. But he was willing to obey.

What has God asked you to do that you are afraid to do? There are many reasons why we hesitate to obey God: fear of failure, the desire to control our own lives, or fear of what God may require of us.

What little thing has God been nudging you about? He wants you to trust and obey Him in the small things. Don't allow your unwillingness to obey God to cause you to miss the blessings He has for you. Every time God asks you to do something, He has something good in store for you.

Father, help me trust You in the small things, knowing You have something good in store for me.

(PATHWAYS TO HIS PRESENCE)

Living Life to the Fullest

SCRIPTURE READING: 1 THESSALONIANS 5:1–14
KEY VERSE: 1 THESSALONIANS 5:5

You are all sons of light and sons of the day. We are not of the night nor of darkness.

What does living life to the fullest mean to you? Some may picture a life-long dream being fulfilled. Others may think of a comfortable retirement, while many more envision what they can achieve if given enough time. But if you really want to start living life to the fullest, begin with Jesus. He is the fulfillment of all your dreams. In Him, you will find the things you need the most—contentment, love, and friendship.

God also commands us to love others—and for good reason. Living life to the fullest includes encouraging and supporting other people emotionally. In fact, without a godly love tucked away inside your heart, you cannot successfully lift someone else's spirits. Let Jesus be the object of your affections; then you will find that loving even the unlovely will bring pleasure and joy to your heart.

When you show unconditional love and acceptance to others, marvelous things can happen. Think about it—that's how God loves us. His merciful love changes us, motivating us to righteous living. So share God's unconditional love with others, both with your brothers and sisters in Christ and unbelievers. Divisions may fade, differences may ease, and fears may subside. Where there once was disagreement, unity can prevail.

God desires His people to enjoy meaningful community, giving and receiving encouragement. In such an environment, we find fullness of joy, despite the pressures of this world. Evaluate yourself. Are you living life to the fullest?

I want to live life to the fullest, Lord, and I know that will happen only as I experience Your love. Give me Your love—even for the unlovely.

(INTO HIS PRESENCE)

A Shining Light

SCRIPTURE READING: GENESIS 6:1–13
KEY VERSE: MATTHEW 5:14

You are the light of the world. A city that is set on a hill cannot be hidden.

Contrasting colors are more noticeable than colors that are similar. For example, a white dot really shows up on a black background; it almost pops off the page.

That's the way Noah was, compared to the society around him. The first few verses of the sixth chapter of Genesis paint a bleak picture of the world, with great evil and sin abounding: "Then the LORD saw that the wickedness of man was great on the earth, and that every intent of the thoughts of his heart was only evil continually" (Gen. 6:5 NASB).

Yet in the midst of this great darkness, Noah was the bright spot: "But Noah found favor in the eyes of the LORD. . . . Noah was a righteous man, blameless in his time; Noah walked with God" (vv. 8–9 NASB). Noah desired to please God in all his ways, and his continual desire was to walk in complete fellowship with Him.

Is that your desire as you live in a world that operates on an entirely different basis? When you focus on abiding in Christ and seeking His purposes every day, your life becomes a shining light in a society of sometimes overwhelming darkness (Matt. 5:14). Of course, you may not be consciously aware that you are being a light, but you can be sure that others are watching what you say and do.

Lord, others are watching what I say and do. Show me how to live in such a way that I will point others to You. Let me be a shining light in this dark world.

(SEEKING HIS FACE)

Making Important Decisions

SCRIPTURE READING: JOHN 16:7–15
KEY VERSE: JOHN 16:1

These things I have spoken to you, that you should not be made to stumble.

God has definite plans for each of our lives and is very interested and involved in our every decision. In light of this fact, how should we go about making important decisions?

The Lord has our interests at heart every single second of our lives. There is no time at which He does not care about us or long for our very best. This is why He has promised in Psalm 16:11 to show us the path of life. Later, in Psalm 32:8, God promises to instruct us in the way we should go, and that He will guide us with His eye.

In his book *What God Wishes Christians Knew About Christianity*, author Bill Gillham reminds us that God has a "helicopter view" above the parade of our lives. While we can only see the parade as it marches by, God sees the beginning, middle, and end of our parade. Why, then, would we not beseech the Lord to give us guidance not only in major decisions but also in our daily choices?

Do you prayerfully submit to the Lord the choices you face? Do you rejoice in the fact that He has given you His Holy Spirit as a pilot in your search for guidance? Or do you navigate without first checking with your pilot, proceeding as if your personal philosophy holds that it is better to ask for forgiveness than permission?

Dear God, thank You for Your Holy Spirit, who provides guidance for my way and gives me wisdom for making decisions.

(PATHWAYS TO HIS PRESENCE)

Unconditional Surrender

SCRIPTURE READING: JUDGES 6
KEY VERSE: JUDGES 6:14

The LORD turned to him and said, "Go in this might of yours, and you shall save Israel from the hand of the Midianites. Have I not sent you?"

What would you say if you were going about your daily business and a stranger walked up and said to you, "The LORD is with you, O valiant warrior" (Judg. 6:12 NASB)?

Chances are, you would be surprised, confused, and maybe a little mistrustful of the stranger. Gideon certainly did not feel that he was a valiant warrior. Like the rest of the Israelites, he was in hiding, desperately trying to conceal his meager portion of grain from the oppressive Midianites.

But Gideon knew it was an angel of the Lord speaking to him, and his stumbling block to obedience was focusing on his personal inadequacy. He could think of many reasons God should choose someone else: "O Lord, how shall I deliver Israel? Behold, my family is the least in Manasseh, and I am the youngest in my father's house" (Judg. 6:15 NASB).

In other words, his family was virtually unknown, and he was the least important member of a group of nobodies. Gideon soon learned that God did not want excuses; He wanted submission, obedience, and a yielded and trusting heart. God promised to be his sufficiency: "Surely I will be with you, and you shall defeat Midian as one man" (Judg. 6:16 NASB).

The Lord wanted Gideon to say yes without reservations, having faith that God would do the job. Only when he surrendered fully did God begin to use him in His plan to save Israel.

Almighty God, You don't want excuses; rather, You desire obedience. I submit my heart and life to You. You are my sufficiency. I say yes—without reservation.

(ON HOLY GROUND)

Your Hopes and Dreams

SCRIPTURE READING: JOHN 16:23–24
KEY VERSE: JOHN 16:24

Ask, and you will receive, that your joy may be full.

Some of the requirements to experiencing God's best include the following:

An open and willing heart. Before you can experience the blessings of God, you must be open to His love and will for your life. He takes joy in blessing those who love Him. Jesus told His disciples, "Ask, and you will receive" (John 16:24). Being open to God's blessings does not mean just being open to receive something good from Him. It means being willing to receive whatever He sends your way. And in some cases, He may send something that you did not wish to receive. However, you can be sure that every gift is ultimately good and sent from a loving Father who has your best interests in mind.

Obedience. This is a key to receiving and enjoying the goodness of God. Many times your faithfulness may not be noticeable to others, but God knows. When you take a step forward in obedience, the Lord always sends His blessings your way.

The ability to dream. God wants you to look forward to His gifts. When you lose the ability to dream and think on the goodness of God, something inside dies. No matter how small your dream for the future appears, refuse to let go of it. Allow God to reshape it if necessary, but always believe in His loving ability to supply answers to your hopes and dreams.

Father, give me an open and willing heart. Make me obedient to Your Word. Give me the ability to dream.

(INTO HIS PRESENCE)

God Has a Plan

SCRIPTURE READING: MATTHEW 6:25–34
KEY VERSE: PHILIPPIANS 4:19

My God shall supply all your need according to His riches in glory by Christ Jesus.

Matthew 6:25–34 is a portion of the Sermon on the Mount. As we read Christ's words to those who had gathered along the hillside, we discover a strong calmness emerging from the Son of God.

Essentially, Jesus told those gathered that it was a waste of time to worry. Why? Because God knew their needs, and He promised to provide for each one. The apostle Paul delivered the same message to the Philippian believers (Phil. 4:19).

The thought of God taking care of us is a victorious thought! We know that He has never failed to keep any of His promises. This fact alone should be the end of all doubt and worry, but it rarely is.

Often we become consumed with doubts and fears. When this happens, we have not transferred the ownership of our anxieties to Christ. Instead, we cling to doubt and fear with the hope of doing something to "help" God solve our problems.

If you want to "help God," try trusting Him. Let Him be God, and you become His faithful servant and friend.

Is there a pressing need in your life? Leave it at the altar of God. God is faithful. He takes into account all that you are facing and all that you will face in the future. He is omniscient, and He loves you perfectly. Whatever you need, God has a plan to solve it.

Lord, I rejoice that You have a plan to solve my every need. You know all I am facing today and in the future. I praise You!

(INTO HIS PRESENCE)

The Sifting Process

SCRIPTURE READING: LUKE 22:24–34
KEY VERSE: 2 CORINTHIANS 12:10

I take pleasure in infirmities, in reproaches, in needs, in persecutions, in distresses, for Christ's sake. For when I am weak, then I am strong.

God has a plan for your life. However, it doesn't snap into place overnight. It takes a lifetime to achieve all He has planned for you. He prepares you for service by giving you spiritual gifts and natural talents, and by allowing you to face many difficulties. He uses the difficulties to sift away the impurities in your life. The difficulties also sand and polish the rough edges of your life until they are smoothed. In the end, you become a reflection of His glory.

When God begins His process of sifting in your life, you may feel as though your entire life is being shaken. Don't worry. He is positioning you for a great blessing. Another indication of the sifting process of God comes when you sense His silence. He is testing to see whether you will trust Him even though He is not making Himself known to you through material blessings.

One of the hardest forms of sifting comes through suffering, whether physical, mental, or emotional. Amy Carmichael, a devoted servant of God, spent the last years of her life confined to her bed. God allowed her to be tested beyond what seemed bearable, especially for one who loved being in contact with others. Most of us will never face that kind of trial. However, the life of Christ burned brilliantly within her. Today her books, written during her time of suffering, are testimonies to God's faithfulness and glory.

Master, help me realize that You work in silence, suffering, and times of shaking to accomplish Your purposes in my life. Use these difficult circumstances to prepare me for the future You have planned.

(ON HOLY GROUND)

Removing the Lock

SCRIPTURE READING: 2 CORINTHIANS 3:1–6
KEY VERSE: 1 CORINTHIANS 3:16

Do you not know that you are the temple of God and that the Spirit of God dwells in you?

When you or I have bad habits that we cannot seem to get rid of no matter how much effort we exert, then those habits or problems have mastery over us. In a very real sense, we are their slaves. Whether it's too much food or television or sports, whatever dictates our priorities has control over us. It may seem as though sin has unlimited power, but that is not true. That is simply our impression when we allow ourselves to be victimized by a false master.

The first step in recovery, besides the obvious one of recognizing the problem, is identifying and understanding your true position in Christ as a redeemed one. With His blood, you were literally redeemed, or paid for, and the ownership of your life was transferred from sin and self to almighty God.

Take hold of this powerful liberation statement: "For the love of Christ controls us . . . and He died for all, that they who live should no longer live for themselves, but for Him who died and rose again on their behalf" (2 Cor. 5:14–15 NASB). If the love of Christ controls you, there is no room for subownership by other passions or desires or people. Living in bondage is an unnecessary condition. It is like staying in prison when the lock is removed.

Are you a slave to anything besides Christ? You can declare your own independence day under His authority.

O God, I want to change. Remove the lock to any area of my life where I have refused You access. I declare my independence day!

(ON HOLY GROUND)

Ask the Father

SCRIPTURE READING: MATTHEW 7:7–11
KEY VERSE: JAMES 4:2

You lust and do not have. You murder and covet and cannot obtain.
You fight and war. Yet you do not have because you do not ask.

When a child needs or wants something, he asks his mother or father for it. It would be silly for the child to assume that his parents automatically know all of his needs. For example, if the child said, "Dad, I was thirsty yesterday, and you didn't give me anything to drink," that parent would shake his head in amazement and say, "Well, son, you should have asked me."

Your heavenly Father knows what you need before you request anything. But even so, He wants you to enter into the experience of asking Him specifically. Jesus told us, "Ask, and it will be given to you; seek, and you will find; knock, and it will be opened to you. For everyone who asks receives, and he who seeks finds; and to him who knocks it will be opened" (Matt. 7:7–8 NASB).

He did not mean that God will automatically hand you everything you request. He is too wise and loving a Father to do that: "If you then, being evil, know how to give good gifts to your children, how much more will your Father who is in heaven give what is good to those who ask Him!" (Matt. 7:11 NASB).

God wants you to ask Him so you will learn the joys of a close relationship with Him. He wants you to feel His loving response and appreciate His care. What have you asked Him for today?

Teach me to ask, Lord. Teach me to keep seeking until I find and to keep
knocking until the door is opened to me.

(SEEKING HIS FACE)

Devoted to Prayer

SCRIPTURE READING: MATTHEW 14:13–23
KEY VERSE: LUKE 5:16

He Himself often withdrew into the wilderness and prayed.

Even with all of the crowds pressing around Him, Jesus sought time alone with His Father. Jesus made clear what He believed is the most important part of fellowship with God. In spite of the demands on His energy, He made communing with God His priority.

Is prayer the first thing on your list for the day? The last? Somewhere in between? Read what the apostle Paul said to the Colossian believers: "Devote yourselves to prayer, keeping alert in it with an attitude of thanksgiving" (Col. 4:2 NASB).

The word *devote* here doesn't convey the complete meaning of the original Greek, which was "giving constant attention to" or "persevering." We are to make the conscious decision to set aside time to talk to the Father and to listen to Him as He works in our hearts by the Holy Spirit and His Word.

It is tremendously helpful to set a specific time to pray. Make an "appointment" with the Lord, and write it down on your list for the day. If you keep in mind that you are making arrangements for a special encounter with God, you will treat this meeting accordingly.

You can combat the clamor of the day to find victory and joy in prayer, and a vital part of doing so is finding freedom from avoidable distractions. Ask God to show you how rich your relationship with Him can be.

Father God, I make a conscious decision today to set aside time to talk with You. Set me free from avoidable distractions. Show me how rich our relationship can be.

(ON HOLY GROUND)

Starting a Prayer Journal

SCRIPTURE READING: 1 THESSALONIANS 5:16–18
KEY VERSE: PSALM 48:9

We have thought, O God, on Your lovingkindness, in the midst of Your temple.

Have you ever considered the value of keeping a prayer journal? It's a record of your prayer relationship with God so that you can remember what you talked about with Him.

It works in this way. After you pray, write in a small notebook what you have said, along with the date. As God answers a particular item, draw a single line through the request, so that you can still read it, and put the date of the answer at the end of the line. When you review the journal, you can rejoice at His provision. You will be able to say, "God loves me. He is interested in me. I am growing in my faith, and He is working in my life."

What a thrill it is to trace His involvement and see your spiritual growth unfold as you trust Him, releasing all of your worries and problems to Him. As you pour out your heart to Him, you feel His tender care.

In addition, prayer is a purification process. God changes more than just your outlook on external things; He opens your eyes to aspects of your behavior and attitude that were not obvious before. As you respond to His conviction and make the appropriate changes through His strength, your character is molded more and more into the likeness of Jesus.

A prayer journal will help you observe and chronicle this process for yourself and others.

Lord, I cherish the ways You've answered me in the past. Thank You for loving me and working in my life.

(ON HOLY GROUND)

The Desires of Your Heart

SCRIPTURE READING: PSALM 37:3–8
KEY VERSES: PSALM 37:4

Delight yourself also in the LORD, and He shall give you the desires of your heart.

Most of us are familiar with the scripture from Isaiah in which God said, "For My thoughts are not your thoughts, nor are your ways My ways" (55:8). Yet many times we fail to see the goodness of this verse. God often takes us places we could never dream of going on our own. His vision is far beyond ours. His might and power open doors for us we thought were permanently closed.

God has a way of providing all we could ever hope for. The problem comes when we fail to trust Him in times of waiting. All of us have done this. We want something to take place so badly that we try to convince God to give us what we want now.

When we fail to see His immediate response, we often think He is not going to provide what we desire to receive. Jesus told His disciples to seek God first and then all the other desires of their hearts would be given to them (Matt. 6:33).

Who plants desires in your heart? Many times God does, especially if you are walking closely with Him. These are the very things He wants to give you as a blessing from Himself. Don't worry about wrong motivations. God knows how to sift away selfish longings and replace them with healthy dreams and goals.

God's blessings are so satisfying, few have ever sought to return them. Therefore, wait for His way to be known, and the blessing you receive will fill your heart with boundless joy.

Father, help me to wait for Your way to be known. Don't let me walk in my own way.

(SEEKING HIS FACE)

A Spokesman of God's Truth

SCRIPTURE READING: HEBREWS 13:20–21
KEY VERSE: MARK 2:17

When Jesus heard it, He said to them, "Those who are well have no need of a physician, but those who are sick. I did not come to call the righteous, but sinners, to repentance."

George Whitefield, an English evangelist who lived from 1714 to 1770, delivered more than eighteen thousand sermons in his lifetime of being a traveling preacher. In England and America, his strong voice carried through fields to the crowds of thousands that gathered wherever he went. He was so passionate to spread the gospel that he continued preaching even in poor health.

The people around him recognized that the Lord gave him almost superhuman energy and drive. In their book *The Light and the Glory*, Peter Marshall and David Manuel described the scene in New Hampshire at his last sermon:

> When the time came to speak, he could barely breathe, and one of them said to him, "Sir, you are more fit to go to bed, than to preach."
>
> "True, sir," gasped Whitefield. Then, glancing heavenward he added, "Lord Jesus, I am weary in Thy work, but not of it. If I have not finished my course, let me go and speak for Thee once more in the fields, and seal Thy truth, and come home and die!"

God answered his prayer. After delivering a more than two-hour sermon, the exhausted Whitefield went to a pastor friend's home; he died the next morning as he gazed out the window at the sunrise. Because one man was willing to be a spokesman of God's truth, two nations were touched with His love.

O Lord, make me a spokesman of Your truth. I have not finished my journey. Don't let me grow weary along the way. Keep me faithful to the end.

(ON HOLY GROUND)

Expect the Unexpected

SCRIPTURE READING: 2 KINGS 3:10–18
KEY VERSE: 2 KINGS 3:18

This is a simple matter in the sight of the LORD; He will also deliver the Moabites into your hand.

Go forward!

As we step out without any sign or sound—not a wave or splash wetting our feet as we take the first step—we shall see the sea divide and the pathway open through the very midst of the waters.

If we have seen the miraculous workings of God in some extraordinary providential deliverance, I am sure the thing that has impressed us most has been the quietness with which it was done, the absence of everything spectacular and sensational, and the utter sense of nothingness that came to us as we stood in the presence of this mighty God and felt how easy it was for Him to do it all without the faintest effort on His part or the slightest help on ours. It is not the part of faith to question, but to obey.

Are you craving a fresh encounter with God? Then expect the unexpected. God has the answer to your heart's deepest request.

A. B. Simpson identifies the great victory of faith:

Our unbelief is always wanting some outward sign. The religion of many is largely sensational, and they are not satisfied of its genuineness without manifestations, etc.; but the greatest triumph of faith is to be still and know that He is God.

The great victory of faith is to stand before some impassable Red Sea, and hear the Master say, "Stand still, and see the salvation of the Lord."

God, You are the answer to my heart's deepest requests. I expect the unexpected today.

(SEEKING HIS FACE)

Our Heavenly Father

SCRIPTURE READING: LUKE 20:1–8
KEY VERSES: MATTHEW 7:28–29

So it was, when Jesus had ended these sayings, that the people were astonished at His teaching, for He taught them as one having authority, and not as the scribes.

The authority of Jesus' teaching staggered the Jews of His day. His miracles of healing and control over nature's forces awed hearers and disciples. But there was nothing more stunning to His audience than His constant reference to God as Father.

God was revealed in the Old Testament through very reverent and awe-inspiring names such as El Shaddai (God Almighty), Elohim (Strong One), and Adonai (Lord of all). The most frequent title given to Him was Yahweh. So sacred was the Jewish concept of this name that the devout Jew would not pronounce it; the scribe who wrote it immediately washed his hands.

Imagine how startled Jesus' hearers were when the Messiah referred to God as "My Father," attesting to the deity of Christ and His oneness with God. When conversing with the disciples, Jesus often called God "your Father," referring to their membership in God's family and their intimacy with Him.

God is your Father. God is not distant, aloof, or impersonal, but longs for the depth of a Father-child relationship with you—no condemnation, no rejection, just unconditional love and acceptance.

You will not trust God greatly unless you love Him. You will not love Him freely until, as a son or daughter, you come to know His fatherly embrace.

No condemnation. No rejection. Unconditional love and acceptance. Thank You, Father!

(INTO HIS PRESENCE)

Healing Our Hurts

SCRIPTURE READING: EPHESIANS 4:26–32
KEY VERSE: EPHESIANS 4:32

Be kind to one another, tenderhearted, forgiving one another, even as God in Christ forgave you.

Whether it is the driver who cut you off in traffic, a relative who gets under your skin, or a coworker who irritates you, there will always be someone in your life who needs forgiveness.

Sometimes the pardon is easily doled out, and anger is soon forgotten. Yet sometimes, deep roots of hurt prevail and the bitterness tightens its grip on your spirit and makes reconciliation very difficult.

Christian author Dag Hammarskjöld wrote, "Forgiveness breaks the chain of causality because he who forgives you—out of love—takes upon himself the consequences of what you have done. Forgiveness, therefore, always entails a sacrifice."

Ephesians 4:32 proclaims, "Be kind to one another, tenderhearted, forgiving one another, even as God in Christ forgave you."

Pardon is most easily given when remembering the immense debt of which Christ has relieved you. Each person knows the wrongs he or she has done, yet Christ freely forgives because of His unmatchable love for His children. He heals your hurts first by forgiving you and then by teaching you how to forgive others. Out of thankfulness to Him, reflect the grace that you have been shown.

Forgiveness is God's grace lived out in a practical way. You will never resemble Christ more than when you do what He did for you: forgive.

Lord, grant me the strength to give up my anger and resentment toward others so that I may be a mirror of Your grace.

(PATHWAYS TO HIS PRESENCE)

Your Greetest Need

Scripture Reading: John 3:1–17
Key Verse: John 3:17

God did not send His Son into the world to condemn the world, but that the world through Him might be saved.

Throughout the Bible, we see God reaching out to His creation in an effort to save and restore. Of course, nowhere is this more evident than in the New Testament, especially in the Gospels through the life of His Son.

Jesus came to earth to seek and save those who were spiritually lost and bound by sin. By His own profession, He made that clear when He told His disciples that He did not come to judge mankind, but to save the lost from an eternal death (John 3:17).

We may be tempted to think that God is too caught up in the details of the universe to be concerned about our problems. But this is not true. Jesus was and still is totally interested in our lives.

Even after His crucifixion, His intimate concern was for those He loved. One example was His compassion for Mary as she searched for Him at the empty tomb. Jesus had not yet ascended to the Father. He witnessed Mary's deep sorrow and was moved with compassion. "Mary!" Jesus called out to her.

"Rabboni!" (which means "Teacher") was her reply (John 20:16). When she saw the Lord, she knew her prayers had been answered. Jesus was alive! That was her greatest need—to know that what He had promised was true.

What is your greatest need? Call out to the Savior, and He will meet that need.

Lord, I bring to You my greatest need today. I know Your promises are true. I wait expectantly for fulfillment.

(INTO HIS PRESENCE)

Spiritual Focus

SCRIPTURE READING: PHILIPPIANS 3:7–14
KEY VERSE: PHILIPPIANS 4:4

Rejoice in the Lord always. Again I will say, rejoice!

If you wear glasses or contact lenses, you know how blurry and fuzzy the world can be when you're not wearing them. A simple task like getting ready in the morning is difficult, maybe impossible, if you've misplaced them somewhere. And it would be ridiculous to think about going through the day without them.

What many don't realize, however, is that trying to operate without spiritual focus is detrimental as well. Your daily circumstances are anything but simple, and it's easy to get lost in a fog of confusion, misaligned priorities, and feelings of being overwhelmed. Before you know it, you're moving in a direction you do not want to go, but you don't know how to slow down and allow God to give you His direction.

When you realize that your spiritual life is out of focus, you need to slow down and spend serious time in prayer and study of His Word. All other goals and activities fall into place when you see Jesus as He is, as your Lord and Savior and dearest Friend. Through His love and grace, He wants to clear the fog away and sharpen your spiritual vision with His eternal perspective.

Paul declared in Philippians 3:8: "I count all things to be loss in view of the surpassing value of knowing Christ Jesus my Lord, for whom I have suffered the loss of all things, and count them but rubbish so that I may gain Christ" (NASB).

Jesus, help me to see You as You are, and keep my focus fixed there.

(SEEKING HIS FACE)

Eternally Secure

SCRIPTURE READING: 1 JOHN 5:10–13
KEY VERSE: EPHESIANS 1:13

In Him you also trusted, after you heard the word of truth, the gospel of your salvation; in whom also, having believed, you were sealed with the Holy Spirit of promise.

Perhaps more than ever, our age is security conscious. We like the reassurance of a healthy savings account. We like the benefits that come from working for a supposedly solid company. We treasure the comfort and strength of a good marriage. Yet we must admit that even the biggest savings account can run dry, the best company can go under, and the healthiest marriage can fragment.

God wants us to look to Him for our security. He alone is the cornerstone, the rock, the stronghold, the fortress, the shelter in whom we can find safety, peace, and protection.

You are secure in your position in Him. You are "in Christ," placed there by God Himself. He will keep you forever. Because you are a joint heir with Christ, all the blessings of heaven are yours.

Your eternal destination is fixed. Heaven is your home; no sin can change that once you place your faith in Christ.

Your past sins and mistakes have been thoroughly forgiven through Christ's shed blood. You are a new creature in Christ. The old things have passed away.

You can carry your present problems and challenges to Him in prayer, and He promises to help and sustain you. He upholds you with His eternal grip of love. If you are looking for security, look to Christ. He never changes.

Precious Lord, I am secure in You; my eternal destination is fixed; my sins and mistakes are forgiven. I can take my problems and challenges to You, and You uphold me with the eternal grip of Your love. Thank You, Father.

(ON HOLY GROUND)

Experiencing God's Love

SCRIPTURE READING: HEBREWS 5:6–10
KEY VERSE: HEBREWS 5:8

Though He was a Son, yet He learned obedience by the things which He suffered.

What happens when you ignore God? In your mind, do you picture Him just walking away, looking forlorn and rejected? Or do you have a mental image of God getting mad at you and banishing you to forty years of wilderness wandering?

Neither is correct. God loves you perfectly. And His love for you is not based on your obedience. Though He tells us in His Word that obedience is better than sacrifice, the thing that God wants most from you is a love that comes from your heart.

He doesn't stop loving you just because you do something wrong. None of us can earn God's love by being good or trying to be perfect. For one, we do not have the ability to do either of these on our own. We need a Savior. And this is why Jesus came to die for you and me. He does the very thing that you cannot do for yourself. He sets you free from sin and makes you acceptable in God's eyes.

When we ignore the Lord, we are the ones who suffer and miss a great opportunity for blessing. God is not a strong and mighty taskmaster who waits for us to do something wrong so He can pounce. He is a loving God who listens for our cry. When He draws you to Himself, He uses love, not a rod of thunder. God knows that once you drink of His love, the world's appeal will fade. Give Him your heart, and you will be blessed by what you receive from Him.

Thank You for Your love, Father. It sets me free from sin and makes me acceptable in Your sight. I rejoice in that!

(PATHWAYS TO HIS PRESENCE)

God's Word at Work

SCRIPTURE READING: ROMANS 7:15–8:17
KEY VERSE: ROMANS 7:22

I delight in the law of God according to the inward man.

One particular believer felt like a failure. He had asked Jesus Christ to be his Savior three years ago, and for a while his life seemed to change. Some of his sinful habits went away, and others were diminishing as he began to understand more of God's Word. But lately, some of those old habits were starting to come back, and even worse, on some days he didn't even mind.

"Maybe I'm not really a believer," he worried. "Or maybe God has given up on me. After all, I was pretty poor material to start with." The more he told himself these lies, the more he believed them, and the more he felt like a failure.

Does this struggle with unresolved sin sound familiar? Perhaps it should—it describes the experience of the apostle Paul. He wrote: "For the good that I will to do, I do not do; but the evil I will not to do, that I practice. . . . O wretched man that I am! Who will deliver me from this body of death? I thank God—through Jesus Christ our Lord!" (Rom. 7:19, 24–25).

That was Paul talking, the one God used to send His Word to countless people. His "secret" was that he understood Jesus was in the process of rescuing him and would never give up on him. Always remember that you have "the Spirit of adoption by whom we cry out, 'Abba, Father'" (Rom. 8:15). God's Word is at work in you today!

Father, thank You for the Spirit of adoption at work in me today. I am so grateful that You will never give up on me!

(INTO HIS PRESENCE)

The World Is Not Winning

SCRIPTURE READING: ROMANS 8
KEY VERSE: ROMANS 8:37

In all these things we are more than conquerors through Him who loved us.

As you go about your daily routine, do you sometimes feel as though the world is winning? From the irritations and conflicts of your personal circumstances to bad news in the marketplace and the media, it's easy to become discouraged and focused on the negative.

The victory over sin and death that Christ won on the cross can seem remote from daily application. But the truth remains: "Whatever is born of God overcomes the world; and this is the victory that has overcome the world—our faith. Who is the one who overcomes the world, but he who believes that Jesus is the Son of God?" (1 John 5:4–5 NASB).

You are more than a conqueror through Jesus Christ (Rom. 8:37). Does this mean that you will feel successful in every encounter and conflict? No. God may allow you to go through times when His truth working within you is obscured to another's eyes. He may need to do more work in the other person's heart before he is ready to listen. God is taking care of the consequences; your job is to trust Him for the outcome.

Ultimately the victory is yours in the Lord. In the meantime, you can cling to this promise: "Commit your way to the LORD; trust also in Him, and He will do it. He will bring forth your righteousness as the light and your judgment as the noonday" (Ps. 37:5–6 NASB).

Thank You, Lord, that I can trust the outcome to You. Victory is mine through You.

(SEEKING HIS FACE)

A Higher Purpose

SCRIPTURE READING: JOB 42:1–6
KEY VERSES: HEBREWS 4:14–16

Seeing then that we have a great High Priest who has passed through the heavens, Jesus the Son of God, let us hold fast our confession. For we do not have a High Priest who cannot sympathize with our weaknesses, but was in all points tempted as we are, yet without sin. Let us therefore come boldly to the throne of grace, that we may obtain mercy and find grace to help in time of need.

Mary Slessor was the daughter of a devout Christian mother and an alcoholic father. Her early years in the mid-1800s were devoted to survival in the slums of Dundee, Scotland. She was beaten frequently by her father and often thrown out of the house.

Yet in this cruel injustice, Mary gained a steadfast spirit, one that God used mightily in the years to come. She came to know Christ at the age of twenty-eight and soon after left for missionary training.

Chronic illness and loneliness brought her to the point of despair, but God gave her strength to answer His call. "Christ sent me to preach the gospel," she said. "He will look after the results." In Africa, she chose to identify with the people to whom she witnessed by eating and sleeping on dirt floors of huts.

As a result of her earlier life, Mary was able to handle the most threatening situations. Her missionary efforts accounted for the rescue of countless twins, babies who were viewed as being children of the devil. She quickly earned the title "Ma Slessor" by the Okoyong tribe.

Adversity molded her for a higher service. Whatever you are facing, give it to Jesus, and allow Him to make something beautiful out of your life. Trust Him for the outcome and all the moments in between.

Lord, take the adversities of my life, and use them to mold me for a higher purpose. Take all that is ugly, and make something beautiful from it.

(INTO HIS PRESENCE)

Profiting from Suffering

SCRIPTURE READING: 1 PETER 4:12–16
KEY VERSE: 1 PETER 5:10

May the God of all grace, who called us to His eternal glory by Christ Jesus, after you have suffered a while, perfect, establish, strengthen, and settle you.

The best way to deal with suffering is to set your eyes on Jesus, not your circumstances. Most of us have little problem following Christ when things are going well, but at the first sign of a storm, we instinctively run for cover.

After Jesus calmed the raging winds, He turned to His disciples and asked, "Why did you doubt?" No one knows the length and depth of suffering. However, we know from Scripture that God wants us to place our entire trust in Him during times of difficulty and heartache.

You may be struggling with a burden that has endured for years. You are tired, doubtful, and angry. Satan is tempting you to give up, but God has not given up on you.

Remember, His purpose for allowing suffering is to mold and shape you into the image of His Son. And nothing so sands and polishes a saint like the fiery trials of adversity.

Peter said, "After you have suffered for a little while, the God of all grace, who called you to His eternal glory in Christ, will Himself perfect, confirm, strengthen and establish you" (1 Peter 5:10 NASB).

Let nothing keep you from trusting Him, no matter how great the winds of affliction. Sink your roots deep into the grace and love of Christ.

Master, when I am tempted to give up, help me remember that You have not given up on me. Conform me to the image of Your Son. Sand and polish my life through the trials of adversity.

(ON HOLY GROUND)

Divine Purposes

SCRIPTURE READING: PSALM 67:1–7
KEY VERSE: PSALM 66:1

Make a joyful shout to God, all the earth!

George Bernard accepted Jesus as his Savior at the age of sixteen. He served for a time in the Salvation Army and was later ordained as a minister, leading many revivals throughout Michigan and New York. Then, in 1913, he experienced a time of extreme crisis.

Bernard did what he had done for years—he turned to the Lord. He spent much time in prayer, worship, and Bible study, meditating deeply about the cross. Wanting to share the truth he discovered, Bernard wrote his thoughts in verse form with music to accompany them. His work is a spiritual legacy to believers everywhere, the beloved hymn "The Old Rugged Cross."

The Lord used His dealings with one man to bless countless others. When God deals with us individually, He has divine purposes in mind. God blesses His children and works in our lives because He loves us dearly, and He wants His goodness to go even further. His plan for you fits perfectly with His plan for the world.

Recognizing God's overall plan is a key to a growing relationship with Him. You see yourself as He sees you, a much-loved child with talents and gifts to use for His service. When you understand His higher purposes for your life, you are a useful tool in His hands as you exercise your talents to glorify Him.

God, I know You have divine purposes in mind in every aspect of my life. Help me to use each experience to leave a spiritual legacy to others.

(INTO HIS PRESENCE)

Resolute Trust

SCRIPTURE READING: HEBREWS 2:14–18
KEY VERSE: ISAIAH 26:3

You will keep him in perfect peace, whose mind is stayed on You, because he trusts in You.

Stock markets rise and fall. Farm prices soar and plummet. Personal health peaks and dips.

Such is the nature of our unstable environment: ever changing, altering, moving, and shifting. But believers have a firm anchor in such fluctuation, a sure faith in an unchanging God who promises to never leave us helpless.

God is sovereign. God is always at work in every detail of our lives, using each setback and victory for His primary purpose: to glorify Himself by conforming us to Christ's image. No event or person is outside the power and rule of God.

God is wise. His wisdom is yours as you humbly ask and expectantly receive. His Word and Spirit will light your path to fulfill His will for your life.

God is loving. Whatever comes, you are kept secure in the love of God. His love ensures He will provide for, guide, and sustain you. He tenderly cares for your innermost needs. Nothing can keep you outside His love.

Because God is sovereign, wise, and loving, you can trust Him without reservation. Resolute trust will quell your fears, calm your quivers, and stabilize your emotions. He holds you fast and will not let go.

Precious heavenly Father, You are an unchanging God who never leaves me helpless. You are sovereign and at work in every detail of my life. Use each setback and victory to accomplish Your purpose of conforming me to Christ's image.

(ON HOLY GROUND)

Getting God's Viewpoint

SCRIPTURE READING: 2 CORINTHIANS 4:16–18
KEY VERSE: 2 CORINTHIANS 4:17

Our light affliction, which is but for a moment, is working for us a far more exceeding and eternal weight of glory.

If you have traveled on an airplane, you have experienced the thrill of liftoff. As the plane surges up and up, the objects on the ground become smaller until the plane finally breaks through the clouds. Then, with the pillowy mist below, you are transported to a tranquil wonderland with a new perspective.

When hardships and problems invade our lives, we often fix our focus on them, looking down as we would from an airplane. The result is that we sometimes forget that God has a completely different vantage point. From His perspective, every event has a purpose that fits perfectly into His plan.

Today's Scripture passage provides additional encouragement, saying that our momentary afflictions are producing eternal glory (v. 17). It also reminds us that, while we are on earth, it is not the visible things but the unseen things that are eternal (v. 18).

What "light affliction" in your life is causing you to look away from God? Has someone hurt you? Are you disappointed? Are discouraging circumstances hindering your joy? God, your heavenly Father, longs to relieve you of these burdens. He wants to show you His perspective.

When you have God's viewpoint, you will be able to face your circumstances with the confidence that He will see you through your difficulty. And as a result, the Lord will allow you to soar past your hardships into a new horizon of spiritual growth.

Heavenly Father, give me Your viewpoint. Help me face my circumstances with confidence that You will be with me through every difficulty.

(PATHWAYS TO HIS PRESENCE)

The Initiator of Love

SCRIPTURE READING: PSALM 18:1–6
KEY VERSE: 1 JOHN 4:10

*In this is love, not that we loved God, but that He loved us and sent His
Son to be the propitiation for our sins.*

From the beginning of time, God has been the Initiator of love. In his
book *Lectures in Systematic Theology*, Henry Thiessen wrote, "He is unlike
the gods of the heathen, who hate and are angry, and the god of the phi-
losopher, who is cold and indifferent." God loves us with a personal and
intimate love.

Those who have yet to discover the intimacy of God often view Him
as being cool and demanding toward His creation. But nothing is further
from the truth. Even in the Old Testament, we find God constantly moving toward mankind in an effort to reveal more of Himself on an intimate
basis. Love motivates Him to do this.

In fact, love is the motivating factor of every true relationship. It
motivated the heart of God not to destroy man in the garden of Eden.
And it was the one thing that motivated Him to deliver Israel from the
Egyptians.

Love brought down the walls of Jericho, and love was the motivation
behind the coming of Christ. Love took our place on Calvary's cross and
later rose from the grave. And love reaches out to us each day with freshness and hope.

God created you to live within the embrace of His love. Many wonder how He could love them so deeply. But He does. He is love, and He
loves you and me.

*Heavenly Father, I thank You that You are not a cold, indifferent God.
Thank You for reaching out to me in love.*

(INTO HIS PRESENCE)

In Awe of His Grace

SCRIPTURE READING: PSALM 43:3–5
KEY VERSE: PROVERBS 14:27

The fear of the LORD is a fountain of life,
To turn one away from the snares of death.

Each time a scribe would come to a passage containing the name of God, he would lay down his stylus and go wash his hands. The scribe did not feel worthy to print God's name without cleansing and humbling himself before the Lord. There was an aspect of godly fear in this action that seems foreign to us today.

Do you fear God for who He is? Are you aware of His awesome power and presence in your life? We miss a great blessing when we fail to give Him His rightful place in our lives.

Satan eagerly entices you to become frightened of God. He lies by telling you God wants to hurt you in some way. Nothing is further from the truth. God loves you completely.

Proverbs 14:27 tells us: "The fear of the LORD is a fountain of life, that one may avoid the snares of death" (NASB). When we fear God, we reverence Him with our lives. We are not frightened. Instead, we acknowledge His holiness and humble ourselves before Him. We also avoid anything we sense will bring sorrow or grief to His Spirit living within us.

When you yield to temptation, be quick to admit your failure, and seek His forgiveness. Because His Spirit lives within you, you can trust that He will lead you away from sin and toward righteousness when your heart is right before Him. Standing in awe of His matchless grace gives evidence that you are on the right spiritual pathway.

Lord, I am in awe of Your grace. Help me to avoid anything that will bring sorrow or grief to Your Spirit living within me.

(SEEKING HIS FACE)

A Fresh Touch from God

SCRIPTURE READING: PSALM 77
KEY VERSES: ISAIAH 43:18–19

*Do not remember the former things, nor consider the things of old.
Behold, I will do a new thing, now it shall spring forth; shall you
not know it? I will even make a road in the wilderness and rivers in
the desert.*

Have you ever felt as if your life were a dry, barren desert? In the opening passage, Israel felt spiritually and emotionally desolate. In their disobedience, they had wandered from God, and He had allowed them to go. When they came to their senses, they cried out in evidence of the burden they bore in their hearts. They were alone and needed a fresh touch from God.

The wonderful thing about Christ is He is never at a distance. He is always beside us. Because faithfulness is a part of His nature, He cannot be unfaithful and still be God. When we are faithless, He is still faithful. And in the case of Israel, He proved true to His nature.

God commissioned the prophet Isaiah to record and report His words to His people. In Isaiah 43:18, God told Israel: "Do not call to mind the former things, or ponder things of the past" (NASB). In other words, "Don't spend a great deal of time looking back over past failures. Today is today. Up ahead is where we are going, and this is what I plan to do."

God always works in the present but looks to the future. Life at its best is not lived in the past, worrying over what happened or what once was. Instead, it is lived in the here and now, aware of one thing: God is a God of love, and He is always at work in your life to do something for your good and His glory.

*Dear Lord, keep my focus off the past and on the future. Up ahead is where
I am going. You are at work in my life, opening the way for me. I embrace
tomorrow with joy and anticipation.*

(ON HOLY GROUND)

Coming out of Hiding

SCRIPTURE READING: GENESIS 3:8–13
KEY VERSE: GENESIS 3:10

He said, "I heard Your voice in the garden, and I was afraid because I was naked; and I hid myself."

Adam and Eve did their best not to give away their hiding places. Soon enough, the familiar voice was calling to them, as it consistently did in the cool of the day. Adam and Eve knew that eventually they would have to face the Lord God. In Genesis 3:10, Adam explained his hiding because he was ashamed of his nakedness.

Perhaps you are not hiding in the bushes or covered with fig leaves, but most people understand what it is to conceal their most private, intimate thoughts, faults, and failures. Afraid that the deepest hurts will be exposed—naked for all to see—a person hides behind defensive responses. You may think, *This is the way I am. I've had a hard life, and I can't change.*

However, the Bible exhorts that each person has a responsibility to live a godly life. In other words, each person has the ability to respond in a God-honoring manner. James Rhinehart admonishes, "I've learned that our background and circumstances may have influenced who we are, but we are responsible for who we become."

God is calling to you, and He wants you to come out of hiding. Will you open yourself up to really knowing the Father?

Lord, I offer You the feeble fig leaves that I use to cover my weaknesses so that I may wear Your garment of righteousness.

(PATHWAYS TO HIS PRESENCE)

A True Friend

SCRIPTURE READING: JOHN 14:1–18
KEY VERSE: PROVERBS 17:17

A friend loves at all times,
And a brother is born for adversity.

Have you ever had a friend who liked you because you were fun to be with and put on a good appearance? However, the moment your life took a turn for the worse, you found him distancing himself from you. If you have experienced such rejection, you're not alone. Jesus experienced all kinds of rejection.

And in some ways that rejection continues. Perhaps He asks something of us that we think is too harsh or requires something we don't want to give up. We back off in hopes that He will leave us alone. Once Jesus began talking about a deeper life commitment, many of His followers left.

The disciples told Him that His words were too severe. But Jesus was not persuaded by human opinion, and He held fast to the message the Father had given Him. His words were meant to convict while separating those who would remain with Him from those who would leave.

What kind of Friend is Jesus? He is the kind who willingly laid down His life as payment for your sins—past, present, and future. Without complaint He bore all your sorrows and suffering, while pledging never to leave or forsake you (John 14:18).

He is a Friend who sticks closer than a brother. And before you whisper your most intimate prayer, He knows your heart and rushes to your side.

Jesus, thank You for laying down Your life for my sin and bearing my sorrow
and suffering. Thank You that You will never leave me or forsake me.

(INTO HIS PRESENCE)

Reverence for God

SCRIPTURE READING: MARK 9:36–37
KEY VERSE: JOHN 17:3

This is eternal life, that they may know You, the only true God, and Jesus Christ whom You have sent.

Your reverence for God needs to be active and operational. Remarks about "the Man upstairs" and other off-the-cuff comments about God fail to communicate the attitude of a grateful heart.

When Moses approached God, he trembled at the sight of the Lord's power and strength. Yet often we easily reduce God's glory to fit within the casual context of human language. God demands our love. We are to honor Him with our lives and the gratitude of our hearts.

In the book *The Pursuit of God*, A. W. Tozer wrote:

I want to deliberately encourage this mighty longing after God. The lack of it has brought us to our present low estate. The stiff and wooden quality about our religious lives is a result of our lack of holy desire. Complacency is a deadly foe of all spiritual growth. Acute desire must be present or there will be no manifestation of Christ to His people. . . .

The shallowness of our inner experience, the hollowness of our worship, and the servile imitation of the world which marks our promotional methods all testify that we know God only imperfectly and the grace of God scarcely at all. . . . We must put away all effort to impress, and come with the guileless candor of childhood. If we do this, without doubt God will quickly respond.

Dear heavenly Father, help me to put away all efforts to impress, and come to You with the guileless candor of childhood.

(SEEKING HIS FACE)

Childlike Faith

SCRIPTURE READING: EPHESIANS 2:1–10
KEY VERSES: MATTHEW 18:3

Assuredly, I say to you, unless you are converted and become as little children, you will by no means enter the kingdom of heaven.

Ask the average person how a person gets to heaven, and you will probably hear something like, "Follow the Ten Commandments" or "Make sure your good deeds outweigh your bad ones." However, the truth is, eternal life is offered freely to all who will receive God's gift of salvation. He wants us to admit our absolute dependency on Him. As long as we think we can somehow work our way into heaven or perform some great deed on our own, we receive very little from the hand of God.

Jesus instructed the disciples to become like children in their approach to God. The issue He was addressing was one of pride. A child looks to his mother or father for support and help. He may try to do things on his own, but when frustration comes, he knows he can turn to his parents for a solution.

A young father told how he secretly watched his three-year-old daughter struggling to put on her shoes. The more she tried lacing and tying the shoes on her own, the more frustrated she became. Finally in desperation, she dropped back on her bed and loudly proclaimed: "Help me, God. I just can't do it."

Nicodemus had a hard time understanding Jesus' concept of a new birth. As a member of the Sanhedrin, he was highly educated. Still the only way he could expect to spend eternity with God was to place his childlike faith in Jesus Christ. It was not a matter of intellect; it was a matter of humble faith and grace. Take time to tell the Savior you need Him more than anything else.

Give me childlike faith in You, dear Lord. I need You more than anything else.

(INTO HIS PRESENCE)

The Great Encourager

SCRIPTURE READING: JAMES 1:1–12
KEY VERSE: JAMES 1:12

Blessed is the man who endures temptation; for when he has been approved, he will receive the crown of life which the Lord has promised to those who love Him.

Though all that surrounds you seems lost in a misty sea of confusion, God is with you. He never leaves your side. Some may say, "There is nothing wrong in my life." However, each of us faces times of uncertainty when sorrow or dread covers the pathway before us and leaves us feeling helpless.

There is no greater blessing than beginning and ending each day with Jesus. Don't let doubts cloud the reality of His indwelling presence in your life. God tests your faith to make sure that it is deeply rooted within His truth. He allows adversity to brush across your life sometimes with great intensity so that the level of your trust will be exposed.

You learn to endure in the testing of your faith. And godly endurance, not human ability, makes you strong. James wrote, "Consider it all joy, my brethren, when you encounter various trials, knowing that the testing of your faith produces endurance. And let endurance have its perfect result, so that you may be perfect and complete, lacking in nothing" (1:2–4 NASB).

To have the faith that conquers all doubts and fears, you must look to Christ as your Hope and Guide in every situation. Don't allow yourself to be drawn off course by the criticism or lack of support of others. God is your greatest Encourager, and when your faith is firmly fixed in Him, you can be sure He will lead you to victory.

Almighty God, give me the faith that conquers all doubts and fears. I look to You as my Hope and Guide in every situation. Don't let me be drawn off course by others. I fix my focus on You.

(ON HOLY GROUND)

The Revelation of God

SCRIPTURE READING: JOHN 13:1–17
KEY VERSE: JOHN 15:15

No longer do I call you servants, for a servant does not know what his master is doing; but I have called you friends, for all things that I heard from My Father I have made known to you.

"The highest proof of true friendship," emphasizes Andrew Murray, "is the intimacy that holds nothing back and admits the friend to share our inmost secrets. It is a blessing to be Christ's servant; His redeemed ones delight to call themselves His servants. Christ had often spoken of the disciples as His servants. In His great love our Lord now says, 'No longer do I call you servants, but I call you friends, for all things I heard from my Father I have made known to you.'"

Since the beginning of time God has sought ways of revealing Himself to mankind—first in the garden of Eden and later to the prophets. With the birth of His Son, God initiated an intimacy with man that can never be destroyed. Jesus' love for us was so great that He laid aside His royal robe in heaven and took up a towel and basin to serve those He came to save.

The next time you are tempted to think that God doesn't care if you hurt or if you are lonely, think about what it cost Him to come to earth. He did not come to judge or condemn; He came to demonstrate His personal love for you. Before He left heaven, He knew there would be a cross, and still He was willing to come to you.

God continues to reveal Himself even when you are captivated by the things of this world. Ask Him to make you sensitive to His great love.

Lord, make me sensitive to Your great love. Thank You for Your personal love for me, for leaving heaven and coming to earth to die for my sin.

(SEEKING HIS FACE)

Engineered by God

SCRIPTURE READING: PSALM 4:1–8
KEY VERSE: PSALM 4:5

Offer the sacrifices of righteousness,
And put your trust in the LORD.

The thought of failing can stir up feelings of anxiety and fear. We wonder, *If I fail, what will others think of me? If I am defeated instead of constantly victorious, how will that reflect upon my life?*

Failure is sometimes engineered by God to bring about a stark revelation about ourselves: we need to trust God in every aspect of our lives. Whether our failure relates to a particular sin that seems impossible to conquer or a venture within ministry or a business or a relationship, it helps us to understand that we need to depend totally upon God. There are times in our lives where we strike out on our own, possibly even attempting to do something for God. But when we try these things in our own strength, failure is imminent.

David understood both failure and victory, experiencing both in many different areas of his life. And it was through his defeats that he recognized how desperately he needed God to permeate every place in his heart.

As we place our dependence upon God, an incredible freedom and peace will begin to rest in our hearts. And reaching that point in our lives makes every failure worth it.

Lord, permeate my being so that in failure I can see victory, and in victory I can see You.

(PATHWAYS TO HIS PRESENCE)

When God Says Go

SCRIPTURE READING: GENESIS 12:1–9
KEY VERSES: GENESIS 12:2–3

I will make you a great nation;
I will bless you
And make your name great;
And you shall be a blessing.
I will bless those who bless you,
And I will curse him who curses you;
And in you all the families of the earth shall be blessed.

Hannah Whitall Smith once wrote, "Sight is not faith, and hearing is not faith, neither is feeling faith; but believing when we neither see, hear, nor feel is faith. . . . Therefore, we must believe before we feel, and often against our feelings if we would honor God by our faith."

As you read the account of Abram's life, you realize he was a man of extreme faith. God asked him to do something many would find difficult, and that was to leave his family and friends and go to an unfamiliar land.

Yet God's reassuring words in Genesis 12:2–3 lessened Abram's fear.

Abram—or Abraham, as he was later called by God—gave little thought to the fact that his name would be made great. The most important thing to him was the exercise of his faith through obedience.

When God calls you to move in a certain direction by faith, He will provide you reassurance. Your responsibility is to obey and follow Him. Abram left everything because he heard God say, "Go." Are you willing to do the same? Pray that your response to the Lord is always one of faith, love, and obedience. That way you will never miss a single blessing.

God, give me the faith to obey and follow You when You say, "Go." I don't want to miss a single blessing You have for me!

(INTO HIS PRESENCE)

Live Free in Him

SCRIPTURE READING: JOHN 15:4–7
KEY VERSE: JOHN 14:23

Jesus answered and said to him, "If anyone loves Me, he will keep My word; and My Father will love him, and We will come to him and make Our home with him."

The young woman spent days working on her presentation, but her superiors only gave a casual nod of approval. Later, in the quiet of her office, she broke down and cried. Why was there not more praise for her work? Had they failed to notice her effort?

Our world is performance crazy. Computers push the limits on technology. The one you buy today will be out of date in six months. This type of thinking leads to a lifestyle that pushes in an effort to get higher and closer to an imaginary goal. But sooner or later, it all comes crashing down.

A child's story tells of a caterpillar longing to find out what was at the top of a huge pile of caterpillars. He pushes and shoves his way to the top, but when he reaches his goal, he finds nothing there. Immediately he returns to what he was before, and a marvelous thing occurs. The desire to become all God intends for him to be takes over, and he becomes a beautiful butterfly.

You may spend years striving and pushing to get more out of life, but all you gain is a sense of being burned-out. The mind-set that adheres to the thought, *I'm good, but not good enough*, is the mark of performance-based living. God's way is life lived to the fullest in the light of His grace and acceptance. Lay down your expectations and fears, and allow Him to bless you abundantly as you live free in Him.

Father, I want to live free in You. Help me lay down my expectations and fears so that You can bless me abundantly. Thank You for unconditional acceptance.

(ON HOLY GROUND)

A New Beginning

SCRIPTURE READING: JOHN 4:1–30
KEY VERSES: JOHN 4:28–29

The woman then left her waterpot, went her way into the city, and said to the men, "Come, see a Man who told me all things that I ever did. Could this be the Christ?"

There is nothing more hope-filled than being given a new beginning, especially after we have suffered a defeat. This is what God gives to those who seek His forgiveness.

He provides a chance to begin again. While it is true that there are consequences to sin, God will never condemn us for our bad choices (Rom. 8:1). Nor will He leave us in the mess that our sin or doubt has created.

The key to living above your circumstances is realizing that God has a plan for your life even when you make a mistake. He never stops loving you, and He will never give up on you. He may not change the results of a poor decision, but He certainly knows how to take a bad circumstance and bring good out of it.

Jesus made a point of meeting with the woman at the well. From a human perspective, her life was filled with failures. Jesus, however, only saw potential. Even though the woman had been married several times, Jesus did not hesitate to express His love for her.

While God's love for us is unconditional, it is not without responsibility. Love like this demands our complete devotion. Jesus came so that this woman—and each of us—might know and experience the eternal love of God. We are transformed when we draw near to God's amazing love.

Oh, Father, Your love is so deep that I cannot comprehend it, yet I know that it is that love that is transforming me. Thank You.

(PATHWAYS TO HIS PRESENCE)

The Love of God

SCRIPTURE READING: PSALM 66:1–9
KEY VERSE: PSALM 66:5

Come and see the works of God;
He is awesome in His doing toward the sons of men.

There are people who find it hard to believe that God is involved in the physical elements of this world. They maintain a false assumption that God is distant from His creation. But this assumption is opposite from the true nature of God. Just as God spoke life into the universe, He is actively involved in every aspect of life.

From the beginning, God's sole intent has been one of revelation, whereby He has sought to manifest Himself to mankind. And while His desire is for all men and women to love Him in return, it has never been His goal to force anyone into loving Him. To be sincere, love must come from the heart and not as a result of obligation, guilt, or other external pressure.

God draws you to Himself by loving you. However, He will never demand your love in return. He desires it, looks for it, longs for it, and welcomes it, but He will never demand it.

What an awesome God we serve! He is so sure of Himself and so confident in His power and mercy that He can trust us to make the right decision.

How do you know you can trust the love of God? One way is by taking time to study His Word. Ask Him to reveal more of Himself to you. Once you encounter God on an intimate level, the need to question His sovereignty fades, and the desire to love Him grows in a wondrous way.

Dear God, draw me to You in love, and reveal Yourself to me.

(SEEKING HIS FACE)

When Others Fail Us

SCRIPTURE READING: 2 TIMOTHY 4:9–18
KEY VERSE: 2 TIMOTHY 4:17

The Lord stood with me and strengthened me, so that the message might be preached fully through me, and that all the Gentiles might hear. Also I was delivered out of the mouth of the lion.

In times of trouble, why are we sometimes forsaken by those we trust? Why do the friends we believed we could count on suddenly disappear during our worst days? These questions are painful to consider, but sometimes they represent harsh reality. Truly, there are many reasons that others fail us. And although examining the cause may not erase our pain, it can help us to process and understand why we are often disappointed by our friends.

Perhaps you have witnessed some of these situations or emotions in the lives of friends who have walked out on you:

- Feeling inadequate to help
- Disassociation from trouble
- Jealousy, insensitivity, or a critical spirit
- Fear of facing a similar problem
- Self-centeredness

The apostle Paul was certainly familiar with this list. As he penned his letter to Timothy, he stood abandoned by his friends and was left to face his final court trial alone. "No one stood with me, but all forsook me," he said in verse 16.

Yet look at what he said in the very next line: "But the Lord stood with me and strengthened me" (v. 17). Paul's faith in the Lord he loved and trusted shone through, despite his discouraging situation.

The good news is that God offers His strength and presence to us in the same way today. Even if all others leave, the Lord will remain faithful.

Father, when others fail me, help me remember that You remain faithful. I rejoice in Your strength and presence. I am not alone.

(PATHWAYS TO HIS PRESENCE)

Come on Back

SCRIPTURE READING: REVELATION 2:1–7
KEY VERSE: REVELATION 2:4

Nevertheless I have this against you, that you have left your first love.

The church at Ephesus was commended for many things. It was a wonderful body of believers, known for their service, sacrifice, perseverance, and suffering. Yet the Lord had a key criticism of them: "I have this against you, that you have left your first love" (Rev. 2:4).

Their "first love" was Jesus Christ. Their activities and demonstrations of grace to others were admirable, but outside of a growing, intimate relationship with Jesus, those things were of no real value.

That is how important Jesus considers your relationship with Him. Whether you slowly drift away from closeness with Him or make the conscious choice to be consumed with other things, the result is the same—a feeling of distance from the Lord and a hollowness to your days.

Rest assured, however, that God has not pulled away from you. He longs for fellowship with you; He sent His Son to die for that purpose. If you feel you have lost your first love, or are somewhere in that process, do not be discouraged. Satan would love nothing more than for depression and thoughts of defeat to drive you away from the Lord.

Don't believe statements such as, "I've wandered too far to come back," or "It will take awhile before God wants to hear my prayers." He wants to talk to you right now. Come on back to the cross!

I'm coming back to the cross, Lord. Renew my first love as I have a divine encounter with the power of the cross.

(SEEKING HIS FACE)

The Voice of Accusation

SCRIPTURE READING: GENESIS 3:1–7
KEY VERSE: JOHN 8:44

*You are of your father the devil, and the desires of your father you want
to do. He was a murderer from the beginning, and does not stand in
the truth, because there is no truth in him. When he speaks a lie, he
speaks from his own resources, for he is a liar and the father of it.*

Jesus called Satan "a murderer" and "the father of lies" (John 8:44 NASB).
In the book *The Bondage Breaker*, Neil T. Anderson observes:

> One of the most common attitudes I have discovered in Christians
> . . . is a deep-seated sense of self-deprecation. I've heard them say,
> ". . . I'm no good." I'm amazed at how many Christians are paralyzed
> in their witness and productivity by thoughts and feelings of inferi-
> ority and worthlessness.
>
> Next to temptation, perhaps the most frequent and insistent
> attack from Satan to which we are vulnerable is accusation. By faith
> we have entered into an eternal relationship with the Lord Jesus
> Christ. . . . Satan can do absolutely nothing to alter our position in
> Christ and our worth to God. But he can render us virtually inopera-
> tive if he can deceive us into listening to and believing his insidious
> lies accusing us of being of little value to God and other people.

When God speaks, He always uses words of hope, encouragement,
direction, and promise. Even in times of discipline, He is quick to restore
and renew our fellowship. If the voice you hear within your heart is one
of accusation, know it belongs to the deceiver. Therefore, take your stand
against the enemy and ask God to fill your heart with His truth.

*O God, the accuser often tries to condemn me, but I realize there is no
condemnation because I am Your child. I reject the accuser's voice and his
deceptive lies.*

(ON HOLY GROUND)

Glorifying God

SCRIPTURE READING: PSALM 63:1−8
KEY VERSE: PSALM 63:4

I will bless You while I live; I will lift up my hands in Your name.

Glorifying God seems to be such a titanic goal that it can frighten us into inaction: "My life is a mess. I am so erratic. How can I ever glorify God?"

Lao-tzu once said, "A journey of a thousand miles must begin with a single step." Glorifying God is an eternal process that begins on earth and continues in heaven. Our heavenly existence will be forever focused on exalting God. Realizing that, we can take the initiative to begin glorifying Him one day, one act, one thought at a time.

Each day is God's gift. You have multitudes of opportunities to honor God through your conduct and conversation. Thus, glorifying God means seeking to maximize each occasion with a deliberate step of obedience. When you falter, which will be often, you confess your disobedience, thank Him for His complete forgiveness, and move on with the task.

What could be more pleasing to your heavenly Father than to daily glorify Him? Establish that lofty aim as your supreme objective, and then live each day in humble dependence on the power of the Holy Spirit and obedience to His revealed truth.

Dear Lord, help me to glorify You today one act and one thought at a time. When I falter, forgive me, and help me to move on with the task.

(INTO HIS PRESENCE)

The Spirit of Truth

SCRIPTURE READING: JOHN 16:7–15
KEY VERSE: JOHN 14:26

*The Helper, the Holy Spirit, whom the Father will send in My name,
He will teach you all things, and bring to your remembrance all things
that I said to you.*

The disciples were worried. Jesus was talking more and more about the time when He would leave them. Who would tell them what to do and how to act? Who would answer the tough questions?

Jesus put their fears to rest: "I tell you the truth, it is to your advantage that I go away; for if I do not go away, the Helper will not come to you; but if I go, I will send Him to you. . . . But when He, the Spirit of truth, comes, He will guide you into all the truth; for He will not speak on His own initiative, but whatever He hears, He will speak; and He will disclose to you what is to come" (John 16:7, 13 NASB).

Jesus was not leaving them to muddle about in confusion and uncertainty; on the contrary, He promised them revelation and understanding of His truth beyond their current experience.

The Holy Spirit is actually the One who takes the words of the printed page of God's Word and reveals the meaning to your heart and mind. He uses many human "tools" as aids in the process, including pastors, teachers, and your personal traits. But without the Spirit, the words would remain just that—words.

If you've ever avoided a difficult passage because you feel you won't understand it, don't turn away. God promises to enlighten your heart (1 Cor. 2:10–16). You are the intended recipient of every meaningful word.

O Lord, how I thank You that You did not leave me to muddle about in confusion and uncertainty. You promised revelation and understanding beyond my abilities. I receive it!

(ON HOLY GROUND)

True Victory

SCRIPTURE READING: ROMANS 12:9–11
KEY VERSE: ROMANS 12:9

Let love be without hypocrisy. Abhor what is evil. Cling to what is good.

When life sends us sprawling, our response is an excellent measuring stick for how mature we are in our relationship with Christ. A response that demonstrates total and complete trust in the Lord is what He desires to see. That is the measure of true victory.

If we are careless, the tragic events that unfold in our lives can leave us jaded. Quickly forgetting who our God is, and the role He plays in our lives, will lead to the wrong responses. When we drift away from a passionate pursuit of God in the midst of adversity, we react in a way that goes against God's Word. We might blame others or God for our current situation. We might search for an escape through drugs and alcohol. We might pity ourselves or just give up.

Turning to the Lord in difficult situations reinforces where our strength and hope reside. Paul, who experienced more than his share of adversity following his conversion, gave us great direction as to how we should respond in adversity, beginning with this: "Cling to what is good" (Rom. 12:9).

As we enter the storms in our lives, clinging to the Lord reveals where our hearts are. Clinging is an action of determined grip, unwilling to let go no matter what the cost. And we know that, with Him, we will be able to endure anything that comes our way in life, and emerge victorious.

Lord, when all else fails, I know that I can count on You. I cling to Your promise that Your goodness will prevail.

(PATHWAYS TO HIS PRESENCE)

Knowing God

SCRIPTURE READING: EPHESIANS 3:14–21
KEY VERSES: EPHESIANS 3:18–19

*[I pray that you] may be able to comprehend with all the saints
what is the width and length and depth and height—to know the
love of Christ which passes knowledge; that you may be filled with
all the fullness of God.*

It's difficult to describe things that are beyond the terms of our immediate visual experience. For example, we know that outer space is immeasurably vast, but we cannot make any concrete comparisons. When numbers get up into billions and trillions and even higher, the effect is staggering, and we lose all sense of their meaning. And there are crevices in the ocean floor that go down so far they cannot be measured.

If we cannot fully grasp the mysteries of our physical world, how much more inept are we at comprehending our all-knowing, all-powerful, eternal Lord? Yet the true wonder is that God wants you to know Him and love Him the way He loves you. He does not want to remain a distant mystery.

That was why Paul stressed the importance of understanding who He is: "[I pray that you] may be able to comprehend with all the saints what is the breadth and length and height and depth, and to know the love of Christ which surpasses knowledge, that you may be filled up to all the fullness of God" (Eph. 3:18–19 NASB).

When you are filled with the knowledge and intimate experience of His love, the rest of life falls into perspective. His clarity and righteousness subdue the confusions and complexities of this world. God is not impenetrable or distant, and He desires your fellowship.

*Dear God, I want to know You and love You the way You love me. Fill me
with the knowledge and intimate experience of Your love.*

(SEEKING HIS FACE)

Abiding in Christ

SCRIPTURE READING: JOHN 15:9–17
KEY VERSE: JOHN 15:17

These things I command you, that you love one another.

In John 15, Jesus instructed us to abide in Him. The visual picture is one of a branch abiding in a vine. Christ taught that God is the Vinedresser, pruning and shaping the branches so that they will bear much fruit. Abiding means "remaining and continuing." It is an active word, even though from a worldly perspective we often view it as a word of passivity. However, nothing is further from the truth. When we abide in Christ, we are in a process of growth unlike anything we have known before.

Notice how the young tender shoots of the grapevine appear in the spring and begin running along the arbor. God tenderly watches over His branches and with the greatest of care and skill cultivates the vine so that it produces a maximum harvest.

The sole purpose of the branches is to bear fruit. They are not destined to live on their own apart from the vine, nor are they allowed to grow wild. They maintain, they continue, and they rest in the vine.

We live under the grace of God and are given full access to His infinite peace as we abide in Him. When turmoil comes, we can go to a place of refuge. It is a place of abiding contentment in the inner chamber of our hearts. You need never fear when you are abiding in Christ. His peace and rest are yours.

Precious heavenly Father, thank You that I have a place of refuge in times of turmoil. Peace and rest are mine when I abide in You.

(ON HOLY GROUND)

The Answer to Your Needs

SCRIPTURE READING: LUKE 8:43–48
KEY VERSE: PSALM 111:4

He has made His wonderful works to be remembered;
The LORD is gracious and full of compassion.

Jesus is holistic. A good example is found in Luke 8 when He heals a woman who has experienced hemorrhaging for twelve years. It's hard to imagine how this woman maintained her hope for healing, especially with the stigma that accompanied her illness. But she continued to look for a cure, and her determination brought her to the feet of the Savior.

A deep longing for love and acceptance is a normal need for any person, let alone someone who has been placed in forced isolation. The cruelty of Jewish tradition blocked this need from being met. Anyone who touched this woman was considered unclean.

The portrait Jesus provided is one of abundant mercy and grace. Not only did He heal her physical disease, but He also healed her spiritually and emotionally. Jesus was not repulsed by this woman's suffering. He saw her need and knew that only He could meet it. This woman believed if she could just stretch out her hand far enough to touch the hem of Christ's outer garment, she would be healed. What a tremendous demonstration of faith!

In His compassion, Jesus turned to her and said, "Daughter, be of good cheer; your faith has made you well. Go in peace" (Luke 8:48). No matter how complex life may appear, God has an answer for your needs. What is your need? Will you place it in the hands of the Savior and trust Him to meet it in His timing?

You are the answer to all my needs! Dear Lord, I place everything in Your hands and entrust it to Your loving care.

(INTO HIS PRESENCE)

God's Blessings

SCRIPTURE READING: PSALM 16
KEY VERSE: PSALM 16:6

The boundary lines have fallen for me in pleasant places;
surely I have a delightful inheritance. (NIV)

The time-worn phrase "Count your blessings" is a good one to remember. It may sound trite, but it's always a good exercise to pause and consider all the wonderful things God has poured into your life.

And don't forget to include events and circumstances that did not seem positive at the moment. From the vantage point of the passing of time, you can probably see how God transformed even those negatives into blessings. Sometimes you appreciate those blessings at an even deeper level.

King David made a habit of viewing his life from a perspective of gratitude and satisfaction. In Psalm 16, he wrote, "The LORD is the portion of my inheritance and my cup; You support my lot. The [boundary] lines have fallen to me in pleasant places; indeed, my heritage is beautiful to me. . . . In Your presence is fullness of joy; in Your right hand there are pleasures forever" (vv. 5–6, 11 NASB).

By nature, are you a grumbler? Do you have a habit of whining about every little thing? A spirit of complaining and dissatisfaction can pervade every facet of your being and even influence how you understand God's involvement in your life.

Instead of grumbling, you can give thanks to God as David did, and that process begins by deliberately and specifically identifying His generous blessings.

Dear Father, help me to give thanks instead of grumbling. Help me this day
to specifically identify Your generous blessings.

(SEEKING HIS FACE)

A Divine Encounter in Prayer

SCRIPTURE READING: MATTHEW 6:9–15
KEY VERSE: MATTHEW 6:6

When you pray, go into your room, and when you have shut your door, pray to your Father who is in the secret place; and your Father who sees in secret will reward you openly.

Prayer's greatest reward is the chance it gives us to experience the heart of God.

The most important activity we can engage in as Christians is prayer. Everything connected with God evolves out of time spent alone with Him in praise, worship, devotion, and petition.

We cannot truly experience the wonder of praise or the peace that comes from meditating on His Word unless we have first spent time with Him in prayer. Without prayer, there is no depth in our relationship with God, and our knowledge of Him becomes empty and stale within our hearts.

Only prayer can revive a weary soul. When David was on the run from Saul, the first place he went was to God in prayer. When Jesus became physically tired, He sought the Father through prayer. Nothing has the potential to change the face of your environment like prayer.

Arrested, thrown into prison, and waiting for execution, Peter prayed, as did those who knew him, and God sent an angel to help him escape. Prayer is not merely coming to God with a wish list. It is, instead, a time when you make yourself available to be used of Him in whatever way He chooses.

Dear heavenly Father, thank You for the privilege of being used by You. I am making myself available.

(SEEKING HIS FACE)

Sifted for Service

SCRIPTURE READING: LUKE 22:31–34
KEY VERSE: LUKE 22:32

*I have prayed for you, that your faith should not fail; and when you
have returned to Me, strengthen your brethren.*

If you want to be greatly used of God, you must be willing to be sifted for
His service. This principle is much like the process of winnowing wheat. In
New Testament times that was done by threshing the grain on high ground.
The chaff was blown away by the wind while what was useful remained.

Peter was no exception to the winnowing process. Jesus told the future
apostle: "Satan has demanded permission to sift you like wheat; but I have
prayed for you, that your faith may not fail; and you, when once you have
turned again, strengthen your brothers" (Luke 22:31–32 NASB).

It was the night of our Lord's arrest. If ever there was a time Peter
wanted to stand firm, that was it. Yet he ended up denying Jesus three
times. What emotional pain and sorrow must have gripped his mind. But
think back to Jesus' words: "When once you have turned again, strengthen
your brothers." This is the hope we have in Christ; that even when we fail
Him, even when He has to winnow us like wheat, He never gives up on us.

By sifting your life through trials and frustrations, God brings to
the surface the things that are impure. Had Peter refused to be sifted,
he never would have been fit for service. If you sense God's sifting hand
in your life, submit your will to Him and allow Him to prepare you for
His service.

*Lord, help me realize that my trials and frustrations are not without
purpose. You are separating the good from the bad, the spiritual grain from
the chaff. You are sifting me for service.*

(ON HOLY GROUND)

Prayer and Anxiety

SCRIPTURE READING: PSALM 69:1–3
KEY VERSE: 1 PETER 5:7

[Cast] all your care upon Him, for He cares for you.

Prayer plays an important role in handling anxiety. Prayer is a demonstration of your trust in God. When you pray in faith, you declare your need to God. Anxiety, however, represents the absence of faith.

Peter instructed us, "[Cast] all your anxiety on Him, because He cares for you" (1 Peter 5:7 NASB). Older saints, such as Charles Spurgeon, Amy Carmichael, and Hudson Taylor would use the term "to roll" all your cares on Him. This act of rolling gives us a mental picture of what it means to give our troubles to the Lord. We actually release them into His care and walk away from the situation in such a way that we are no longer anxious over the matter. We say, "Lord, I want to roll this problem onto You." What a great sense of encouragement awaits you when you give Jesus the problems and trials of your heart!

He is your Burden Bearer, and He will accept every care perfectly onto Himself. He is sovereign. All-powerful. Holy. Righteous. Infinite in wisdom. His mercies never cease, and He has an eternal love for you that will never end. Sounds like someone you can trust? Try Him and you will see!

Lord, You are holy, righteous, and infinite in wisdom. Thank You that Your mercies never cease.

(SEEKING HIS FACE)

Standing in the Storm

SCRIPTURE READING: PSALM 62:1–12

KEY VERSES: PSALM 62:1–2

Truly my soul silently waits for God;
From Him comes my salvation.
He only is my rock and my salvation;
He is my defense; I shall not be greatly moved.

This moving passage can bring to mind many images, but a favorite may be a photograph of a tiny bird wedged into a small crevasse within a rocky cliff. Just outside his hiding place, a brutal storm rages. Strong winds and rain beat down, upturning leaves and breaking tree branches. Yet the bird is safe and still and his life is spared, thanks to the solid rock around him.

Can you recall a time in your life when it seemed as if you would be blown away by a physical or emotional storm? Think back to what you did in response to this trial. Did you venture out into its midst or retreat into the shelter of God's protective arms?

When the next storm blows into your life, remember the words of Psalm 62. Give special attention to the phrase, "my soul silently waits for God." In the photograph mentioned above, the bird was not chirping and fretting. Instead he was resting quietly until the storm passed. His confidence was in the source of his protection, and he did not need to panic.

Though God always hears our cries of distress, we can be assured that once we call for Him, He will be with us. We can release our anxieties and rest in Him until the storms die down and we emerge once again victorious from our hiding place.

Lord, as the birds calmly seek shelter to wait out the storm, let me also be
quick to seek shelter in You when life buffets me about.

(PATHWAYS TO HIS PRESENCE)

Facing Life's Challenges

SCRIPTURE READING: 2 CHRONICLES 20:1–30
KEY VERSE: 2 CHRONICLES 20:12

O our God, will You not judge them? For we have no power against this great multitude that is coming against us; nor do we know what to do, but our eyes are upon You.

Jehoshaphat had a choice. In 2 Chronicles 20, we read how a tremendous army had come against the nation of Israel with one intention: destroying the people of God. Most armies in Israel's position would have been plotting their survival. Wisely, Jehoshaphat chose to lead the people in a prayer that confessed their total dependence on the Lord: "O our God, will You not judge them? For we have no power against this great multitude" (v. 12).

You may think that you do not have an option when facing a difficult challenge, but you do. You can choose to turn to God and bow down before Him, or you can turn and run away in fear.

If Israel caved in to fear, the people would be running for the rest of their existence. Jehoshaphat was wise enough to know that his nation wouldn't survive without God's intervention.

The enemy has one goal for your life, and that is discouragement—to influence people to give up and become ineffective for God. You are called to follow Christ for a purpose. When challenges come, go to God in prayer. Confess your inability and your need for Him. Humility is a sign of great strength, not weakness.

Then trust God to do the impossible in your situation and give you the victory.

Heavenly Father, You have a solution for the challenges I am facing today. I trust You to do the impossible and bring the victory.

(PATHWAYS TO HIS PRESENCE)

His Deeds and Greatness

SCRIPTURE READING: PSALM 150:1–6
KEY VERSE: PSALM 95:6

Oh come, let us worship and bow down;
Let us kneel before the LORD our Maker.

Two basic truths can lead to sincere worship, changing the perspective on problems and giving hope for endurance:

"Praise Him for His mighty acts" (Ps. 150:2a). God created the heavens and earth. He created you. He sent His Son to earth to bear your sin so you might receive eternal life. He has filled you with the Holy Spirit, who always extends the mercy and grace of God for your every need. The list goes on. Think of those special times when God answered your prayers, provided guidance in critical situations, protected you from harm, and specifically worked in your life. Thank Him that He is still working in your present circumstances to bring about positive future results, even though that may seem impossible right now.

"Praise Him according to His excellent greatness!" (Ps. 150:2b). God never changes. He is always loving, always caring, always working for your good. His power stands firm in the midst of any storm. Spend time thanking Him for who He is.

Praise lights the candle of hope and encouragement in the midst of blackness that no ill wind can snuff out. Worship is the way to put your problems in God's capable hands.

I praise You for Your mighty deeds, Father. I thank You that You have answered prayer and that You are working in my present circumstances to bring positive future results.

(INTO HIS PRESENCE)

Confidence in Prayer

SCRIPTURE READING: PSALM 40:1–8
KEY VERSE: PSALM 40:8

*I delight to do Your will, O my God,
And Your law is within my heart.*

"I know God hears my prayers," you may say, "but how do I know my requests are according to His will?"

That sentiment can do more to undermine our confidence in prayer than any other thought. If we knew God's will to begin with, we reason, we would have no problem trusting God for the answer. Actually we know more about God's will than we think.

It is God's will to give thanks in all things (1 Thess. 5:18). Do you have a grateful heart no matter your circumstance? Giving thanks acknowledges His sovereignty and expresses a steadfast faith in Christ.

It is God's will to walk in purity and holiness (1 Thess. 4:3). Do you walk on a thin edge of immorality, giving place to impure thoughts? Don't.

It is God's will to be filled with the Spirit (Eph. 5:18). The verb tense emphasizes such filling as a continuous action, stressing our complete dependence on the Spirit and our unceasing need for His help and guidance.

Prayer is precisely the place where we discover the will of God. We seek His mind, sift through His Word, and thank Him that God is faithfully at work in our lives.

Lord, give me renewed confidence in prayer through increased knowledge of Your will.

(SEEKING HIS FACE)

The Ground of Victory

SCRIPTURE READING: PSALM 96
KEY VERSE: PSALM 96:4

The LORD is great and greatly to be praised; He is to be feared above all gods.

General Norman Schwarzkopf revealed after the Persian Gulf War that the one-hundred-hour battle was decided in the very first minutes when Allied planes savaged Iraqi air defenses.

"When I saw our planes knock out their radar, I knew at that very moment we had them," Schwarzkopf said.

There is a very distinct parallel for Christians. Although we are in a very real war, with enticements to sin and an adversary who harasses us, the outcome of the conflict has been decided.

That occurred at Calvary when Jesus "disarmed the rulers and authorities, [making] a public display of them, having triumphed over them through Him" (Col. 2:15 NASB). Jesus defeated Satan on the cross. He took away the sting of death by bearing our sins, making reconciliation between God and man possible.

The man or woman who has believed in Him and received His forgiveness of sins is on the winning side. But we deal with our foe on the ground of victory. We are not helpless, frightened little children but sons and daughters of God who triumph over Satan "through Him."

Don't shrink from the battle. It was won at Golgotha, and you share in its victory through your union with the Victor, Jesus Christ.

O God, thank You that the battle was already won at Golgotha. I share in its triumph through my union with Christ. I praise You that I deal with the enemy on victory ground!

(ON HOLY GROUND)

The Rewards of Waiting

SCRIPTURE READING: 1 SAMUEL 1:1–28
KEY VERSE: 1 SAMUEL 1:20

It came to pass in the process of time that Hannah conceived and bore a son, and called his name Samuel, saying, "Because I have asked for him from the LORD."

You've just finished gathering all the ingredients for baking, and you mix them together carefully in a large bowl. Then you pour the batter evenly in two round pans and slide them gently onto the oven rack. You set the timer and sit back for a while to enjoy the delicious smells coming from the kitchen.

Suppose that twenty minutes before the timer rings you decide you want to take the cake out of the oven anyway. It's only partially baked, with gooey spots everywhere, and obviously isn't fit for consumption.

Such a decision would be ridiculous, wouldn't it? Yet in an interesting way that scenario parallels what we do as believers when we try to outrun God's timing and take ourselves out of His preparation time too soon. We do not give Him time to reveal His purposes in the way He knows is best.

Hannah is an inspiration in the area of spiritual patience. She knew that God was the One in charge of whether she would conceive a child, and she took her sorrows and fears to Him daily. We don't know how long Hannah waited on the Lord. All the Bible says in 1 Samuel 1:7 is "year by year." What a wearying process, especially with the taunts of Peninnah.

God knows what you need. Don't give up and try to satisfy that need your own way. Wait on Him, and He will take care of you according to His goodness.

Heavenly Father, I thank You that I can rest in the assurance that You know exactly what I need.

(INTO HIS PRESENCE)

God Is Good

SCRIPTURE READING: ROMANS 8:35–39
KEY VERSE: PSALM 33:5

He loves righteousness and justice;
The earth is full of the goodness of the LORD.

Here is the truth about God's goodness: it always seeks to encourage and lift up rather than tear down or condemn. Romans 8:1 reminds us that "there is therefore now no condemnation to those who are in Christ Jesus." God knows the times you struggle, and He longs to pour out His encouragement and hope over your life.

In the light of this goodness, nothing has the power or ability to separate you from the love of God (Rom. 8:35, 38–39). His power securely keeps you. Nothing is strong enough to deter His help when you call to Him. Does this mean that you will never face hardship? No, but it does mean that in times of difficulty, God will be near enough to hear even the whispers of your heart.

Never view Christ as a stern, unloving judge. Jesus was very quick to point out that He came to save, not to judge the world. Once you accept Him as your Savior, the only judgment you will ever attend is the one where God rewards your faithful love and devotion toward Him and His Son.

Can you step away from God's goodness? Yes. Because the Lord has given each of us a limited free will, we can choose to turn from God. However, God will never turn away from you. You may be troubled by a situation that seems uncontrollable, but God holds the solution, and He will provide the hope you need as you turn to Him.

Lord, I am so grateful that You will never turn away from me. You hold the solution to every situation. You will provide the hope I need.

(SEEKING HIS FACE)

Faith to Cling To

Scripture Reading: Genesis 7
Key Verse: Hebrews 11:7

By faith Noah, being divinely warned of things not yet seen, moved with godly fear, prepared an ark for the saving of his household, by which he condemned the world and became heir of the righteousness which is according to faith.

It is an old saying that people are "creatures of habit." Of course, we love occasional variation in the routine, but we strive for stability as much as possible.

If you ever feel stressed when dealing with the unknown, then you have a small idea of how Noah felt when God told him to build an ark. An ark? He probably didn't have a clear idea of what it even looked like until God's blueprint began to take shape.

In a single encounter, Noah's vision of the future changed dramatically. Though he was surrounded by a self-serving, sensual society with no interest in God, he knew where he and his family stood. But what would the world be like if they were the only people alive?

Hebrews 11:7 notes that in spite of the questions: "By faith Noah, being warned by God about things not yet seen, in reverence prepared an ark for the salvation of his household . . . and became an heir of the righteousness which is according to faith" (NASB).

Faith was all he could cling to; God was truly his only port in the storm. When your circumstances turn upside down, when you don't have the answers, trust the Lord. His plan is perfect.

Almighty God, You are my port in every storm of life. When my circumstances are confusing, when I don't have all the answers, help me trust You. Your plan is always perfect.

(On Holy Ground)

Oh, the Wonderful Cross!

Scripture Reading: Romans 5:1–8
Key Verse: Romans 5:6

When we were still without strength, in due time Christ died for the ungodly.

The cross is where love became a five-letter word. Incomprehensible, eternal, unconditional love is spelled C-R-O-S-S.

Romans 5:1–8 explains this great love and how God expressed it by sending His Son, Jesus Christ, to die on the cross for our sins. The cross is the turning point in history, where a holy God made a way for fallen, sinful man to have a relationship and fellowship with Him.

In one awesome, indescribable moment, justice and mercy met at the cross. There was enough justice at the cross to punish every sin of all humanity. There was enough mercy at the cross to envelop all of humanity in God's wonderful, loving forgiveness. God not only poured out His wrath on sin—which is justice—but He even exhibited mercy by lovingly providing Jesus so we would not have to face the death penalty of sin.

God also demonstrated His wisdom at the cross. His goal was the redemption of mankind, the forgiveness of mankind's sins. God's plan and purpose are always the very best, and He chose the best route to accomplish His plan when He sent Jesus to die on the cross.

Was there any other way in which a holy God could breech the divide between Himself and sinful man and still remain just? Think about it. No other plan could so perfectly accomplish His will and yet direct all of the honor and glory to God and not one shred of glory to man.

Lord, thank You for demonstrating Your love at the cross. Thank You, Lord, that Your mercy was great enough to envelop all of humanity—including me!

(Pathways to His Presence)

Waiting to Act

Scripture Reading: Psalm 139:1–8
Key Verse: Psalm 55:22

Cast your burden on the LORD,
And He shall sustain you;
He shall never permit the righteous to be moved.

The toddler climbed to the top step of the plastic slide in the backyard and lifted one leg onto the top platform. With one leg on the top of the slide and the other on the top step, his undeveloped coordination left him trapped. He couldn't move either leg.

"Daaaaaddyyyyy!"

The toddler knew exactly what to do next. In his moment of complete helplessness, with fear setting in as he was stranded several feet above the ground, he called for his daddy. Watching nearby, the dad moved in to save the day. What father wouldn't act quickly in such a situation?

When hit with a trial or when bad news comes our way, our most effective response is to immediately cry out, "Father!" Not only does this immediately stunt the problem from growing into something that over-whelms us, but it reminds us of our rightful position as children of God.

Our Father says He will never leave us or forsake us. Armed with such a promise, we know that God is under His divine obligation to provide us guidance and direction. There will be many times when life will leave us stretched into an awkward position. We should always remember that our Father is watching nearby, ready to act when called.

Father, I thank You that You will never leave me or forsake me. Help me remember that You are always nearby, just waiting to act in my behalf when called upon to do so.

(INTO HIS PRESENCE)

This Grace Is Yours

SCRIPTURE READING: JOHN 1:19–29
KEY VERSE: JOHN 1:29

The next day John saw Jesus coming toward him, and said, "Behold! The Lamb of God who takes away the sin of the world!"

One of the most encouraging things you can receive from God is the hope that comes from being given a second chance. This is especially important when you have yielded to temptation or feel that you have fallen short of His plan and purpose for your life. The truth is that God never limits the opportunity for forgiveness.

Second chances encourage us to go on and not to give up even when the whispers of the world around us seem to say the opposite. After his denial of Christ, Peter was in need of a second chance, and Jesus, through His grace, provided this (John 21:15–17).

How many of us have longed for God's cleansing touch when we become trapped by our wrongful actions? The only cure for sin or failure of any kind is God's grace applied to our lives. This is what changes the stumbling sinner into a person living victoriously for Jesus Christ.

Even before you knew Him, Jesus knew and loved you. It was His love that saved you, and it is His love that will keep you throughout eternity. "God demonstrates His own love toward us, in that while we were still sinners, Christ died for us" (Rom. 5:8).

Are you struggling with the idea of grace and how it applies to your life? Realize that God loves you. He stands beside you and is pleased to call you His own. This grace is yours.

Lord, thank You for Your grace—Your love and kindness toward me even when I don't deserve it. I accept Your extended grace.

(PATHWAYS TO HIS PRESENCE)

Saved by Grace

SCRIPTURE READING: I JOHN 5:7–13
KEY VERSE: I JOHN 5:11

This is the testimony: that God has given us eternal life, and this life is in His Son.

Have you ever wondered about your salvation? Many people do. They worry that they have done something to cause Jesus not to love them. They struggle with feelings of doubt, confusion, and fear. In 1 John 4:18 we read, "There is no fear in love; but perfect love casts out fear, because fear involves punishment" (NASB). The apostle John also reminded us that we are able to love God "because He first loved us" (v. 19).

Even before you were born, God knew what you would look like—the color of your hair, the sound of your voice, and the successes and failures you would face. In spite of all you have or have not done, God continues to love you with an everlasting love.

Jesus came to earth with a clear goal in mind, and that was to save those who are lost. He never said, "Be perfect and receive My salvation." Salvation comes to us one way, by the grace of God. When we accept His Son in faith, we receive eternal life.

You can work a lifetime to be good and perfect and not be any better off than when you first started. Salvation is based not on your works but on the finished work of Jesus Christ at Calvary. He is the One who bore your sins—past, present, and future.

Thank Him for the work He has done, confess any sin that comes to mind, and accept His forgiveness and unconditional love as a blessing.

O God, before I was born, You knew me. You knew my strengths and weaknesses, my successes and failures. Yet You love me with an unconditional, everlasting love. How I thank You!

(ON HOLY GROUND)

A Bright Beginning

SCRIPTURE READING: ACTS 1:1–14
KEY VERSE: ACTS 1:8

You shall receive power when the Holy Spirit has come upon you; and you shall be witnesses to Me in Jerusalem, and in all Judea and Samaria, and to the end of the earth.

The crucifixion left the disciples stunned and bewildered. When they were sure all hope was gone, Jesus came to them. All that He had told them was true! He was with them again, only this time it was even better. Then came the day that He returned to heaven.

The Bible tells us that the group gathered at Christ's ascension stood gazing into heaven. Do you wonder what they were thinking? Whatever it was, God knew they needed immediate direction and hope.

Two angels appeared and spoke to them, "Men of Galilee, why do you stand gazing up into heaven? This same Jesus, who was taken up from you into heaven, will so come in like manner as you saw Him go into heaven" (Acts 1:11).

As they dispersed and went back to their homes, Jesus' last words filled their thoughts: "You shall be witnesses to Me in Jerusalem, and in all Judea and Samaria, and to the end of the earth" (Acts 1:8).

They had heard the words of Christ and understood His desire, yet it took angels from heaven to move the disciples to the next step.

Don't let the disappointments of this world discourage you. What you see as an ending, God sees as a bright and glorious beginning. Therefore, as you go, share His love and hope with everyone.

Dear heavenly Father, I thank You for endings that are really new beginnings. Help me move on by faith to take the next step.

The Value of Defeat

SCRIPTURE READING: PSALM 98:1–9
KEY VERSE: PSALM 98:1

Oh, sing to the LORD a new song!
For He has done marvelous things;
His right hand and His holy arm have gained Him the victory.

Paul tried to do the right thing, but, like us, sometimes he failed. In his letter to the Romans, Paul seemed to agonize over his inability to triumph over sin at every confrontation in his life. Don't we all feel like Paul at times? We want to do what's right, but our actions don't always represent our true desires.

However, Paul learned that failure didn't disqualify him from serving God—in fact, it taught him an invaluable lesson about victory: Christ's strength could shine through any situation, no matter how weak that situation may have made Paul (2 Cor. 12:10).

Here are some things to remember about defeat:

1. Defeat is often engineered by God. He isn't after self-improvement. He is after death—death to our flesh, which leads to life in Him.
2. Defeat is often essential for God to fulfill His purposes in our lives. When we are broken to the point that the only place we can look is up, and see Him, then we begin to see the purposes and plans He has for our lives.
3. Defeat exposes our weaknesses and inadequacies. Our best efforts never match what God can—and wants to—do in us and through us.

Defeat in our lives doesn't mean we are defeated. It is merely God's way of pointing us to ultimate victory.

Lord, let me realize that defeats are simply signposts along the road to point me to ultimate victory.

(PATHWAYS TO HIS PRESENCE)

The Cycle of Blessing

SCRIPTURE READING: PSALM 145
KEY VERSE: PROVERBS 10:22

The blessing of the LORD makes one rich, and He adds no sorrow with it.

Nature's cyclical pattern marks God's scheme of blessing. All blessings come from above (Gen. 49:25; Eph. 1:3). As Creator of all, the Lord is the Giver of life along with what sustains us (Ps. 145:15–16).

Heat from the sun, moisture from the rains, and oxygen in the atmosphere originated in His mind and exist through His wisdom and power (Gen. 1:1–2:3). He is the Designer of our bodies—organs, bones, tissues, muscles, nerves.

Our Father is also the Originator of our spiritual blessings. We can know God only because He first chose to reveal Himself through His creation; His Son, our Lord Jesus Christ; and the Bible (John 1:18).

When we receive the blessings of God through faith, the cycle continues as we share His presence in our conversation and our deeds. God told Abraham: "I will bless you . . . and so you shall be a blessing" (Gen. 12:2 NASB).

The Lord favors us with His encouragement, hope, and joy. In turn we encourage the fainthearted, revive the sagging soul, and bring cheer to the afflicted.

Are you participating in God's cycle of blessing? Look to Him as your Resource; then look to help others.

Precious heavenly Father, You are the Originator of all my spiritual blessings. Help me to plug into Your divine cycle of blessing. Let me look to You as my divine Resource in every situation, and then reveal ways I can bless others.

(ON HOLY GROUND)

Words of Encouragement

SCRIPTURE READING: HEBREWS 10:19–25
KEY VERSE: PROVERBS 12:25

Anxiety in the heart of man causes depression,
But a good word makes it glad.

Have you ever hesitated to speak words of encouragement because you weren't sure how they would be received? Being an encourager means reaching out even when you're not sure.

You never know the impact you might have. In his book *The Power of Encouragement*, Dr. David Jeremiah explains:

> I can be encouraged by what I hear. If I sense someone genuinely cares about me, that person's words can be powerful. As the adage goes, "Nobody cares how much you know until they know how much you care."
>
> The Book of Proverbs speaks often about encouragement. Here's one example: "Anxious hearts are very heavy but a word of encouragement does wonders!" (Proverbs 12:25 TLB). Have you ever been weighed down by anxiety when someone came along and spoke a good word which lifted your spirit?
>
> During one of the deepest, darkest times in my life, a fellow pastor called me just to say, "David, I want you to know I love you, and I know you are going through some hurt. I want you to know I'm here if you need me. I want to pray with you." And he prayed with me on the phone. He called me every week for several weeks with a word of encouragement. He poured courage into my heart. . . . Believe it or not, two or three sentences can turn a person's life around.

Lord, give me the spiritual maturity to help others. I want to be an encouragement and blessing to those with whom I come in contact today.

(PATHWAYS TO HIS PRESENCE)

Experiencing God's Best

SCRIPTURE READING: PSALM 138:1–8
KEY VERSE: PSALM 138:8

The LORD will perfect that which concerns me;
Your mercy, O LORD, endures forever;
Do not forsake the works of Your hands.

As we make decisions every day, our choices determine the quality of our lives. This is why it is very important to seek God's guidance in order to experience His best. How do we discover God's best? The answer is two-fold. We must first realize that God's way is the best way, and then we must learn to listen to His voice.

Realizing that God's way is better than our way is a difficult process for many of us, because we like to think that we can figure things out on our own. We pridefully tell ourselves that we don't need help from anyone else as we struggle and toil with burdens and decisions. Yet we must understand that God longs to help and bless us. There is truly no one who knows our needs better than He does.

When we understand these things, our spirits are fertile ground to receive His guidance and instruction. We begin to welcome the promptings of the Holy Spirit and to find practical insight for our daily lives as we read God's Word.

A true indicator of hearing God's voice will be a new and complete sense of peace. Jesus said that He gives peace "not as the world gives" (John 14:27), but a peace that passes understanding (Phil. 4:7). His peace, therefore, must be the governing force of each decision we make.

Choose to let the peace of God guide you in your next important decision, while keeping in mind that God's best will far exceed any good thing you could create on your own.

All of history tells the story of those who let You guide them, Lord, and those
who didn't. Help me open the pages of my life to Your instruction.

(PATHWAYS TO HIS PRESENCE)

Investing in Eternity

SCRIPTURE READING: COLOSSIANS 3:1–4
KEY VERSE: COLOSSIANS 3:2

Set your mind on things above, not on things on the earth.

Have you ever seen the devastating effects of an earthquake? Maybe you are even a survivor of an earthquake. The terror of such an experience is overwhelming: the ground shakes, and structures bend, warp, explode, and fall. Things that seemed so permanent are heaps of rubble. Towers that seemed solid and substantial are on the ground. It is a sobering reminder of the impermanence of earthly things.

That's why it is so critical to set your focus on the things that don't change, the things that cannot be destroyed. Paul urged, "If you have been raised up with Christ, keep seeking the things above, where Christ is, seated at the right hand of God. Set your mind on the things above, not on the things that are on earth. For you have died and your life is hidden with Christ in God. When Christ, who is our life, is revealed, then you also will be revealed with Him in glory" (Col. 3:1–4 NASB).

Your identity in Christ places your true citizenship in heaven. In a real sense, you don't belong here, where things pass away and change continually. It's been said that the only two things that are eternal are God's Word and people. When you invest your time in the eternal, your time is not wasted. And best of all, one day you'll see the investments of your life come to fruition in heaven.

Lord, I want to invest my time in eternal things. I want to see the investments of my life come to fruition in heaven.

(SEEKING HIS FACE)

The Ultimate Victory

SCRIPTURE READING: REVELATION 19:1–8
KEY VERSE: JOHN 16:33

These things I have spoken to you, that in Me you may have peace. In the world you will have tribulation; but be of good cheer, I have overcome the world.

Jesus Christ has been ascribed many fitting names. He is the Lamb of God, sacrificed for our sins. But He also is the Lion of Judah. One day He will return as King of kings and Lord of lords. His power will be displayed in all its fullness, and those who have rebelled against Him will reap the consequences.

In one instant at his Second Coming, Jesus will return to earth not as a gentle, nurturing Savior but as victorious Judge, Ruler, King, and Lord. He will destroy the evil world system propagated by the Antichrist. He will bind Satan and cast him into hell. Those who have aligned themselves with Christ through the ages are assured victory. We can have confidence that the spiritual battle has already been won—and Jesus is the Victor. No matter how evil our age becomes, we know that ultimately, justice will reign over all the earth. The wicked will be punished and righteousness will be rewarded.

Let the assurance of Jesus' victory motivate you to serve Him with your life. One way you can do this is to share your faith. Think of someone you can tell about Him today. Now imagine how rewarding it would be to meet that person in heaven and realize God used you to help get him or her there. Ask God for an opportunity to share His love with that person today.

Heavenly Father, please use me today to tell others about You. Help me direct others to Your Son, Jesus Christ.

(INTO HIS PRESENCE)

Don't Let Him Pass By

SCRIPTURE READING: MATTHEW 8:1–3
KEY VERSE: PSALM 3:4

I cried to the LORD with my voice,
And He heard me from His holy hill.

Read the description of this scene: "When He had come down from the mountain, great multitudes followed Him. And behold, a leper came and worshiped Him, saying, 'Lord, if You are willing, You can make me clean.' Then Jesus put out His hand and touched him, saying, 'I am willing; be cleansed.' Immediately his leprosy was cleansed" (Matt. 8:1–3).

Jesus wants us to see Him as our only Source of help in every situation. Although the multitudes pressed in on Him, compassion rose up from within Him at the sight of the approaching man with leprosy who was deeply despised by others.

Leprosy was a curse. All who associated with people having leprosy were considered ceremonially unclean as well. Yet the man dared to venture into the city in hopes of talking to Jesus. When Christ came near, the man immediately knelt before Him. It was a demonstration of his adoration of God. Next he told Jesus: "If You are willing, You can make me clean." They were words of tremendous faith spoken by a man who did not doubt God's ability but feared that somehow he might be overlooked.

Some who read these words have suffered for a long time. Jesus can heal your infirmity. He may choose to do so completely, or He may change the circumstances so that you can find peace and rest in your suffering. Don't let the Savior pass by; step forward in worship and allow Him to work in your life.

Don't pass me by, Lord. Work in my life as I humbly bow in worship before You.

(INTO HIS PRESENCE)

Jars of Clay

SCRIPTURE READING: 2 CORINTHIANS 4:7–18
KEY VERSE: 2 CORINTHIANS 4:7

We have this treasure in earthen vessels, that the excellence of the power may be of God and not of us.

The apostle Paul knew true success in ministry, but he also knew something about pain and turmoil. During his ministry, he was hunted, imprisoned, beaten, shipwrecked, and mocked. His fellow Jews branded him a traitor, and he was often scorned or not trusted by his Christian brothers. Paul faced the worst that life had to offer, yet he retained the joy that comes from a relationship with Jesus.

Unfortunately, many new believers assume that the saving work of Christ in their lives will prevent them from experiencing times of trials and troubles. Paul, however, disagreed. In 2 Corinthians 4:7–18, Paul illuminated the pain often associated with discipleship. Dispelling the illusion that Christians are spared hardships, Paul instead praised God for those times in which His power is revealed in human weakness.

In verse 7, Paul wrote about earthen vessels and the power of God. The New International Version translates "earthen vessels" as "jars of clay." The image here is of the unimaginable power of God being poured into fragile, cracked containers: you and me.

God's glory is not revealed *in spite of our* brokenness, but rather *through* our brokenness. Just as a cracked jar will seep water, so will the power of God leak out from our fractured lives.

Do not be ashamed of your "cracks." Rather, examine yourself to discover how God may be more fully revealed to you and others through your hardships.

Dear heavenly Father, let me realize that the "cracks" in my jar of clay provide openings for Your light to shine through. Reveal Yourself through me today.

(PATHWAYS TO HIS PRESENCE)

The Servant Spirit

SCRIPTURE READING: JOHN 13:1–20
KEY VERSE: MATTHEW 20:27

Whoever desires to be first among you, let him be your slave.

Why was Peter so stunned and overcome with shame when Jesus knelt to clean his feet? Foot washing was servant's work, a menial and dirty task, certainly not a job for an esteemed and beloved Leader. In one humble and brilliant gesture, Jesus demonstrated what their attitude and actions should be: "If I then, the Lord and the Teacher, washed your feet, you also ought to wash one another's feet. For I gave you an example that you also should do as I did to you" (John 13:14–15 NASB).

This servant's spirit should characterize everything you do. Of course, it's easy to think of a hypothetical situation and say, "Yes, I would do anything to help out." But the real test of your willingness to serve comes when you are confronted with the actual need.

You see trash all around a picnic site. Do you pick up the litter, or do you eat and walk away, hoping that someone who is paid to do it will clean up?

Your elderly neighbor needs a driver to take her to the store and the doctor. Would you volunteer?

The key to overcoming hesitation to serve is keeping the right attitude. When you see others as Jesus sees them, you want to meet their needs with enthusiasm. You discover the joy of serving when you follow the Savior's lead.

Heavenly Father, I want to serve others with joy, touching their lives with Your love, extending my hands to a hurting world. Make me a servant.

(ON HOLY GROUND)

Rest in His Care

SCRIPTURE READING: LUKE 15:1–7
KEY VERSE: LUKE 19:10

The Son of Man has come to seek and to save that which was lost.

The Pharisees were appalled that Jesus associated with sinners. They publicly grumbled about Jesus' actions to show their disgust for what they called loose, disreputable behavior. Sometimes He even ate meals with sinners and social outcasts.

Jesus responded immediately. He wanted them to understand that His real mission is to save lost mankind, all who recognize that they are separated from God by their sin and believe that He pays the price for them. Jesus wanted the Pharisees and scribes to know how much each lost soul means to Him, how much He is willing to do to restore the person to fellowship with God.

Jesus, the true Shepherd, compared His love for sinners to a shepherd boy searching for one lost sheep. This shepherd boy left his other ninety-nine sheep safe in the fold to seek the missing one. The shepherd was personally responsible for each sheep in his care. If something happened to one of them, he had to give an account to the owner of the flock. Imagine this boy's relief and joy when he finally carried the wandering one home.

Jesus has this same love for you. He wants you to know your infinite value, to come to Him and rest in His care.

Thank You for Your love, Lord. I rest in Your care today.

(SEEKING HIS FACE)

Deliverance Is Near

SCRIPTURE READING: HEBREWS 12:1–4
KEY VERSE: HEBREWS 11:39

All these, having obtained a good testimony through faith, did not receive the promise.

It's hard to read Hebrews 11:39 without feeling sorrow. In chapter 11, the writer of Hebrews recounted the faithfulness of the Old Testament saints. He told of the faith exhibited by Sarah and Abraham, of Jacob and Joseph, of King David, and many in between. There's a passage about Enoch and Abel—two names we rarely mention in our day-to-day conversations.

Each had one thought in mind, and that was to receive God's promise. Their eyes were turned to the future with the expectation that their generation might witness Messiah's arrival. However, the writer of Hebrews told us that each died without seeing or physically touching His hand. But in Hebrews 12:1, our dismay is turned into great joy: "Therefore we also, since we are surrounded by so great a cloud of witnesses, let us lay aside every weight . . . and let us run with endurance the race that is set before us."

Were these Old Testament saints disappointed because they missed Jesus' arrival? Not in the least. Their prayers were answered the moment they entered the presence of God. The burden you bear, the tears you shed, the sorrow you carry—God knows it all, and He has assembled a great and mighty host of experienced witnesses to cheer you on to victory.

Therefore, you can praise Him today and wait for Him in peace and joy, for His deliverance is near.

I praise You, Lord, because my deliverance is near. You know my burdens, tears, and sorrows. I humbly bow before You and worship.

(INTO HIS PRESENCE)

Trusting in God

SCRIPTURE READING: GENESIS 39
KEY VERSE: GENESIS 39:23

The keeper of the prison did not look into anything that was under Joseph's authority, because the LORD was with him; and whatever he did, the LORD made it prosper.

People who have spent time in prison talk about the mind-numbing effects of incarceration. Days slide into days, months into months, and an inmate's perception of time and reality may become stunted. It is easy to lose motivation or the will to live without hope, a goal, something to work toward.

If ever anyone had a reason to be bitter, it was Joseph. He did not even deserve to be in jail. Joseph could have allowed his frustration to deepen into resentment and then taken it out on his fellow prisoners and the guards. He could have made life miserable. Instead, Joseph chose to trust God:

> But the LORD was with Joseph and extended kindness to him, and gave him favor in the sight of the chief jailer. The chief jailer committed to Joseph's charge all the prisoners who were in the jail; so that whatever was done there, he was responsible for it. The chief jailer did not supervise anything under Joseph's charge because the LORD was with him; and whatever he did, the LORD made to prosper (Gen. 39:21–23 NASB).

Joseph understood that God's plans for him extended beyond the negatives of the here and now; in faith he could look past the present pain. As a result, God turned his circumstances into a beautiful testimony of His love and provision.

I trust You, Master! By faith, I look beyond the past and present into the tremendous future You have planned for me. Turn my negative circumstances into a testimony of Your love and provision.

(ON HOLY GROUND)

The Process of Beautification

SCRIPTURE READING: EPHESIANS 5:1–14
KEY VERSE: EPHESIANS 5:2

Walk in love, as Christ also has loved us and given Himself for us, an offering and a sacrifice to God for a sweet-smelling aroma.

Have you ever seen "before and after" photos in magazines? Cosmetics companies and weight-loss plans often use this advertisement technique. Of course, sometimes the changes seem just a little too remarkable. Yet that's what people love to see and experience, something that makes a change for the better.

The fifth chapter of Ephesians is a kind of spiritual "before and after" snapshot. It helps you understand what Jesus' grace actually does in your heart and mind as you grow in your relationship with the Savior: "Do not be partakers with them [the evildoers]; for you were formerly darkness, but now you are light in the Lord; walk as children of Light (for the fruit of the Light consists in all goodness and righteousness and truth), trying to learn what is pleasing to the Lord" (Eph. 5:7–10 NASB).

Can you remember what you were like before you accepted Christ as your Savior? For some people the transformation was radical and easily visible to others. But no matter what your story, you can certainly recall areas of darkness that were opened up to the light of Christ and made new.

The good news is that "beautification" is still taking place. You don't have a final "after" picture because you are always in the process of becoming more like Him.

Thank You that You are changing me, Lord. I humbly submit to the beautification process that is making me more like You.

(SEEKING HIS FACE)

Enjoying God

SCRIPTURE READING: JEREMIAH 32:39–41
KEY VERSE: DEUTERONOMY 30:9

*The LORD your God will make you abound in all the work of your hand,
in the fruit of your body, in the increase of your livestock, and in the
produce of your land for good. For the LORD will again rejoice over you
for good as He rejoiced over your fathers.*

The *Westminster Shorter Catechism* encapsulates the Christian's purpose in
this terse statement: "The chief end of man is to glorify God and to enjoy
Him forever."

Most committed followers of Christ passionately seek to honor Him.
Fewer, however, really know how to enjoy God. Perhaps this is due in
part to the misunderstanding of how God feels about you. He takes great
pleasure in you.

John Piper wrote in *The Pleasure of God*: "God is rejoicing over my
good with all His heart and with all His soul. He virtually breaks forth
into song when He hits upon a new way to do me good."

Piper continued:

But the promise is greater yet. Not only does God promise not to run
away from doing good to us, He says, "I will rejoice in doing them
good" (Jer. 32:41). "The LORD will again take delight in prospering
you" (Deut. 30:9). There is a kind of eagerness about the beneficence
of God. He does not wait for us to come to Him. He seeks us out,
because it is His pleasure to do us good.

God is not waiting for us, He is pursuing us. . . . I have never
forgotten how a great teacher once explained it to me. He said God is
like a highway patrolman pursuing you down the interstate with lights
flashing and siren blaring to get you to stop—not to give you a ticket,
but to give you a message so good it couldn't wait till you get home.

*Set me free to enjoy You, dear Lord. Thank You for Your goodness and the
blessings You bestow upon me each day.*

(INTO HIS PRESENCE)

Characteristics of True Believers

SCRIPTURE READING: EPHESIANS 1:1–14
KEY VERSE: EPHESIANS 1:11

In Him also we have obtained an inheritance, being predestined according to the purpose of Him who works all things according to the counsel of His will.

A life of enduring holiness (reflecting the mind and character of God) is possible only when we first are convinced of our identity in Christ. The Scriptures describe believers with these remarkable statements:

We are the salt of the earth. We are children of God.
We are saints. We have peace with God.
We are joint heirs with Jesus. We are free from condemnation.
We are justified by faith. We are the temple of God
We are ambassadors for Christ. We are complete in Christ.
We are eternally secure in Christ. We are triumphant in Christ.
We are citizens of heaven. We are accepted in the Beloved.
We are blessed with every
    spiritual blessing.

Many other benefits are already yours through faith in Christ. They are gifts from the Father, bestowed upon every disciple for effective service.

Knowing who you are in Christ is the starting point for abundant living. You can live a holy life because you are holy in Christ. Today agree with God concerning your new identity in Christ.

O God, I declare my new identity in Christ: I am the salt of the earth, a child of God, a saint who has peace with You. I am joint heir with Jesus, free from condemnation, and justified by faith. I am the temple of God, an ambassador for Christ, eternally secure, triumphant, complete, and accepted in Christ. I am a citizen of heaven and blessed with every spiritual blessing!

(ON HOLY GROUND)

Simply Be Still

SCRIPTURE READING: PSALM 46:1–11
KEY VERSE: PSALM 46:10

Be still, and know that I am God;
I will be exalted among the nations,
I will be exalted in the earth!

"Don't just stand there! Do something!" This is a familiar call to action in our modern world. However, there is something inherently dangerous when we try to force this way of thinking into our spiritual lives.

Too often, whether we voice the belief or not, we act as though God needs our help. We wrestle with God for some degree of control over the events in our lives. In effect, we make a proud stand and proclaim, "Okay, God. I think this is what You want to happen, so I'm going to work and work and work and make it come about."

Somewhere in the back of our minds, we hear the time-honored counsel, "God helps those who help themselves." In fact, the vast majority of Christians believe that this word of advice is in the Bible. It is not.

Actually, this statement is 100 percent contrary to the Word of God, which instead tells us to be still. The Father knows that we cannot help ourselves. That is the very reason He sent His Son to die—because we were utterly helpless to improve our sinful condition (Rom. 5:8).

While we seek to do God's will, we must not forget His fundamental call to stillness before Him. When we are still and quiet in His presence, we put ourselves in the most teachable position possible.

Are you too busy trying to keep up with God? Lay down your efforts and simply be still. What you discover in the stillness may revolutionize your call to Christian service.

Lord, I cease from my own efforts. I wait in stillness before You.

(PATHWAYS TO HIS PRESENCE)

A Man After God's Heart

SCRIPTURE READING: 2 SAMUEL 23:13–17
KEY VERSE: ACTS 13:22

When He had removed him, He raised up for them David as king, to whom also He gave testimony and said, "I have found David the son of Jesse, a man after My own heart, who will do all My will."

Hidden within the text of 2 Samuel 23:13–17 is a revealing detail of King David's life. The Philistines had captured Bethlehem, David's birthplace, and established a garrison there. The city was shut up: no one could go in and no one could leave. David was in his stronghold in the nearby cave of Adullam. There with selected members of his mighty men, David plotted the next attack against the enemy.

There he longingly expressed a desire for a drink of water from the well of Bethlehem. As his men listened to his words, their devotion for their commander was stirred. Three of the men risked their lives by crossing enemy lines to bring a single cup of Bethlehem's water to David. When he saw what they had done, David's heart was humbled. He refused to drink the water, choosing instead to pour it out as a drink offering to God.

David recognized the valor of his men, but he also understood that only God was worthy of such devotion. The other aspect to the story is that David refused to elevate himself above the others.

The entirety of David's heart was humbly committed to God. That is why God called David "a man after My own heart." In God's eyes, humility is a sign of greatness and obedience a characteristic of those who intimately walk with God.

Dear God, help me walk humbly and obediently with You. Make me a person after Your own heart.

(INTO HIS PRESENCE)

Amazing Grace

SCRIPTURE READING: EPHESIANS 2:1–10
KEY VERSE: EPHESIANS 2:13

Now in Christ Jesus you who once were far off have been brought near by the blood of Christ.

It is little wonder that the hymn "Amazing Grace" is sung so resoundingly in churches across the world. Its vivid imagery reminds us of the preeminence of grace and its indispensable role in our salvation and sanctification. But what makes grace so amazing?

God's grace is amazing because it is free. No currency exists that can ever purchase grace. We are usually suspicious of anything free, but God's offer is without any hidden strings. He bore the cost for our sins (therefore, it is not cheap grace) so that He could extend it freely to any man on the basis of faith—not intellect, status, or prestige.

God's grace is amazing because it is limitless. His grace can never be exhausted. Regardless of the vileness or number of our sins, God's grace is always sufficient. It can never be depleted; it can never be measured. He always gives His grace in fullness.

God's grace is amazing because it is always applicable. Do you need wisdom? God's grace provides it through His Word. Do you need strength or guidance? God's grace sustains you by His Spirit. Do you need security? God's grace supplies it through His sovereignty.

The amazing grace of God! Full and free! Without measure! Pertinent for your every need!

It's free! It's limitless! It is applicable to my every need today! O Lord, thank You for Your amazing grace. I praise You that it flows full and free in my life.

(ON HOLY GROUND)

The First Step to Victory

SCRIPTURE READING: ROMANS 8:26–28
KEY VERSE: ROMANS 8:28

*We know that all things work together for good to those who love God,
to those who are the called according to His purpose.*

Our pride deceives us into thinking that failure is for the weak, not for us. We assume that God is working through our victories. But what does God's Word say?

Paul wrote, "And we know that all things work together for good to those who love God, to those who are the called according to His purpose" (Rom. 8:28). In relation to failure, this verse explains that God works through our failures for His glory. Failure is actually the first step to victory.

God's ultimate goal is to transform us into His image so that we more vividly reflect His glory, and He will do whatever is necessary to achieve that within our hearts. And sometimes, failure in our lives is essential for God to bring about a greater purpose.

We may wonder why failure is happening in our lives. We ask ourselves, "What am I doing wrong? Doesn't God love me? Doesn't He want me to be victorious?"

Above achieving victory, God wants to transform us into His likeness. And when we fail, self-reflection occurs. We look upon our hearts and wonder what we could have done differently.

If we are willing to ask God what He is trying to teach us through our failures, He gladly will reveal lessons. We begin to recognize that failure leads to victory—the triumphant transformation of our hearts to totally trust God with control of our lives.

Lord, take my victories and my failures and shape them into paths that lead to You.

(PATHWAYS TO HIS PRESENCE)

Worthy of Praise

SCRIPTURE READING: PHILIPPIANS 4:5–23
KEY VERSE: PSALM 147:1

Praise the LORD!
For it is good to sing praises to our God;
For it is pleasant, and praise is beautiful.

Whenever you read a passage of Scripture concerning suffering, you almost always find an exhortation to praise God.

It seems an odd mix—the moment when you are enduring the greatest internal stress is the time when you least feel like offering praise and thanksgiving. In her book *31 Days of Praise*, Ruth Myers explains the connection:

> Why do I at times feel reluctant to praise in the midst of everyday trials: when I hear news that makes me anxious about someone I love, or when I face a major disappointment, or when I'm angry or under a lot of pressure?
>
> Could it be that one of Satan's major strategies is to divert us from praise? After all, he knows that God delights in our praise, and that doesn't exactly make him happy. He also detests the rich benefits praise brings to us and others. Or is it simply that our flesh prevails over our spirits, dampening our desire to glorify God? Might it be some of both? . . .
>
> Praise flourishes as you weed and water and fertilize your spiritual garden in which it grows. It becomes more constant as you nurture your soul on God's Word and walk in His ways, depending upon the Holy Spirit. It gets richer and more spontaneous as you grow in your knowledge of how worthy the Lord is to receive honor and glory and praise.

You are worthy to receive praise, O Lord. I praise You today with my whole heart.

(INTO HIS PRESENCE)

Gifts of Eternal Value

SCRIPTURE READING: EPHESIANS 4:29–32
KEY VERSE: PROVERBS 10:20

The tongue of the righteous is choice silver;
The heart of the wicked is worth little.

One of the most important components of the Christian life is the way we communicate with one another. Paul told us: "Let no unwholesome word proceed from your mouth, but only such a word as is good for edification according to the need of the moment" (Eph. 4:29 NASB). Our words can be powerful tools of encouragement and hope or, if thoughtlessly delivered, weapons of emotional devastation.

Few people truly understand the depth of shame and guilt of the woman at the well (John 4:7–39). More than likely, she was the focus of local gossip and malicious accusations. No one took the time to look into her heart—no one, that is, until Jesus.

Instead of rejection, Christ's words brought hope and forgiveness. The result was a changed life. Many of the people we meet and pass each day need to hear of God's love and eternal forgiveness. Rather, they are often met with disapproving stares and whispers.

Those trapped in sin already know the reality of their shame. What they really need is a way out of the mess they are in. Do as Jesus did. Accept them as people dearly loved by God while refusing to justify their sin. Let your words be gifts of eternal value instead of arsenals of pain.

Lord, let my words be gifts of eternal value instead of arsenals of pain.

(SEEKING HIS FACE)

Pray Without Ceasing

SCRIPTURE READING: PSALM 5:1–3
KEY VERSE: 1 THESSALONIANS 5:17

Pray without ceasing.

What did the apostle Paul mean when he wrote, "Pray without ceasing"? For one, he was indicating that we can live in an attitude of prayer even though we are engaged in everyday activity. That does not mean we walk around mumbling prayers to God, though there will be days when we pray much more than others.

Instead, the indication here leans to one of opportunity. We can have a natural attitude of prayer surrounding our lives. Prayer is a sign that we are dependent on the Lord and not on ourselves. Should you pray about trivial matters? Yes. God listens to every prayer. A prayer to find lost glasses or to mentally retrieve forgotten information is a worthy request.

God has called us to be people of prayer. Communication on this level is one of intimate fellowship with the Savior. Through prayer, we discover the goodness and personal devotion of God. Though taking time to be alone with God is the ideal, we don't have to limit ourselves. God hears our prayers no matter where we pray.

Oswald Chambers spoke to this issue: "So many of us limit our praying because we are not reckless in our confidence in God. In the eyes of those who do not know God, it is madness to trust Him. But when we pray through the power of the Holy Spirit we realize the resources of God. He is our perfect heavenly Father, and we are His children."

Dear Lord, give me reckless confidence in You as my loving heavenly Father, one who is concerned about my every need.

(INTO HIS PRESENCE)

Restoration for Your Soul

SCRIPTURE READING: ROMANS 7:15–25
KEY VERSE: ROMANS 7:22

I delight in the law of God according to the inward man.

How can we possibly restore our lives to victory when we have just experienced a particularly difficult time? The best way to restoration is through focusing on God's truth. This means refusing to listen to the nagging voice of the enemy.

Satan tempts us to doubt God's goodness by telling us that we are not worthy of God's love. The enemy interjects thoughts of doubt, worry, and anxiety into our minds so that we will become paralyzed and melt with fear. The enemy also assaults our minds with lies, but God's truth brings hope and restoration to our souls.

Are you facing a time of intense pressure? If so, you may wonder how you will get through it. Christ has the answer. When the storms of life hit, you can retain a strong sense of peace and calm by meditating on the fact that God is in control, and He has nothing but good in mind for your life. He wants you to be victorious spiritually.

When the burden you are carrying becomes too heavy, give it to God. He is your source of strength. In *Telling Yourself the Truth*, author William Backus wrote that there are three steps to becoming a person of contentment and peace:

1. Locate your misbeliefs, those things that the enemy uses to discourage you.
2. Ask God to help you remove them.
3. Replace misbeliefs with God's truth.

Lord, I give all doubt and fear to You. For me, they are insurmountable roadblocks, but in Your hands, they are nothing.

(PATHWAYS TO HIS PRESENCE)

When in Need

SCRIPTURE READING: HEBREWS 4:12–16
KEY VERSE: 2 TIMOTHY 2:26

They may come to their senses and escape the snare of the devil, having been taken captive by him to do his will.

We are likely to think of the obvious—hatred, lust, immorality—as Satan's primary weapons of temptation and defeat. But our accuser possesses a far more deadly and cleverly disguised agent of spiritual destruction—discouragement.

In times of need, he causes us to dwell on our mistakes, our repeated failures, our constant confession of sins, and our general lack of holiness and unrighteousness. It doesn't take much on the devil's part to disillusion us. We are all too well acquainted with our infirmities. Allowed to linger, discouragement breeds despair, which engulfs any sense of godly hope and confidence. Like a battle tank out of gas, we are neutralized on the spiritual battlefield.

If you have experienced this bewildered state, you can disarm the deceiver with this unchanging Bible truth: God's grace will never fail you.

Christ's grace saved you. His face smiles upon you even when you stumble. His grace has reserved a place in heaven for every believer that no sin or sins can alter.

His throne is adorned with grace and mercy. As the Son of man, Christ understands your plight. He will never turn you away. The instant you call on Him and thank Him for His forgiveness, discouragement has no room to stand. Go boldly to Him.

Father God, I take authority over the enemy's tool of discouragement in my life. I give You all my mistakes, failures, and recurring sins. Thank You for grace that will never fail.

(ON HOLY GROUND)

The Basics of Faith

SCRIPTURE READING: 2 CORINTHIANS 5:1–8
KEY VERSE: 2 CORINTHIANS 5:7

We walk by faith, not by sight.

Until we discover what it means to have faith, we cannot begin to walk by faith. Faith in God is more than just believing He exists; it is living with confidence that He will fulfill all His promises and bring salvation to us. We must discover whether we have placed our faith in God or if we only are wishing His Word is true. As our faith is tested, the true spiritual state of our hearts is revealed.

A situation is presented before us where we can act within our own strength, doing whatever we can to manipulate the outcome, or we can trust in God's strength, taking our hands off the problem and allowing Him to enter the scene.

As we begin to walk by faith, there will be times when we stumble and fall. However, falling and getting up is part of learning how to walk. Once we get up and dust ourselves off, we take our next step with more wisdom, more strength, more faith.

Walking by faith is a lifestyle, a way in which we conduct ourselves. As God molds and shapes us more into His image, He desires for us to live a life of faith, a life that relies upon Him for everything we need. Paul wrote, "For we walk by faith, not by sight. . . . Therefore we also have as our ambition, whether at home or absent, to be pleasing to Him" (2 Cor. 5:7, 9 NASB).

Lord, guide me to that place where I go beyond just believing You are real but, rather, rely on Your wisdom for every detail of my life.

(PATHWAYS TO HIS PRESENCE)

The Message of the Cross

SCRIPTURE READING: MARK 15:33–39
KEY VERSE: MARK 15:39

When the centurion, who stood opposite Him, saw that He cried out like this and breathed His last, he said, "Truly this Man was the Son of God!"

Two men of different faiths sat across from each other at a restaurant table. In an effort to understand the other's views, the first man asked, "Can you sum up the essence of Christianity in one word?"

Without pause, the second man replied, "Forgiveness."

Would you have given the same answer? There are so many words that could have been said: *love, sacrifice, joy, assurance, eternity.* Yet *forgiveness* seems to carry the most meaning and power. What other religion offers its believers the ability to be set free from sin with no penance to pay?

We can count ourselves among the most fortunate in the world. When we pledge our lives to God and accept the Lord Jesus Christ as our personal Savior, we are guaranteed forgiveness and eternal life.

Though none of us is exempt from the storms and trials of life, we can live with inner joy and peace. We will never pay the penalty of eternal death for our sins. That price was paid for us at the cross by a loving God who is merciful and longsuffering.

The blood that Christ shed upon the cross is truly the key to heaven for those who believe. Today, why not reach out to someone who may not be aware of the gift God gave to the world through the atoning death of His only Son?

Lord, Your blood shed on the cross spelled forgiveness for me. I cannot repay You, but I can share this key to heaven with others.

(PATHWAYS TO HIS PRESENCE)

Never Alone

SCRIPTURE READING: 2 TIMOTHY 4:16–18
KEY VERSE: 2 TIMOTHY 4:16

At my first defense no one stood with me, but all forsook me. May it not be charged against them.

Most of us can identify with Paul's words in 2 Timothy. In fact, as we read them, we probably can sense the heaviness and thoughtfulness with which they were written: "At my first defense no one stood with me, but all forsook me" (4:16).

Have you ever been in a position where you had to take a stand for something that you knew was not right, and no one was willing to stand with you? Maybe you had to say no to a project that was in the process of being developed. You knew that if things continued, the company you worked for would suffer.

Or perhaps your son or daughter came to you and asked permission to do something you felt was not best. All the other moms and dads had said yes, but for some reason, you sensed that you should say no, and this is what you did. Suddenly, you were very unpopular. Those who had once supported you now felt you were being prudish and legalistic.

The Spirit of God leads us in the way that we should go. Godly decisions require godly courage. From a human perspective, Paul was alone. No one was with him. But he was not alone. Jesus was beside him and with him.

You are never alone. Life's trials provide a wonderful opportunity for God to display His power and wisdom in your life. Be courageous and do not fear. The Lord your God is with you, and He will give you strength, wisdom, and victory (Josh. 1:9).

Lord, I need Your courage in order to stand strong when I feel forsaken or alone. Let me not forget that my strength comes from You.

(PATHWAYS TO HIS PRESENCE)

God's Provision

SCRIPTURE READING: 2 KINGS 6:8–23
KEY VERSE: PSALM 27:1

The LORD is my light and my salvation;
Whom shall I fear?
The LORD is the strength of my life;
Of whom shall I be afraid?

Do you remember looking through a microscope for the first time? Your eyes were opened to a teeming world of protozoan life. You had to look at the droplet in a new and different way to perceive another dimension of the physical world.

Elisha's servant had to learn to look at their circumstances in a new way. Things looked bad for them on the surface. The king of Syria and his men were angry with Elisha because they knew God told Elisha their attack strategies in advance; and of course, Elisha told their plans to the king of Israel.

It's no surprise that the Syrians wanted to do away with Elisha. So one night, the king of Syria sent horses and chariots and an army to surround the city where Elisha was staying. At first sight, Elisha's attendant went outside and saw the army circled to attack.

He ran to Elisha and cried, "Alas, my master! What shall we do?" But Elisha wasn't panicked. He said, "Do not fear, for those who are with us are more than those who are with them" (2 Kings 6:15–16). The attendant must have been mightily confused. The only people he saw were the ones with weapons pointed at them.

Then Elisha prayed for God to open his eyes, and the attendant saw an angelic host with horses and chariots of fire surrounding them. God had already arranged for their protection, but the attendant had to learn to see His provision.

Father, I thank You that You have already arranged for my protection.
Open my eyes to Your provision.

(INTO HIS PRESENCE)

Biblical Weakness

SCRIPTURE READING: JOHN 10:7–18
KEY VERSE: JOHN 10:10

The thief does not come except to steal, and to kill, and to destroy. I have come that they may have life, and that they may have it more abundantly.

The late Traian Dorz was an influential Christian leader in Communist Romania following the Second World War.

As such, he was beaten on many occasions by Communist authorities seeking to weaken his faith. After each beating by one particular guard, he would look into the guard's menacing face and say, "I want you to know that God loves you very much, and I love you very much too."

The guard returned one evening for what Dorz thought was yet another pummeling. Instead, the guard reported he had found Jesus as his Savior.

Traian Dorz modeled the biblical idea of weakness. Contrary to the world's definition, weakness is not fear, cowardliness, or defeat. Weakness is a rational appraisal of our strength versus God's strength. We are finite; He is infinite. We are erratic; God is unchanging.

In view of this truth, it is foolish not to trust in God for help and guidance, to come to Him in solid anticipation that He can and will handle our problems.

Draw on the inexhaustible reservoir of God's wisdom, grace, and mercy. In your limitations, you have the power of an unlimited God to sustain you.

Almighty God, I receive by faith Your wisdom, grace, and mercy. Thank You that in my limitations, I have Your unlimited power to sustain me.

(ON HOLY GROUND)

Captive Thoughts

SCRIPTURE READING: PHILIPPIANS 4:4–9
KEY VERSE: 2 CORINTHIANS 10:5

[We are] casting down arguments and every high thing that exalts itself against the knowledge of God, bringing every thought into captivity to the obedience of Christ.

A clear conscience brings peace to the heart and a sense of contentment to the mind. People who are continually rushing and running in and through trouble shouldn't be surprised to find it hard to relax and forsake feelings of anxiety.

One of the roles of the Holy Spirit is to lead us into all truth, an essential element in gaining a clear conscience. The apostle Paul wrote, "Whatever is true, whatever is honorable, whatever is right, whatever is pure, whatever is lovely, whatever is of good repute, if there is any excellence and if anything worthy of praise, dwell on these things. The things you have learned and received and heard and seen in me, practice these things, and the God of peace will be with you" (Phil. 4:8–9 NASB).

The verses immediately preceding these also add insight: "Rejoice in the Lord always; again I will say, rejoice! . . . The Lord is near. Be anxious for nothing, but in everything by prayer and supplication with thanksgiving let your requests be made known to God. And the peace of God, which surpasses all comprehension, will guard your hearts and your minds in Christ Jesus" (vv. 4–7 NASB).

When your thoughts are captivated with things that are not of God, it is difficult to experience the hope of His truth. Only when you are in tune with His loving Spirit can you sense His grace and mercy at work in your life.

Lord, help me to be in tune with Your loving Spirit so I can sense Your grace and mercy at work in my life.

(SEEKING HIS FACE)

God's Faithfulness

SCRIPTURE READING: PSALM 102
KEY VERSES: HEBREWS 13:5–6

Let your conduct be without covetousness; be content with such things as you have. For He Himself has said, "I will never leave you nor forsake you." So we may boldly say: "The LORD is my helper; I will not fear. What can man do to me?"

At times in our spiritual walk we feel as though all of heaven is shut up before us. We find ourselves wondering whether God has forgotten us or we have done something to disappoint Him. But nothing we do surprises God. He is omniscient and perfectly in tune with our every thought.

God has chosen to love you, even in sin, with an unconditional love. His love is based not on your performance but on His grace. You could never in your own strength perform up to God's standards. He loves you just as much when you stumble and fall as He does when you closely follow Him. This is not an excuse for sin but an opportunity to learn to love Him better.

Along the pathway of faith, each of us can expect to face times of trials and difficulty when it appears that God is distant and removed from us. Yet we walk not by sight but in the reality of the promise that He will never leave or forsake us (Heb. 13:5–6). Faith always looks beyond the immediate to the eternal.

The times you feel God is doing nothing in your life are usually the very times He is doing His greatest work. Be of good courage; He may simply have you protected under the cover of His hand while He works out the necessary details for your advancement. Trust Him, and you will find Him faithful.

Almighty God, even when I feel You have forgotten me, You are still there. Thank You for Your unconditional love. I know You love me just as much when I stumble and fall as when I follow closely. Thank You for the great work You are doing in my life.

(ON HOLY GROUND)

Ask, Seek, Knock

SCRIPTURE READING: 2 TIMOTHY 2:11–13
KEY VERSE: 2 TIMOTHY 2:13

If we are faithless, He remains faithful; He cannot deny Himself.

Those who ask will receive answers. Those who seek will find. Those who knock will find the door opened for them. It is God's acrostic: A-S-K: Ask, Seek, Knock.

The Lord wants us to pray to Him, not only because it honors Him, but also because it helps us to grow in Him. Furthermore, prayer taps us into His work in the world. At any given moment, you can pray for anyone anywhere on earth and have confidence that the Lord of the entire universe will hear you and respond in the most effective fashion.

For this reason, prayer is one of the best ways to get involved in God's mission. What a wonderful privilege it is to be able to participate in the expansion of God's kingdom by asking the Lord to help His children and work in the lives of unbelievers.

Another reason the Lord bids us to pray is to build our faith in Him. Even sinful men give gifts to their children. How much more does the holy God enjoy giving good gifts to those who ask Him? (Matt. 7:11). He enjoys helping us along in our faith as we learn His Word, practice His presence, and stay so close to Him that His thoughts become our thoughts. He also loves to answer our prayers and see us become bolder in our walk and witness.

God's Word tells us that He is faithful because He cannot deny Himself (2 Tim. 2:13). Be certain to set aside time daily to talk to Him, and you will learn this truth firsthand.

Father, teach me to ask, seek, and knock—to persevere in prayer until I receive an answer.

(PATHWAYS TO HIS PRESENCE)

Growing Your Faith

SCRIPTURE READING: MATTHEW 17:14–20
KEY VERSE: MATTHEW 17:20

[Jesus said to them,] "Assuredly, I say to you, if you have faith as a mustard seed, you will say to this mountain, 'Move from here to there,' and it will move; and nothing will be impossible for you."

How do you respond when presented with a challenge that calls for a surge of faith in God? Hesitantly? Tentatively? Fearfully? Optimistically?

The key to breaking the faith barrier and anchoring our trust in God is an exalted view of God Himself.

"But I thought to have more faith, I had to work at it more," you say. You do, but your work is to see God for who He really is, not to struggle to obtain more faith or have a more positive mind-set.

When the disciples thirsted to have more faith, Jesus told them all that was necessary was faith the size of a mustard seed. "Use what you have," Jesus was saying, "and your faith will grow in the process."

We use what faith we have, as little as it may seem, by magnifying the heart's view of God. When Moses was scared to go to Pharaoh, God dealt with Moses' fears by revealing Himself more fully: "Thus you shall say to the sons of Israel, 'I AM has sent me to you'" (Ex. 3:14 NASB).

We grow in faith by seeing God in a new light. Our faith is as big as our God. If your notion of God is grand, your faith will soar. If it is little, your faith will sag. How big is your God? See Him as He is, and the faith barrier will shatter before you.

Dear God, let my faith soar. Grow faith in me that is as big as You are. O God, I want to see You as You are. Shatter the obstacles of fear, disobedience, and faithlessness in my life. I want to break through the faith barrier.

(ON HOLY GROUND)

The Pathway of Faith

SCRIPTURE READING: GENESIS 12:1–9
KEY VERSE: GENESIS 12:1

Now the LORD had said to Abram: "Get out of your country, from your family and from your father's house, to a land that I will show you."

No one would have blamed Abram if he immediately began making to-do lists upon hearing the Lord's command to leave his country. After residing in Haran for seventy-five years, Abram would have had extensive details to care for and many ties to resolve.

The task for both Abram and Sarai must have been dizzying. Not only was the overall mission overwhelming, but they were also responsible for the daunting duty of caring for their entourage.

Great missions and trials are always accompanied by mountains of details. In fact, sometimes it is the smallest issue that is the most devastating discouragement to the believer. However, God cares for everything in our lives. R. A. Torrey counsels, "If our troubles are large enough to vex and endanger our welfare, they are large enough to touch God's heart of love."

You may believe that your situation is too small to bring before God. However, the pathway of faith is trusting God for every facet and feature of your life. Have confidence that He cares for you even in the smallest issues, and you will find how abundant His great love for you really is.

Lord, thank You for caring about the small details of my life. I get lost in all the miniscule tasks, but You have room in Your heart for all of them.

(PATHWAYS TO HIS PRESENCE)

Constant Communion

SCRIPTURE READING: PSALM 63
KEY VERSE: PSALM 63:8

My soul follows close behind You;
Your right hand upholds me.

When we think about the good things in life, one thing overshadows all the rest, and that is fellowship with God. No one can take His place in our lives. As much as we love our family members and friends, the greatest friendship we will ever experience is with Jesus Christ.

He knows your heartache and your joys. He never tires of you but is always excited to hear your voice calling out to Him in prayer. He has promised good things for those who seek Him. If you want to find the key to the good things in life, discover the fellowship that God has waiting for you through Jesus Christ.

In *My Utmost for His Highest*, Oswald Chambers wrote,

> To be so much in contact with God that you never need to ask Him to show you His will, is to be nearing the final stage of your discipline in the life of faith. When you are rightly related to God, it is a life of freedom and liberty and delight; you are God's will, and all your commonsense decisions are His will for you unless He checks. You decide things in perfect delightful friendship with God, knowing that if your decisions are wrong He will always check; when He checks, stop at once.

Chambers describes life lived in constant communion with God. It is not the life of a reclusive servant, but the life of a child of God who is living in perfect fellowship with Jesus Christ.

How thankful I am, dear Lord, that You know my heartache and my joys. You never tire of me. You are always excited to hear my voice calling out to You.

(SEEKING HIS FACE)

Viewing Eternity from Here

SCRIPTURE READING: 2 CORINTHIANS 4:1–18
KEY VERSES: 2 CORINTHIANS 4:16–18

We do not lose heart. Even though our outward man is perishing, yet the inward man is being renewed day by day. For our light affliction, which is but for a moment, is working for us a far more exceeding and eternal weight of glory, while we do not look at the things which are seen, but at the things which are not seen. For the things which are seen are temporary, but the things which are not seen are eternal.

In the book *Shadow of the Almighty: The Life and Testament of Jim Elliot,* Elisabeth Elliot wrote of the last time she saw her husband alive:

> Jim slung the carrying net across his forehead, and started for the front door. As he put his hand on the brass handle I almost said aloud: "Do you realize you may never open that door again?"
>
> He swung it open, followed me out and slammed it, striding down the bamboo trail in his usual firm, determined gait. As we reached the strip, the plane was circling to land, and it was only a matter of minutes before Jim kissed me, hopped in beside the pilot, and disappeared over the river. On Sunday, January 8, 1956, the men for whom Jim Elliot had prayed for six years killed him and his four companions.

Jim Elliot's life was one of total commitment to Jesus Christ. At the age of twenty-two, he wrote, "He is no fool who gives what he cannot keep to gain what he cannot lose."

He saw life from a different angle. His goal was to be remembered not as someone who had done a great work but as one who exemplified total love of and devotion to his Savior. Because of his devotion to his Savior, his martyrdom at age twenty-eight remains an inspiration to all who would dare to live and die by the cross of Jesus Christ.

O God, give me an eternal perspective. I want to live and die by the cross of Your Son, Jesus Christ.

(INTO HIS PRESENCE)

Nothing Is Wasted

SCRIPTURE READING: JOHN 11:1–45
KEY VERSES: JOHN 11:25–26

Jesus said to her, "I am the resurrection and the life. He who believes in Me, though he may die, he shall live. And whoever lives and believes in Me shall never die. Do you believe this?"

By the time Jesus reached Bethany, Mary and Martha were overwhelmed by the reality of their brother's death. Jesus loved Lazarus too, and He was not ashamed to display His sorrow. God is sensitive to our needs and doesn't hesitate to weep with us when we hurt.

Jesus also had a greater plan in mind for the sisters and all who were present. He used this tragedy to point others to Himself. Jesus told those who had gathered at the tomb: "I am the resurrection and the life. He who believes in Me, though he may die, he shall live. And whoever lives and believes in Me shall never die. . . . Did I not say to you that if you would believe, you would see the glory of God?" (John 11:25–26, 40).

You may wonder why a certain tragedy had to happen, but you need never doubt the goodness of God's sovereign will. He sees the beginning and the end of your life, and only He can transform your tragedies into something of lasting value.

In Jesus Christ, Mary and Martha found the hope of eternal life. Author and speaker Elisabeth Elliot says nothing is a waste with God. He takes everything, even the slightest detail, and works it all together for our good. No matter what you are facing, the Lord has a plan in mind for the future. Tell Him of your doubts, fears, and inadequacies, and He will strengthen and encourage you.

How I thank You, Father, that nothing is wasted in Your divine economy. You take everything and work it together for my good.

(INTO HIS PRESENCE)

The Difficulties of Life

SCRIPTURE READING: PSALM 57
KEY VERSE: PSALM 57:1

*Be merciful to me, O God, be merciful to me! For my soul trusts
in You;
and in the shadow of Your wings I will make my refuge,
until these calamities have passed by.*

If God is good, why does He allow bad things to happen? This important
theological question has mystified people throughout the ages. But as
believers, we can be confident that God always has a purpose for allowing
adversity:

Spiritual cleansing. Nothing exposes sin like pain and suffering. If there
is something in your life that needs His forgiveness, go to Him immediately. Ask Him to restore the sweetness of the fellowship you once shared.

Companionship. God is not the author of evil, but He uses it to bring
you into a closer relationship with Himself. Any sin in your life needs to
be removed because it blocks the flow of God's love.

Conformity. Adversity purifies your motives and strips away the dross
in your life so that you reflect His love to others with an even greater
brilliance.

Conviction. After Christ's death, the disciples had to hold fast to what
they believed concerning God's Son. In the end, the adversity they faced
led to an increased joy that came through the reality of living in harmony
with the Holy Spirit.

Comfort. When God becomes your only Source of comfort in times of
trials, you will experience an inner peace like nothing you have felt before.

*Dear Lord, thank You for the supernatural purposes that You are
accomplishing in me through the difficulties of life. Strip away the dross in my
life so that I can reflect Your love to others with an even greater brilliance.*

(INTO HIS PRESENCE)

Victory Through Faith

SCRIPTURE READING: 1 SAMUEL 17:12–37
KEY VERSE: PHILIPPIANS 1:6

He who has begun a good work in you will complete it until the day of Jesus Christ.

As a young shepherd boy, David did not possess all the qualities of a strong, conquering faith. God took years to train him for his future role as a king of Israel. However, he never lost sight of God's goal for his life by fretting over the future.

When facing his first major challenge with Goliath, David mentally went through several steps to ensure himself of the victory through faith. These will keep you encouraged in the midst of your battles:

Recall past victories. Remember how God has been faithful to you.

Reaffirm the reasons for the conflict. Make sure your motives and heart are pure before God.

Reject discouragement. Always be wary of pessimism. Instead, practice recalling God's promises to you.

Recognize the true nature of the battle. Claim your position in Christ as a joint heir and a beloved child of God.

Respond with positive confessions of faith. God is in control, and He will give you the victory.

Rely on God. All your hope and security is in Christ. You struggle with human abilities and limitations, but God knows no limits.

Reckon the victory. David did, and you can too! Whether the victory comes today or in ten years, God will complete what He has begun in your life (Phil. 1:6).

Dear Lord, thank You for past victories. As I face the battles of life, make my motives pure. Help me resist discouragement and claim my position as a joint heir with Christ. Your power knows no limit, and You will complete what You have started in my life.

(ON HOLY GROUND)

Walking by Faith

SCRIPTURE READING: PSALM 27:11–14

KEY VERSE: PSALM 27:14

Wait on the LORD;
Be of good courage,
And He shall strengthen your heart;
Wait, I say, on the LORD!

In our excitement to see God work in our lives, we oftentimes forget that He knows the big picture, and He also knows what is best for us. Our zeal, apart from His divine knowledge, can send us racing into the unknown, when it's best for us to wait upon Him for guidance.

However, learning to walk by faith teaches us to stand firm while awaiting God's direction. Our mentality that places a disproportionate amount of emphasis on works can incite us to go forward. We forget that some of our greatest personal growth as believers, and the preparation necessary for God's next step in our lives, takes place in the stillness of our hearts.

David believed strongly that waiting upon God was vital to walking in His ways. In fact, twice in one verse, he implored us to wait: "Wait for the LORD; be strong and let your heart take courage; yes, wait for the LORD" (Ps. 27:14 NASB).

While we are anxious to tackle the next obstacle thrust in our path, God knows that we need time to grow—time learning to trust in Him— in order to conquer that obstacle. As we discover that our strength truly comes from God alone, we will wait patiently; for we understand that a deep faith in Him trusts that, with Him alone, we will succeed in walking victoriously by faith.

Lord, thank You for being there in the still, quiet places. Please calm my
racing heart so that I may have the patience to wait and hear Your voice.

(PATHWAYS TO HIS PRESENCE)

Waiting on God

SCRIPTURE READING: PSALM 27:1–4
KEY VERSE: PSALM 62:1

Truly my soul silently waits for God;
From Him comes my salvation.

When you think about the principles of God, there is one you don't want to overlook. It is the principle of waiting. Many times it is something we fail to understand and enjoy. Impatience can come from the feverish pace set by our society. Cell phones, e-mail, and the Internet have changed the way we live and communicate. No longer do we take time to be still and listen to the dreams and hopes of a friend. Instead, we hurry away and shout over our shoulders, "E-mail me and I'll get back with you!"

This attitude can have disastrous results. God created us for fellowship with Him and with others. Certain principles hold eternally true, and learning how to wait before the Lord is one of the wisest and healthiest things you can do.

A. B. Simpson once confided to a friend, "I am nothing without time alone with God." No one is at his best when he lays aside time alone with God in order to meet a deadline or pursue another activity.

Learning to be still before God is not just a devotional dream. Those who do it discover the deep richness that is theirs at the feet of Jesus. If you are having difficulty finding time to be alone with the Lord, ask Him to open up your heart and mind to His plan. He is very creative, and you will be surprised at the opportunity He provides.

God has a plan for your life. If you will maintain your course of faith, He will reward your obedience. The only way you can continue to go forward is to maintain a spiritual gaze that is set on Jesus, the Lover of your soul.

Teach me how to wait, Lord. I set my spiritual gaze on You, the Lover of my soul.

(SEEKING HIS FACE)

Supernatural Strength

SCRIPTURE READING: HEBREWS 12:1–3
KEY VERSE: GALATIANS 6:9

Let us not grow weary while doing good, for in due season we shall reap if we do not lose heart.

Spiritual fatigue hits everyone. In the race to know and serve Christ, our bodies, minds, and hearts can reach an overload point, causing us to drop back. If severe enough, spiritual fatigue can discourage us from continuing the race.

God enables us to endure when we "lay aside every encumbrance and the sin which so easily entangles us" (Heb. 12:1 NASB). Cast your burdens on the Lord (1 Peter 5:7). Keep short accounts with Him, daily confessing your sin.

God's strength comes when we recognize that "in due time we will reap if we do not grow weary" (Gal. 6:9 NASB). Your efforts will pay off. Harvesttime will come. God promises that your toil will be rewarded.

God strengthens us to finish the race if we do not "worry about tomorrow; for tomorrow will care for itself" (Matt. 6:34 NASB). Do not be unduly concerned about the future; instead, take life one day at a time. This spiritual race is not won instantaneously—it must be run step-by-step.

God's ability flows through us when we let Him be strong in areas where we are weak. Isaiah 40:29 says, "He gives strength to the weary, and to him who lacks might He increases power" (NASB).

When you are weary, draw from almighty God's unlimited power supply. Faint not. Fear not. Fret not. He gives supernatural strength to finish the race.

Dear God, transform my human weakness into supernatural strength. Let me faint not, fear not, and fret not. Give me supernatural strength to finish the race.

(ON HOLY GROUND)

A Passion to Know Him

SCRIPTURE READING: JOHN 4:1–42
KEY VERSE: JAMES 4:8

Draw near to God and He will draw near to you. Cleanse your hands, you sinners; and purify your hearts, you double-minded.

If you have ever had a best friend, you know what it feels like not to be able to get enough time with him or her. When you thoroughly enjoy someone's company, it is no trouble at all to arrange ways to spend time with that person. Going a season of time without seeing your friend can be a real emotional letdown.

The same is true of your relationship with the Lord. Jesus is your most intimate Friend, the One who loves you with agape love. If you go a period of time without fellowshipping with Him, you will experience the effects of separation from your very lifeline—an inner sadness and loneliness that can be satisfied only by drawing near to Him again (James 4:8).

The more time you spend with the Lord and in meditation on His truth, the greater your passion to know Him. The Samaritan woman at the well discovered this principle in the short amount of time she spent talking with Jesus.

When Jesus offered her living water, her curiosity was piqued. She was flooded with many emotions, including surprise and wonder. The woman was so excited about this new relationship that she left her water pot and ran to tell others in town (John 4:1–42).

That is what happens when you know the Lord; your excitement grows and, with it, your fervor for sharing His good news with others.

Give me a passion to know You better, dear Lord. Then give me fervor for sharing the good news of the gospel with others.

(INTO HIS PRESENCE)

Quality Time

SCRIPTURE READING: I THESSALONIANS 5:14–24
KEY VERSE: I THESSALONIANS 5:24

He who calls you is faithful, who also will do it.

Ours is a world of satellites, lasers, cell phones, and ATMs. Faxes zoom across telephone lines, and computers arrange daily schedules with supreme accuracy. Because of all these things, we have learned to demand instant results.

The tendency to try to become super Christians within a very short time is grave. It is almost as if we believe that to please God, we must become "better" quickly. However, God does not work this way.

Over time, our love and devotion for God will increase naturally. Spiritual growth cannot be forced. The maturation process takes time, quality time, spent with God.

This is how God weeds out old, sinful habits and plants His renewing truths within our hearts and minds. He knows that to produce maximum growth there must be maximum care and nurturing. God slowly reshapes our lives until they are molded into the image of His Son.

Never become discouraged by the apparently slow process of your spiritual growth. God's schedule is not ours. And if you will seek Him above everything else, you will receive all He has for you within His timing.

Lord, I want a relationship with You above all else. I want to receive all that You have for me.

(SEEKING HIS FACE)

The Priority of Prayer

SCRIPTURE READING: DANIEL 6:1–28
KEY VERSE: DANIEL 6:10

When Daniel knew that the writing was signed, he went home. And in his upper room, with his windows open toward Jerusalem, he knelt down on his knees three times that day, and prayed and gave thanks before his God, as was his custom since early days.

Sometimes it doesn't take much to throw you off track when it comes to spending time in prayer. You finally get by yourself and bow your head, and the phone rings. You suddenly remember another obligation. One of the children runs in with a question or a problem that cannot wait. Or maybe you can't concentrate, and you decide to give up and try again later.

For Daniel, not even the threat of becoming lunch for lions deterred him from his daily habit of prayer. The edict to worship the king was handed down, and the rulers waited with delight to catch Daniel in the act of defiance. Of course, they did not have to wait long. Daniel continued to pray before God three times a day, as he always did.

What gave Daniel his determination and resolve? He believed without a shadow of a doubt that God would honor his commitment to prayer and take care of any trouble. Daniel did not concern himself with who might see or what others would think; he focused on the Lord alone.

In the end, Daniel was saved, the king was awed, and the rulers got to meet the lions. And here is the good news: God protects and uplifts you, too, when you trust Him to handle the consequences of obedience in prayer.

Dear Lord, give me the determination and resolve to make prayer a priority. Make it the consuming passion of my life.

(INTO HIS PRESENCE)

How to Count Your Blessings

SCRIPTURE READING: PSALM 34
KEY VERSE: PSALM 34:8

Oh, taste and see that the LORD is good; blessed is the man who trusts in Him!

When you are asked to count your blessings, your list may not be overwhelming. You struggle to make ends meet; your days are hard. You are grateful for much, but weariness clouds your vision.

Pause to think of this: when you have the Lord Jesus Christ, you have the greatest blessing possible. That is not spiritualizing; it is the bedrock of your existence now on earth and one day in heaven.

In Christ you have the guarantee of eternal life. Life may be unsettling, but a place of unparalleled beauty and joy awaits the one who knows Christ as Savior, Lord, and Life. Heaven is real, and its blessings are sure.

In Christ Jesus you have the Source of true life. He gives love, joy, peace, strength, comfort, hope, and patience. He nourishes your soul and energizes your spirit. Possessions are nice, but they cannot impart life— only Jesus can.

In Christ you have a Friend for all seasons. He understands your disappointments, rejoices in your triumphs, and stands with you in your trials. You can confide in Him, weep before Him, and celebrate with Him.

Begin with all you have in Jesus Christ when you count your blessings. Then you will lose count.

Jesus, You are my greatest Source of blessing. You are my life. You give love, joy, peace, strength, comfort, and hope. You nourish my soul and energize my spirit. Thank You, Lord!

(ON HOLY GROUND)

Blessed Assurance

SCRIPTURE READING: 1 JOHN 3:18–24
KEY VERSE: 1 JOHN 3:23

This is His commandment: that we should believe on the name of His Son Jesus Christ and love one another, as He gave us commandment.

It is easy to look across the church sanctuary and see someone whose salvation you would not question. Perhaps you also can identify someone you believe is struggling even more in his walk with Jesus than you are.

One of the enemy's traps is to get us to compare ourselves to others. It is a way that he deceives us into thinking we do not measure up.

At other times he gets us to think we're better than the next person so we become complacent in our faith. The only true measuring stick resting in a church pew is in the book rack. It is the Bible, the inerrant Word of God.

Listen to what God says about assurance of salvation: "For God so loved the world, that He gave His only begotten Son, that whoever believes in Him shall not perish, but have eternal life" (John 3:16 NASB); "Believe in the Lord Jesus, and you will be saved" (Acts 16:31 NASB); and "This is His commandment, that we believe in the name of His Son Jesus Christ" (1 John 3:23 NASB).

The common thread in these scriptures is that salvation comes only through belief in Jesus Christ as the Son of God. There is no other itinerary or requirement, no need for comparisons: "These things I have written to you who believe in the name of the Son of God, so that you may know that you have eternal life" (1 John 5:13 NASB).

Father, thank You for the blessed assurance You have given me. Let me continually use the measuring stick of Your Word to check my spiritual growth.

(SEEKING HIS FACE)

Triumph Against All Odds

SCRIPTURE READING: JUDGES 7:12–15

KEY VERSE: JUDGES 7:12

Now the Midianites and Amalekites, all the people of the East, were lying in the valley as numerous as locusts; and their camels were without number, as the sand by the seashore in multitude.

Do you need special encouragement today? Does it feel as though all your sources of security have crumbled around you? Gideon understood feeling as if all the odds were against him. He faced the challenge of his life: fighting the mighty battalions of Midian with an army of only three hundred men.

Judges 7:12 reported that the Midianites and the Amalekites appeared as numerous as locusts. Their camels appeared as plentiful as the sand on the seashore. Can you imagine how Gideon's heart must have sunk upon seeing the awesome view? However, God did not allow Gideon to remain discouraged. When he returned to the camp, he heard two men discussing a dream that, being interpreted, was of God giving Midian over to the Israelites. Upon hearing this, Gideon worshiped God.

Gideon's boldness was renewed. Yours can be too. Such courage is available to you, though all the odds appear stacked against you. This is because you can know for sure that God will not leave you to face your foes alone. No matter what you face today, God is greater. Trust Him, and He will use you in a mighty, wonderful way to effect victory.

Thank You, Lord, that You will use me today to effect victory in Your name. I move forward with confidence and trust.

(PATHWAYS TO HIS PRESENCE)

Clothed with Power

SCRIPTURE READING: LUKE 24:44–49
KEY VERSE: JOHN 6:63

It is the Spirit who gives life; the flesh profits nothing. The words that I speak to you are spirit, and they are life.

After Jesus rose from the dead and ascended to the Father, His disciples were zealous to spread His message of salvation. Yet Christ commanded them to wait until they were "clothed with power from on high" (Luke 24:49 NASB) on Pentecost, when the Holy Spirit would come for a new, indwelling ministry.

Think seriously about this fact: If the Holy Spirit was necessary for the apostles to live and minister effectively, do we not need His power as well? The Christian life is started by the Holy Spirit in the new birth experience and continued by the same Holy Spirit.

We need God's Holy Spirit to enable us to live in victory over our circumstances. Only He gives us His hope, strength, and peace in the midst of crises. Only He supplies the mind and life of Christ when our emotions and situations are unpredictable and unstable.

We need the Holy Spirit to carry out the commands of Scripture through us. We can love our enemies, give thanks in heartache, deny ourselves, and turn the other cheek when we are ridiculed—only as He expresses Christ's life through us.

The Lord gives you His all-sufficient Holy Spirit to glorify Himself through you. Let Him complete what He started in you at salvation by yielding to His reign daily.

Dear Lord, I yield to Your reign in my life so that You can complete what You started in me at salvation. Enable me to live in victory over my circumstances. Give me the mind of Christ when my emotions and situations are unstable.

(ON HOLY GROUND)

Pouring Forth Your Heart

SCRIPTURE READING: 2 CHRONICLES 20:1–12
KEY VERSE: 2 CHRONICLES 20:3

Jehoshaphat feared, and set himself to seek the LORD, and proclaimed a fast throughout all Judah.

Jehoshaphat had a huge problem. This good king of Judah had just received some bad news. The armies of the Moabites and Ammonites were about to march on them. It was a time of national emergency, and most leaders would have called their advisors or mustered the army, but not King Jehoshaphat.

Jehoshaphat was afraid and sought the Lord. He didn't falter, complain, or waste time in pessimistic thinking. Instead, he immediately called the people together for a time of prayer with fasting.

Notice the attributes of God he named at the beginning of his prayer: "O LORD God of our fathers, are You not God in heaven, and do You not rule over all the kingdoms of the nations, and in Your hand is there not power and might, so that no one is able to withstand You?" (2 Chron. 20:6).

The king recognized God's ultimate power and authority; therefore, he was not afraid of what mere men might do to him. Furthermore, he showed that he was willing to be involved in the process of God's answer. The king didn't mouth a halfhearted, unemotional statement; he prayed with passion and sincerity.

Have you ever poured forth your heart to the Lord? He wants you to cry out to Him and actively seek His deliverance.

Lord, I pour out my heart before You right now. Hear my cry. Deliver me!

(INTO HIS PRESENCE)

A Safe House

SCRIPTURE READING: PHILIPPIANS 4:4–7
KEY VERSE: PSALM 31:3

You are my rock and my fortress;
Therefore, for Your name's sake,
Lead me and guide me.

In her book *Seeking God,* Joni Eareckson Tada explained what turning to
God as a refuge means to her:

> I know something about fortresses. I have happy childhood memo-
> ries of my sister Kathy and me constructing a tree house on the farm.
> Our little fortress was some distance from the farmhouse, so it was
> private and far away from adults . . .
>
> To my childlike way of thinking, that tree house was a fortress.
> Not just a shelter or a place to hide, but a safe house that would pro-
> tect us from the rain beating on the tin roof and the wind shaking
> the branches of the tree. We were safe. We felt secure. . . .
>
> There's a lot more safety and security in the Lord than in safe
> houses of our own making and design. . . . Now that I'm an adult,
> I put childish activities behind me and go . . . to a place, a Person,
> who is the Everlasting Rock.

Where do you go when you feel burned-out, overcommitted, used
up? Do you run to the Lord, or to your own devices? All other sources of
relief—friends, hobbies, sports, vacations—are ultimately disappointing.
Once they're out of the picture, the pressures return.

Take your tensions and troubles to Jesus in prayer. He gives lasting
peace that is beyond your comprehension.

You are my safe house, O God. Help me turn to You in prayer for strength
in difficult times.

(INTO HIS PRESENCE)

When Things Go Wrong

SCRIPTURE READING: JAMES 1:2–4
KEY VERSE: MATTHEW 6:34

Therefore do not worry about tomorrow, for tomorrow will worry about its own things. Sufficient for the day is its own trouble.

Have you ever heard the expression "hitting the wall"? It sounds painful, doesn't it? "The wall" is sometimes used among individuals who have recently begun a new athletic endeavor, most often jogging. Symptoms include a racing heart rate, perspiration pouring down, and lungs gasping for breath in loud, painful inhalations. This is the point at which the runner feels he or she simply cannot go another step.

After experiencing this sensation, many people give up running. After all, exercise is supposed to make you feel good, right? The problem for these new runners is that they have not yet reached the point of physical endurance. This is what enables runners to continually grow stronger and better able to jog farther each day. Endurance is the result of determination, discipline, and the willingness to suffer in order to achieve results. This is true in your spiritual life as well as on the racetrack.

James 1:2–4 shows the progression of spiritual stamina. In the passage, joy in the face of extreme trials produces endurance, the end result of which is maturity, or "perfection." Pray for God's help in meeting your everyday trials with the joy that comes from Christ, so that you may develop spiritual endurance and, ultimately, victorious maturity in Christ.

Lord, help me to respond properly as I face my trials today. Enable me to rejoice, knowing that You are developing spiritual endurance that will result in victory.

(PATHWAYS TO HIS PRESENCE)

The Favor of God

SCRIPTURE READING: 1 SAMUEL 3:1–10
KEY VERSE: PSALM 90:12

Teach us to number our days,
That we may gain a heart of wisdom.

Does God care more for you than He does anybody else? No. Does He care less for you than He does anybody else? No.

God cares for you in precisely the same manner He does for each of His children—with complete justice, fairness, goodness, and equality.

His forgiveness is offered to you personally. His love is custom designed to meet your most excruciating emotional and spiritual needs. His Word speaks to you intimately.

He calls you by name as He did Samuel (1 Sam. 3). He is intimately acquainted with every single one of your peculiar ways (Ps. 139) and has numbered each of your days on planet Earth (Ps. 90:12).

Yet you are not to stand still and bask in all this attention lavished on you. God takes care of you, His workmanship, so that you may engage in a lifetime of extending His goodness to others.

Assured of Christ's unstinting, unreserved grace and favor toward you in every circumstance, you may wake up each day with a positive outlook and the knowledge that He is at work through you to accomplish His objectives.

God has designed good works for you today that no one but you can do.

Thank You, dear Lord, that You know me by name. You are intimately
acquainted with every one of my ways and have numbered each of my days.

(INTO HIS PRESENCE)

Second Chances

SCRIPTURE READING: 1 JOHN 1:7–9
KEY VERSE: 1 JOHN 1:9

If we confess our sins, He is faithful and just to forgive us our sins and to cleanse us from all unrighteousness.

The love Jesus demonstrated at the cross is unconditional. True love reaches out to the unlovely.

The woman caught in adultery sought affection, but reaped a scandal. As the scribes and Pharisees brought her before Jesus, they demanded that her punishment be stoning. Jesus reacted in love. Stooping down, He began writing something in the sand.

Then Jesus related the basic truth that only the sinless have a right to cast stones. Knowing that sinlessness was not something they could claim, the crowd of religious men dispersed. Only Jesus was left, and He refused to condemn her (John 8:1–11).

Jesus' ministry always allowed for second chances. His interest was not to hold on to records of wrong, but to give people the chance to accept Him and do right. We do well to reflect His love by giving others second chances. Our greatest acts of love may be offering forgiveness to someone who has wronged us or to reach out to someone others have judged as unlovely.

Always remember the love and forgiveness God has shown you as you deal with other people. You will be less likely to cast stones and more likely to give second chances.

Father, thank You for the offer of a second chance. I accept. Thank You for Your love and forgiveness.

(PATHWAYS TO HIS PRESENCE)

A Changed Life

SCRIPTURE READING: COLOSSIANS 3:12–17
KEY VERSE: COLOSSIANS 3:17

Whatever you do in word or deed, do all in the name of the Lord Jesus, giving thanks to God the Father through Him.

After we are saved, the constant pressure to conform to the world's standards can give us spiritual amnesia. We have to pay the electric bill on time, fight the rush-hour traffic, mow the yard, and wash the dishes just as everyone else does. The danger is that the familiar routine can cause us to lose sight of the radical transformation that occurred when we were born again.

At salvation, we received a new spirit, the Holy Spirit, who works through our ordinary experiences to accomplish the supernatural goal of conforming us to the image of Christ. In our bill paying, we can depend on His provision. In the irritating traffic snarls, we can meditate on Scripture. (Try it, it works!) In the yard work, we can enjoy His creation. In the kitchen, we can give thanks for His many gifts to us.

As new creatures with a new spirit, we have a new purpose—to honor God in all we do: working, eating, drinking, driving, playing, and thinking.

If your Christian experience borders on boring, remember the monumental change that occurred when you were saved and the divine dimension that is now yours to enjoy by faith and obedience.

Heavenly Father, thank You for the tremendous change that occurred when I was saved. Thank You for the divine dimension that is mine to enjoy in every area of my life. I want to honor You in all I do.

(ON HOLY GROUND)

A Love for the Word

SCRIPTURE READING: NEHEMIAH 8:1–9
KEY VERSE: PSALM 119:105

Your word is a lamp to my feet
And a light to my path.

One of the most beneficial prayers you can pray is to ask God to give you a love for His Word. Many try to read and study the Word of God through human effort. They struggle through Genesis, fight their way through Exodus, but lose momentum in Leviticus.

However, when there is a deep, abiding love for God's Word, even the genealogies take on a life of their own. God's principles lift off the pages and fill your heart with insight and hope. After all, God inspired His Word to be written so you would have proof of His loving desire toward you.

The psalmist exclaimed, "How I long for your precepts!" (Ps. 119:40 NIV), and "Your word is a lamp to my feet and a light for my path" (Ps. 119:105 NIV).

Something about the Word of God changes lives. According to the book of Nehemiah, after the walls of Jerusalem had been rebuilt, the book containing the Law of Moses was brought out and read to the people.

For years, they had thirsted to hear God's Word read aloud. Memories of their exile in a foreign land made that moment in time like none other. The nation of Israel—what was left of it—stood together "as one man" (Neh. 8:1), and as Ezra read God's words, the people began to weep.

Have you uncovered the sweetness of God's presence through His Word? It's there, and it awaits your discovery.

Thank You for Your Word, Lord. It is a lamp unto my feet and a light to my path.

(SEEKING HIS FACE)

The Fabric of Your Life

SCRIPTURE READING: PSALM 119:169–176
KEY VERSE: PSALM 119:175

Let my soul live, and it shall praise You; and let Your judgments help me.

Amy Carmichael made a habit of collecting short prayers written throughout the Bible. When a need arose, she would pray God's Word to Him. One of her favorites is found in Psalm 119:175: "Let my soul live, and it shall praise You; and let Your judgments help me."

Two things immediately happen when you use God's Word as a prayer source. First, you are strengthened within your soul. God's Word is powerful (Heb. 4:12). It reveals the message of His heart written just for you. If you are weary from the battles of life, the Word of God is a minister of hope and truth. It is God breathed; therefore, it has the ability to refresh and renew the downtrodden.

Second, you experience intimate fellowship with the Lord by reading His Word. In picking it up, you are telling Him that you want to know more about Him, your life, and the situation at hand. He honors your devotion just as He honors the promises in His Word.

Too many people wait until desperation hits before they turn to God for guidance. But you don't have to wait until the alarm sounds. God's Word is a standard of truth. When you weave it into the fabric of your life through prayer, your trust level rises, and you can see clearly the hope that is given to you by a faithful, loving God.

Lord, help me weave the fabric of my life with prayer. Lift the level of my trust so I can see clearly the hope that You have given me.

(INTO HIS PRESENCE)

Does Your Prayer Honor God?

SCRIPTURE READING: I THESSALONIANS 5:16–22
KEY VERSE: I THESSALONIANS 5:17

Pray without ceasing.

The believer's two most important spiritual disciplines are Bible study and prayer. It is impossible to grow continually in Christ without practicing both. Prayer is the primary means by which we talk to God, and also a way He grows us: it is through prayer that we petition the Lord and trust Him for the answer. In this way, we learn to listen to Him, just as we learn to wait for His answer. And He loves for us to put Him in His proper place of honor through the spiritual act of worship called prayer.

Indeed, prayer is one of the best ways in which we can honor God. When we pray to our heavenly Father, we are acknowledging that He is God, that He truly is the high and exalted One who lives forever and whose name is Holy. God alone deserves glory, and we ascribe honor to Him when we pray continually—that is, maintain a Godward attitude throughout the day, asking Him to govern every detail of our lives (1 Thess. 5:17).

Our heavenly Father dwells both on a high and holy place and also with the contrite and lowly in spirit. This means that our motives and the condition of our hearts are very important in prayer. Simply wanting to "get our way" is not the spirit of prayer that honors God. Furthermore, it does not produce prayers that God will answer. The Lord longs for an intimate relationship with us, and time spent in communication is the best way to grow close to Him.

Lord, examine the motives and condition of my heart. I want to exalt You in Your proper place of honor. Make me lowly in spirit.

(PATHWAYS TO HIS PRESENCE)

Molded by the Master

SCRIPTURE READING: JEREMIAH 18:1–6
KEY VERSE: JEREMIAH 18:4

*The vessel that he made of clay was marred in the hand of the potter;
so he made it again into another vessel, as it seemed good to the potter
to make.*

Young Christians often complain that the Christian growth process is slow
and tedious. They become discouraged and stop growing because they want
instant knowledge without exerting any effort. Seasoned Christians have
some of the same difficulties, only in a different way. They perceive themselves as having all the knowledge necessary to live the Christian life, so
they stop growing and risk becoming hardened to the intimate love of God.

The Lord has a solution for both of these spiritual abnormalities. It is
called being molded into the likeness of Christ, and it's much more than
a one- or two-year process. It is a process through which we grow abundantly as children of God. There is no time for boredom or pride because
we are too much in love with Christ.

Elisabeth Elliot wrote: "God will never disappoint us. He loves us
and has only one purpose for us: holiness, which in His kingdom equals
joy." Holiness is a priority with God. When we seek to be like Christ, we
seek holiness.

But to become holy, we must submit ourselves to the shaping and
molding of God's loving hands. The clay of your spiritual being cries out
to be molded into something of beauty. The Potter longs to mold and
shape your life. Allow Him to take whatever time He needs to create in
you joy and devotion of immeasurable worth.

*Heavenly Father, mold me into the likeness of Your Son. Make me into
something of beauty.*

(ON HOLY GROUND)

Sufficient Provision

SCRIPTURE READING: MATTHEW 14:22–34
KEY VERSE: MATTHEW 14:31

Jesus stretched out His hand and caught him, and said to him, "O you of little faith, why did you doubt?"

The storm the disciples encountered in the Scripture was tenacious. Even though several of them were seasoned fishermen, they thought they were about to die. And if that wasn't enough, they looked out over the raging sea and saw what appeared to be a ghost walking toward them.

How many times have you found yourself in a frightening situation and seen things differently from what they actually were? When you are fighting fear and anxiety, it is easy to be carried away by your emotions.

Jesus sent His disciples on before Him across the Sea of Galilee for a purpose. He knew the storm was coming. He also knew how they would respond to the thundering skies. They trusted Him as their Teacher; now they were going to learn about His lordship. Their faith had to be tested, and nothing tries faith like trouble and difficulty.

When we feel stretched to the limit and have no place to go, Jesus wants us instinctively to run to Him. However, instead of crying out to God, the disciples vainly struggled with oars and sails. They were captivated by fear and did not recognize Jesus even when He crossed over the waves of the sea to save them.

No matter what you face, you can trust Jesus to be your peace amid the storm. When you lay aside your human efforts, you will find His provision infinitely sufficient and true.

You are my peace, O God. You are my provision. You are sufficient for every need today.

(INTO HIS PRESENCE)

Cherish the Word

SCRIPTURE READING: DEUTERONOMY 6:1–9
KEY VERSE: DEUTERONOMY 6:6

These words which I command you today shall be in your heart.

Are you a list maker? Most people at least jot down their grocery items on a piece of paper before heading to the store. It's so easy to forget the little details that we need to keep checklists to help us remember.

We're just as "forgetful" concerning God's Word many times too. The Lord understands our natural weaknesses and our tendency to mentally push aside thoughts we don't deem urgent at the moment. That is why He commanded His people to keep His words ever before them:

> These words, which I am commanding you today, shall be on your heart. You shall teach them diligently to your sons and shall talk of them when you sit in your house and when you walk by the way and when you lie down and when you rise up. You shall bind them as a sign on your hand and they shall be as frontals on your forehead. You shall write them on the doorposts of your house and on your gates (Deut. 6:6–9 NASB).

In other words, they were to put God's Word in the paths of their daily lives, everywhere they went, and as a part of all they did. How can you do the same today? Find some verses that pertain to your personal circumstances, and write them out on cards. Keep the cards with you or in a prominent place in your home. You'll be surprised how quickly they become a part of your everyday thinking.

Write Your Word on my heart, O Lord, and teach me to cherish it.

(SEEKING HIS FACE)

Strength in Weakness

SCRIPTURE READING: JOB 23:8–10
KEY VERSE: PSALM 66:12

You have caused men to ride over our heads;
We went through fire and through water;
But You brought us out to rich fulfillment.

A certain businessman knew he was a poor speaker. He always got so nervous standing up before a crowd that his voice quivered, his face flushed red, and he could barely remember what to say. When his manager asked him to give a product demonstration to some potential clients, he was less than thrilled. He was too embarrassed to decline the opportunity, and everyone was counting on him.

The night before his talk, he knelt beside his desk chair to pray and give the problem to God: "Dear Lord, You know that I am weak in this area. Like Moses, I don't even want to try to speak before important people, but I'm trusting You for the strength and ability. Father, show Your power tomorrow through me. Give me the words. Fill me with Your calm and peace, and guide my every syllable. In Jesus' name, amen."

The next morning when he began the presentation, he could feel the Lord answering his prayer. He spoke slowly and distinctly, and his voice didn't shake once. After it was over, a colleague gave him a slap on the back in approval. The man replied, "Hey, it wasn't me—God handled this one."

That is the truth of 2 Corinthians 12:10 in action: "Therefore I take pleasure in infirmities, in reproaches, in needs, in persecutions, in distresses, for Christ's sake. For when I am weak, then I am strong."

Dear Lord, in my weaknesses today, demonstrate Your strength. Help me
remember that when I am weak, You are strong.

(INTO HIS PRESENCE)

Your Perfect Friend

SCRIPTURE READING: JOHN 15:12–15
KEY VERSE: JOHN 15:15

No longer do I call you servants, for a servant does not know what his master is doing; but I have called you friends, for all things that I heard from My Father I have made known to you.

Where did you meet your best friend? Often you make friends in your own neighborhood. Sometimes you find them at school, in college, or at work. The friendship isn't perfect, yet it is an integral part of your life.

But if you could find the perfect friend, what would be your blueprint? You would probably choose someone who loves you just as you are, someone who overlooks every negative act and still loves you without condition. You'd pick someone who accepts you without regarding qualifications or stature.

No doubt, your friend would understand you fully and know why you're hurt, discouraged, or tempted, and he would understand even when you err. He doesn't agree with it, but he understands because he's been tempted too.

Your ideal friend would be someone to whom you could tell your innermost desires and secrets without fear of rejection or criticism. The person would be committed to you, no matter the circumstance, and would be completely open with you.

Your new friend would be selfless, showing you love every day and encouraging you to love others. He would offer inspiration and comfort simply by listening before answering. If you haven't met such a friend, it's time for an introduction.

This is Jesus Christ. He is your perfect Friend!

You are the perfect Friend, Jesus. You offer inspiration and comfort. Thank You for being my Friend.

(SEEKING HIS FACE)

Unshakable Faith

SCRIPTURE READING: PSALM 16:1–11

KEY VERSES: PSALM 16:8

I have set the LORD always before me . . . I shall not be moved.

Clinging to your faith in times of trouble is not a casual undertaking. To stand strong in faith, unwavering in your stance, takes determination, purpose, and intentional action. In the life of David, we see the determination and resolve it took for his own mind to stay on the Lord rather than on the enemies that hotly pursued him. In Psalm 16:8, David shared, "I have set the LORD always before me . . . I shall not be moved."

That's determination. He purposed to concentrate on who the Lord is instead of on who was chasing him. He intentionally acted on faith rather than on fear. Did David ever experience moments of fear? He wouldn't be human if he didn't. Yet the key is, how did David respond? And what does that tell us about how we should respond?

If we believe God is truly in control, we need not worry about tomorrow (Matt. 6:33–34). The first step in responding to times of uncertainty is to focus on God. Get in His Word and learn about His character.

That sovereign character of the Lord Almighty is what will remind you that this life is all about Him. His purpose is always at hand. You will not experience any trial, hardship, or even loss of life on earth until the Lord has allowed it. Will you trust that the sovereign God knows what is best for your life?

Lord, help me be focused on Your kingdom, determined in my purpose, and intentional in my actions as I serve You.

(PATHWAYS TO HIS PRESENCE)

Unhappiness

SCRIPTURE READING: I TIMOTHY 6:6–11
KEY VERSE: I TIMOTHY 6:6

Godliness with contentment is great gain.

Written into our country's famous Declaration of Independence is the noble idea that each citizen possesses inalienable rights, among which are "Life, Liberty and the pursuit of Happiness." In the past few decades, that pursuit has become more frenzied than ever. We, a nation of millions who seek the good life, "grab all the gusto" we can.

The framers of our document of freedom did not explain that while we may have a right to happiness, finding it—and maintaining it—is another matter altogether. The more we look, the more elusive happiness seems.

Moses endured millions of Israelites who were anything but happy campers. Jeremiah and Noah preached for a lifetime under oppressive conditions with little effectiveness. Paul spent many years imprisoned, whether in jail or under house arrest.

Yet we cannot say these and other Bible personalities were sad, disillusioned men. Anything but that. Despite their conditions, they radiated joy.

Perhaps they defined happiness differently. Contentment would best describe them.

Searching for happiness is a roller-coaster experience. However, you can consistently attain contentment.

Father, I want to consistently radiate Your joy, despite my circumstances. Instead of seeking the "good life," let me focus on You. Let me learn to be content.

(ON HOLY GROUND)

Loneliness

SCRIPTURE READING: PSALM 139
KEY VERSE: ISAIAH 43:5

Fear not, for I am with you.

The thought of loneliness usually stirs visions of being physically alone. Yet many feel lonely even in a crowd of people. Loneliness is an experience of the heart and cannot be simply chased away by material gain or the wealth of possessions. Only Jesus can truly satisfy a lonely heart.

Corrie Ten Boom wrote of her time spent in isolation in a concentration camp:

> A solitary cell awaited me. Everything was empty and gray. . . . Here there was nothing, only an emptiness, a cold gray void. "O Savior, You are with me, help me; hold me fast and comfort me. Take away this anxiety, this desolation. . . . Take me into Your arms and comfort me," I prayed. And peace stole into my heart. The weird noises still surrounded me, but I fell quietly asleep.
>
> I soon grew accustomed to the cell, and when worries threatened to overwhelm me I began to sing. What a change in my life! I talked with my Savior. Never before had fellowship with Him been so close. It was a joy I hoped would continue unchanged. I was a prisoner— and yet—how free!

No matter how dark your loneliness appears, God will bring light, hope, and a sense of total security if you will call out in faith to Him.

Dear heavenly Father, when I am overwhelmed with loneliness, let me realize that no matter how dark it may seem, Your light of hope and love still penetrates. I am not alone. You are with me.

(ON HOLY GROUND)

Loving Acceptance

SCRIPTURE READING: EPHESIANS 1:1–6
KEY VERSE: JOHN 15:16

You did not choose Me, but I chose you and appointed you that you should go and bear fruit, and that your fruit should remain, that whatever you ask the Father in My name He may give you.

The youngster ran out the door to join his friends. Twenty minutes later he was back. "I thought you were meeting your friends down at the ball field," his mother commented. But before he could answer, she noticed the look of hurt on his face and asked, "Honey, what happened?"

"Mom, they didn't choose me to play on either one of their teams. Nobody likes me." This disappointment may seem trivial from an adult's perspective, but it's not. Rejection can leave a person feeling left out and disillusioned. Such an incident has the power to shape one's personality and self-image.

"I'm sorry you weren't chosen," replied the boy's mother. "Sometimes things happen that are hurtful, but always remember you mean a lot to me and your dad."

One of the greatest needs of our society is the need to belong. We want to know we matter to someone else. How we choose to meet this need is critical to our sense of self-worth and to our relationship with God.

Jesus Christ holds the greatest amount of acceptance you could ever hope to find. No matter what turns your life has taken or who has rejected you, God promises to love and accept you when you come to Him. And the fact remains that He will always choose you to be on His team!

Dear Lord, please heal the emotional scars left by rejection. Thank You for loving and accepting me just as I am.

(INTO HIS PRESENCE)

Neglect

SCRIPTURE READING: 2 SAMUEL 5:1–12
KEY VERSE: 2 SAMUEL 5:12

*David knew that the LORD had established him as king over Israel,
and that He had exalted His kingdom for the sake of His people Israel.*

Have you ever been passed over at work for a promotion that you felt you deserved? Or have you ever not received due recognition for your work?

If so, you will be excited to know about a dynamic principle that runs through the life of David that kept him in line for God's blessing in similar circumstances. Though anointed as king, David spent many years on the run from his former boss, King Saul. On several occasions David had opportunity to kill Saul and seize the kingdom. In each instance he refused.

When Saul ended his life on a remote battlefield, David could have declared himself king over all of Israel. Instead he initially ruled over the single tribe of Judah. Seven and a half years later, the remaining tribes of Israel asked David to rule them.

The principle is this: David allowed God to promote him in His way and in His time. He refused to take the bull by the horns. David allowed God to give him credit. He waited until "the LORD had established him as king over Israel" (2 Sam. 5:12).

Wherever neglect occurs in your life, remember that God will exalt you in due season.

Father God, cleanse me from selfish ambition. Establish and promote me in Your perfect timing. Give me the patience to wait.

(ON HOLY GROUND)

A Refuge and Rock

SCRIPTURE READING: PSALM 18:1–6
KEY VERSE: PROVERBS 23:19

Hear, my son, and be wise;
And guide your heart in the way.

King David often used words such as *refuge* and *rock* to explain his relationship with God. For him, God was a refuge—a place where he could go anytime to find encouragement and understanding.

Encouragement and hope are crucial to our well-being, especially when we deal with the pressures of this world. Before we know it, we can become drained mentally and physically. This is perhaps how the psalmist felt when he wrote:

I will lift up my eyes to the hills—
From whence comes my help?
My help comes from the LORD,
Who made heaven and earth.
He will not allow your foot to be moved;
He who keeps you will not slumber. (Ps. 121:1–3)

If your hope is in anything other than Jesus Christ, it is temporal hope and will not last because our world changes daily. It is passing away.

People come and go. Disappointments can leave us floundering and wondering how we ever got into such positions. But God is tenacious in His affections toward us.

Nothing is too small for you to bring to Him in prayer. He has the answer you seek to every question. Solving problems on your own leads only to more frustration and wrong decisions.

Lord, I thank You that You have the answer to all my questions, the provision for all my needs. You are my refuge and rock.

(INTO HIS PRESENCE)

Brokenness: The Way to Blessing

SCRIPTURE READING: JOHN 12:24–26
KEY VERSE: PSALM 119:75

*I know, O LORD, that Your judgments are right, and that in faithfulness
You have afflicted me.*

Rub some seed corn between your fingers, and instantly you will be struck
by its hardness. You can step on it, throw it, or try to crush it, and the
seed will remain intact in most instances. An abundant source of life is
stored within this rigid outer husk. The potential for thousands of kernels
is bound up in one tiny seed corn.

As any farmer or gardener knows, prolific life is released only when
the corn is buried several inches beneath the turned soil. There it lies in
darkness and seeming oblivion for many days. The rains come, and the
seed waits. The sun shines, and the seed waits.

Then one day the waiting is over. A small green shoot thrusts through
the earth. In the months to come, the plant will grow, tassel, and produce
ample food for man and beast. The joy of harvest would never be realized
apart from the breaking of the seed's protective shell.

There is a corresponding spiritual process at work in Christians. It is
brokenness—the principle by which God gloriously works to liberate us
for abundant living. It is a hard way, but it is God's way to blessing, joy,
and abundant life.

*Precious Lord, thank You for the process of brokenness, which is at work in
me. Let me realize that despite its pain, it is the road to blessing.*

(ON HOLY GROUND)

Your Source and Supply

SCRIPTURE READING: MATTHEW 6:25–34
KEY VERSE: ACTS 17:28

In Him we live and move and have our being, as also some of your own poets have said, "For we are also His offspring."

What is your most pressing need today? Money for the mortgage, college tuition, or Christmas gifts? A new direction for your career? Peace with your children? Unity in your marriage? Whatever your need, God has an answer: seek first His kingdom and His righteousness (Matt. 6:33).

What does God have to do with schools, cars, relationships, money, or investments? Everything. As the Source and Supply of all your needs—material or otherwise—God is the Ultimate Giver. His wisdom, love, and sovereignty work on your behalf, regardless of the complexity, urgency, or practicality of your needs.

You seek God to meet your needs because He knows them even before you ask. He is fully aware of the problems you face and the demands they place on you. When you seek God first, He promises to supply every necessity, just as He does for the birds of the air (Matt. 6:26).

You seek Him first by depending upon His answer, refusing to manipulate your circumstances. When you want God's way—His path above all else—mortgage, school, and family fit into His plan and purpose. Therefore, He will provide in His time; He will meet every possible need. Anxiety over the future is replaced by confident trust in God's absolute goodness.

Lord, I have confident trust in Your goodness. I know You will provide all I need in Your time.

(INTO HIS PRESENCE)

Submission to God

SCRIPTURE READING: PHILIPPIANS 2:1–11
KEY VERSE: PSALM 51:10

Create in me a clean heart, O God,
And renew a steadfast spirit within me.

In *Beyond Ourselves*, Catherine Marshall wrote of spiritual renewal:

One morning I was particularly discouraged. I was caught between all my blessings: A wonderful husband, three lovely children at home and a fourth in and out, a big new house, and my daily writing. I was, quite frankly, exhausted.

So once more we took the situation to God. . . . "Lord, we've tried everything we can think of. Every road has seemed a dead end. . . . Tell us what it is."

God showed her that she was "dictating the terms" of her life:

A thought stabbed me. What if—for this period of my life—I was supposed to give up the writing? Immediately this possibility brought tears. Why should I have to relinquish something which I had from the beginning dedicated to God and something from which I also got such intense satisfaction?

Resolutely she submitted her desires to God:

Though my emotions were in stark rebellion, I knew that sooner or later they would fall into line. When the relinquishment was complete, the breakthrough occurred.

The way to a renewed mind is the way of submission. When you submit your desires to Christ, He transforms your will and prepares you for a great blessing.

I submit to You, Lord. Transform my will and prepare me for Your blessings.

(SEEKING HIS FACE)

Walking Worthy of Your Calling

SCRIPTURE READING: EPHESIANS 4:1–2
KEY VERSE: EPHESIANS 4:1

I, therefore, the prisoner of the Lord, beseech you to walk worthy of the calling with which you were called.

In coming to the United States shortly after her release from a Nazi concentration camp, Corrie Ten Boom, author of *The Hiding Place*, was answering the call of God for her life.

However, that calling did not go unchallenged. Time after time Corrie's presence in the United States was questioned. The little support she had in the beginning dwindled. She was tempted to become discouraged but refused. Beneath any thoughts of rejection were a peace and a hope that God would honor her obedience.

When others rejected her, Corrie held fast to the promises of God. Finally her commitment paid off. A door of opportunity opened through a well-known Christian evangelist. Soon Corrie Ten Boom became one of the most recognized Christian speakers of our time. She weathered life's most severe storms and was found worthy of God's call.

God has called you to be a light of His love and forgiveness to a world locked away in utter darkness. Therefore, walk worthy of His call. When discouragement comes, stand firm in your faith, and God will mold you into an instrument of His love to others.

Dear Lord, You have called me to be a light as I travel through this world. Use me to minister to others I encounter on my journey.

(ON HOLY GROUND)

Always Ready to Answer

SCRIPTURE READING: 1 PETER 3:13–18
KEY VERSE: 1 PETER 3:15

Sanctify the Lord God in your hearts, and always be ready to give a defense to everyone who asks you a reason for the hope that is in you, with meekness and fear.

John really stood out at his company. When other coworkers were complaining, he quietly went about his business with a smile. He did not abuse company property or time, and he always had a moment to spare to listen to a problem or give encouragement. His team leader could always count on him to finish a task, and everyone could tell by the way he spoke on the phone to his family that he had excellent relationships at home.

That is why one day Brian walked into his office just before closing time and said, "You know, there's something about you that's different. It's not just how you do things; it's your attitude. You don't get your feathers ruffled. How do you keep it all under control?"

John asked Brian if he would like to have dinner with him and hear his answer. Brian was so intrigued by this man that he said yes, and that night he was open to hearing whatever John had to say about spiritual matters.

That is the way God intends for us to operate as believers. "Always be prepared to give an answer to everyone who asks you to give the reason for the hope that you have" (1 Peter 3:15 NIV). You don't have to seek a listening ear. God will bring open ears to you as He leads, and He will give you the words to say under the guidance of the Holy Spirit.

Dear Lord, open the ears of those around me so I can share Your Word with them.

(SEEKING HIS FACE)

Unlimited Vision

Scripture Reading: Isaiah 6:1–8
Key Verse: Psalm 33:11

The counsel of the LORD stands forever, the plans of His heart to all generations.

"Illness destroyed Helen Keller's sight and hearing when she was not yet two years old, leaving her cut off from the world," wrote William Bennett in *The Book of Virtues*. For nearly five years she grew up, as she later described it, wild and unruly.

Anne Sullivan's arrival at the Kellers' Alabama home from the Perkins Institution for the Blind in Boston changed Helen's life. . . . Through the sense of touch she was able to make contact with the young girl's mind, and within three years she had taught Helen to read and write Braille. By sixteen, Helen could speak well enough to go to preparatory school and college. She graduated cum laude from Radcliffe in 1904, and devoted the rest of her life to helping the blind and deaf-blind, as her teacher had done.

In recalling the first day she spent with Anne Sullivan, Helen wrote, "It would have been difficult to find a happier child than I was as I lay in my crib at the close of that eventful day and lived over the joys it brought me, and for the first time longed for a new day to come."

Anne Sullivan had a vision without boundaries, and she shared it. Are your goals limited by fear or doubt? God has a plan for your life that is broad and full of hope. Even now He waits to reveal it to you.

Almighty God, I repent of the fear and doubt that limit my vision. Your plan for me is greater than I can imagine. Even now, You wait to reveal it to me. Lord, I am ready to receive it.

(ON HOLY GROUND)

Savoring God's Gifts

SCRIPTURE READING: LUKE 12:22–32

KEY VERSE: LUKE 12:31

Seek the kingdom of God, and all these things shall be added to you.

Everything we do in life requires a decision. Some have said that even when we refuse to make a decision, we have decided what we will or will not do. The same is true when it comes to experiencing God's best for our lives.

Jesus taught us that it was God's good pleasure to give us the kingdom of God. This means that all we could ever hope or want is ours to enjoy. Of course, there are guidelines for us to follow.

For example, God will never give us things simply to gratify our self-indulgence and greed. On the other hand, there are many Christians living in spiritual poverty because they have never learned to enjoy the goodness of God's blessing.

This in no way solely focuses on financial wealth, though God may choose to bless many in this area. Nor does it mean that we should feel guilty when God blesses us in some area of material value. God's blessings are not limited to any one category. They are endless, and it is our responsibility to enjoy them when they come.

Therefore, instead of denying the gifts He sends your way, ask the Lord to help you correctly handle them so that He will be glorified in your life. Jesus taught us that God gives good things to His children. Therefore, never refuse His gifts when they come because each one is wrapped in eternal love for you.

Thank You for Your precious gifts to me, dear Lord. They are wrapped in Your eternal love for me. I praise You for each one!

(INTO HIS PRESENCE)

Our Eternal Home

SCRIPTURE READING: 2 CORINTHIANS 5:1–9
KEY VERSE: 2 CORINTHIANS 5:1

For we know that if our earthly house, this tent, is destroyed, we have a building from God, a house not made with hands, eternal in the heavens.

There is something special about home. Built on God's wisdom, it is a refuge from the storm, a greenhouse for maturity and growth, a haven of unconditional love. During special seasons, such as Thanksgiving and Christmas, home is a magnet, attracting adults back to their childhood roots with warm simplicity.

That is what makes heaven so wonderful. It is not just a place of pearly gates, golden streets, and angelic hosts. It is more than tearless perfection, sheer ecstasy, and freedom from all want. It is home—blissful, sweet, unending, eternal, blessed home.

At last we can end our earthly pilgrimage, lay down our burdens and pain, kick off our shoes of suffering, and rest forever in our eternal abode. Even now our hearts yearn for home. Home is where the heart is, and the man who has given his life to Jesus has transferred the deed of his heart to Christ. He is our Owner, and He is preparing a place for us in heaven that we can finally call home.

Enjoy your present home and its delights now. But remember, your dream home is in heaven, awaiting those who have built their lives on the foundation of Christ's death, burial, and resurrection.

Lord, thank You for Your promise of an eternal home.

(INTO HIS PRESENCE)

Three Principles of Victory

SCRIPTURE READING: JOSHUA 1:1−9
KEY VERSE: JOSHUA 1:9

Have I not commanded you? Be strong and of good courage; do not be afraid, nor be dismayed, for the LORD your God is with you wherever you go.

Jesus calmed the raging sea not so that the disciples could witness another miracle, but so that they might be caught up in the reality of His strength and personal care for them. Jesus allowed fear to captivate their hearts briefly so they could learn of Him. After the first few opening chapters of the book of Acts, we see His principles come to life in the lives of His followers. They found their strength in Jesus.

Joshua faced a similar situation as he prepared to lead Israel into the promised land. Chosen by God to complete the task, Joshua struggled with thoughts of fear and failure.

The angel of the Lord gave him three principles to keep him focused on the victory of God's strength: (1) meditate on the Word of God daily; (2) focus, be watchful and not distracted by the turmoil around him; and (3) do exactly what God told him to do.

When you begin to realize who Jesus Christ is and how much He cares for you, your faith level will increase. The greater your faith level, the clearer His strength will become.

Remember what the angel of the Lord said to Joshua: "Have I not commanded you? Be strong and of good courage; do not be afraid, nor be dismayed, for the LORD your God is with you wherever you go" (Josh. 1:9).

Master, I choose to meditate on Your Word today instead of my own circumstances. I want to be watchful and not distracted by the turmoil around me. Help me to do exactly what You tell me to do. Increase my faith level today.

(ON HOLY GROUND)

Finding God

SCRIPTURE READING: PSALM 16:7–11
KEY VERSE: PSALM 16:11

You will show me the path of life;
In Your presence is fullness of joy;
At Your right hand are pleasures forevermore.

Men often have a bad reputation for refusing to request directions while driving. At the root of the issue is the fact that we do not like to admit that we do not know something. Even if it means going in circles for hours, many of us would rather stumble upon the right answer ourselves than to ask for help. This method works for us as long as we know the general area. However, if we must get to a specific destination in a strange town, we need to know how to get there!

The same can be said of our lives. We may believe that God has something specific set aside for us, and yet we may not seek His guidance for leading us safely into His plan. How can we arrive at God's destination if we do not consult the only One who can see where we are going?

The Lord has promised to give us direction. Psalm 16:11 says, "You will show me the path of life; in Your presence is fullness of joy; at Your right hand are pleasures forevermore." God's will is not something that we find "out there" through trial and error. Rather, it is something that we find "in Him," through prayer and Bible study as we strive to know His heart more clearly.

If you have been on a quest to "find God," stop your searching and simply talk to Him. He knows where you are, and He knows exactly where you need to go. No roadmap could promise more.

May I not waste precious time wandering, Lord, when I can come directly to You and seek direction for my life.

(PATHWAYS TO HIS PRESENCE)

You Are a Minister

SCRIPTURE READING: ZECHARIAH 4:5–7
KEY VERSE: COLOSSIANS 1:27

To them God willed to make known what are the riches of the glory of this mystery among the Gentiles: which is Christ in you, the hope of glory.

One man, a believer, often prayed for God to allow him to work for a Christian organization. However, the years went by, and that opportunity never came. Eventually he began to wonder, *How can God use me in a place like this?*

Too often we look at those who work for churches and ministries and think what they are doing is the most important work for the kingdom of God. It is important, but so is what you are doing right where you are. Only you can accomplish what God has given you to do. Working in a Christian organization is no more sacred than working in a factory or department store as long as your motive is to honor God.

You may work with someone who is trapped in sin. You don't know it, but he feels helpless and longs for a way out. Because you know the Way, you also know the person who can break through his darkness with the light of eternal hope.

You are a minister of the gospel right where God has planted you. Praise Him for giving you this opportunity, and make every effort to take advantage of it. You can be a part of taking eternal hope to a lost and dying world (Col. 1:27).

Almighty God, thank You for the opportunity to be a minister. Show me how to take advantage of it. Use me today—right where I am!

(ON HOLY GROUND)

Open Your Heart to God

SCRIPTURE READING: LUKE 2:25–40
KEY VERSES: LUKE 2:36–38

There was one, Anna, a prophetess, the daughter of Phanuel, of the tribe of Asher. She was of a great age, and had lived with a husband seven years from her virginity; and this woman was a widow of about eighty-four years, who did not depart from the temple, but served God with fastings and prayers night and day. And coming in that instant she gave thanks to the Lord, and spoke of Him to all those who looked for redemption in Jerusalem.

Anna's husband died when she was quite young. They had been married only seven years before death took his life. Alone she took up the mantle of prayer and devoted herself to seeking God about the coming of the Messiah, never even leaving the temple (Luke 2:37).

How many of us would have done this? There's no mention of worrying about her state of widowhood or how her needs would be provided. No record of anger over being left without her husband, her friend, and her beloved at such an early age. These elements are especially important when we look at her life in the context of Judaism.

Most women were married and had children—to be barren was a disgrace. Anna didn't concern herself with what others thought. Her devotion was solely to the Lord. Day and night, her heart's desire was to seek audience with almighty God through prayer. Times of fasting gave her a spiritual sensitivity that few experience.

When Christ came to earth, one of the first places He went was to the temple. Even as a baby, Jesus was God. He had heard this woman's fervent petition, and with His birth God answered her call.

Prayer transports us into the presence of God. Anna did not concern herself with the talk and gossip of her day. She was focused on the coming of the Messiah. Have you made the decision to open your heart only to God?

Lord, I focus my attention upon You right now as I kneel in Your presence. I open my heart to You.

(INTO HIS PRESENCE)

Free to Live God's Way

SCRIPTURE READING: GALATIANS 5:1–15
KEY VERSE: GALATIANS 5:1

*Stand fast therefore in the liberty by which Christ has made us free,
and do not be entangled again with a yoke of bondage.*

When approving an inmate for parole, prison officials are supposed to consider the likelihood of recidivism, or repetition of the offense. People who have committed certain crimes, especially the more violent ones, have a higher rate of recidivism than others. The sad fact is that some prisoners are never able to escape their pattern of criminal behavior.

Why? Until their thinking changes, the resulting actions stay the same, no matter how good rehabilitation efforts might be. The same is true for a sinful habit in your life. Before you can shake off its negative influence, you must alter your mind-set.

Romans 12:2 explains the bondage-breaking process: "Do not be conformed to this world, but be transformed by the renewing of your mind, so that you may prove what the will of God is, that which is good and acceptable and perfect"(NASB).

As you read God's Word and study His principles carefully, they gradually become a natural part of your thought process. When the new comes in, the old is tossed out. The Lord is then able to work His truth into your innermost being, establishing new, Christlike habits.

You don't have to be confined by the restrictions of an old sin problem. Whether you are in a jail that is real or one of your own making, Jesus wants to set you free to live in His ways.

Almighty God, set me free to live Your way. Remove the restrictions of sin. Toss out the old. Make room for the new.

(ON HOLY GROUND)

Positioned to Hear His Voice

SCRIPTURE READING: 2 SAMUEL 5:22–25
KEY VERSE: PSALM 62:5

My soul, wait silently for God alone, for my expectation is from Him.

David had just been anointed king over Israel when the Philistines attacked. The first thing he did was to go to God in prayer and inquire: "Shall I go up against the Philistines? Will You give them into my hand?" (2 Sam. 5:19 NASB). The Lord affirmed the victory to David.

Israel captured the Philistine camp. In desperation, the Philistines attempted another raid. David could have looked at the situation from a human perspective. His army easily won the first victory; what was there to stop them from repeating the same action? Plenty, and David knew it. Joshua failed to seek God at Ai and lost to a much smaller army than the one David faced (Josh. 7:1–12). Making decisions such as that one apart from God invited defeat. David immediately went back to God for the solution.

The Lord told him not to attack the enemy! Instead, he was to wait until he heard the sound of marching in the tops of the balsam trees. Try to imagine what David felt. He knew the enemy was poised and ready to strike, but he had to wait for God's timing.

Times of waiting are times of great blessing. When we learn to wait on the Lord, we position ourselves to hear His voice. God's timing is always perfect. And when you commit yourself to following His lead, you will never be disappointed.

O God, help me wait for Your timing, even when I frantically feel I must do something. I commit myself to follow You. I know I won't be disappointed.

(ON HOLY GROUND)

The Measure of God's Grace

SCRIPTURE READING: ROMANS 5:20—6:6
KEY VERSE: ROMANS 6:6

Our old man was crucified with Him, that the body of sin might be done away with, that we should no longer be slaves of sin.

Imagine the most beautiful waterfall you've ever seen. Now, in your mind, stand at its base and hold a thimble under the crashing water. This illustrates the measure of God's grace in your life, covering your sin. You can no more contain a waterfall in a thimble than you can contain God's love and forgiveness for you.

If you have accepted Christ as your Savior, then you have accepted His atoning work on the cross. God set no limits on the effects of Jesus' sacrifice, so why should you? If you are wracked with guilt over sin, whether it happened long ago or is ongoing, and you can't seem to escape its snare, remember you cannot out-sin God's grace.

While God will judge sin and will discipline a wayward believer, He also will forgive any transgression. And if you do it again tomorrow, He'll forgive you. This is not a license to sin but an invitation to accept God's grace humbly and repent into an obedient walk with Jesus.

The believer's goal should be to greet God's grace and forgiveness with genuine thanksgiving and contrition. We could never produce one achievement that would warrant our Lord's grace, and we could never produce enough failures for Him to take it away.

When you hold that thimble under Christ's cross and catch one drop of His blood, you have enough.

I humbly accept Your grace, Lord. I revel in its sufficiency.

(SEEKING HIS FACE)

True Contentment

SCRIPTURE READING: JOHN 4:3–18
KEY VERSES: JOHN 4:13–14

Jesus answered and said to her, "Whoever drinks of this water will thirst again, but whoever drinks of the water that I shall give him will never thirst. But the water that I shall give him will become in him a fountain of water springing up into everlasting life."

In talking to the woman at the well, Jesus spoke of life-giving water. The water of the world can never satisfy the God-shaped void that is in the heart of each lost person. However, there is an even starker reality: even after we become believers, the things of the world cannot bring true, lasting contentment. No matter how much money we have, we are never satisfied apart from Jesus Christ.

He waters your heart with His unfailing hope. He fills you with His blessed presence so that you do not fear as the world fears. He comforts you in times of sorrow and holds you close when disappointment and rejection strike. He is your ever-present Savior and Lord.

God does not want you to live a life that feels empty and unrewarding. When you feel either of these, you may end up taking great risks with the hopes that something along the way will fill the void inside. The woman at the well had tried in vain to find true happiness. Yet nothing worked before she met the Savior.

Today, Jesus stands waiting to touch your life with fresh hope. Drink of Him, and be blessed by His unconditional love for you.

Dear Lord, thank You for Your unfailing hope that waters my heart. Thank You for Your presence that alleviates my fears. Thank You for Your comfort in times of sorrow.

(INTO HIS PRESENCE)

An Infinite Treasury

SCRIPTURE READING: EPHESIANS 1:17–19
KEY VERSES: 2 PETER 1:2–3

Grace and peace be multiplied to you in the knowledge of God and of Jesus our Lord, as His divine power has given to us all things that pertain to life and godliness, through the knowledge of Him who called us by glory and virtue.

The elderly couple had lived modestly for years on their small farm. The land was not the best, but they always had raised enough to survive. They eventually sold the farm to a developer. Working on a hunch, the new owner drilled for and discovered oil—a well worth millions of dollars. For years, the couple had lived on top of untold wealth and never knew what they had been missing.

Many believers do not understand the vast riches they already possess in Jesus Christ, an infinite treasury of wisdom and knowledge and all good things. The moment you accept Him as your Savior you receive everything God is, everything He does, and everything He provides. You lack nothing; God's immeasurable, overflowing love and power are available to you by His grace for every trial, every decision, every challenge.

The apostle Peter explained how God gives you these astounding resources: "Grace and peace be multiplied to you in the knowledge of God and of Jesus our Lord, as His divine power has given to us all things that pertain to life and godliness" (2 Peter 1:2–3). Today, you can embrace the fullness of His grace and live the abundant life He has planned.

Lord, I embrace the fullness of Your grace today. I choose to live the abundant life You have planned for me.

(INTO HIS PRESENCE)

The Faithfulness of God

SCRIPTURE READING: LAMENTATIONS 3:19–26
KEY VERSES: LAMENTATIONS 3:22–23

Through the LORD's mercies we are not consumed, because His compassions fail not. They are new every morning; great is Your faithfulness.

The first verse of the hymn "Great Is Thy Faithfulness," by Thomas Chisholm, speaks to God's faithfulness:

Great is Thy faithfulness, O God my Father!
There is no shadow of turning with Thee;
Thou changest not, Thy compassions, they fail not:
As Thou hast been Thou forever wilt be.

These famous words summarize a foundational truth: God is faithful, and He does not change (Heb. 13:8). Theologians call this God's "immutability." Have you ever thought about why it is so important to understand this aspect of God's character? God's unchanging nature is the basis for everything we believe about Him.

If God could change on a whim, then every promise He made in Scripture would be invalidated. He would be untrustworthy. He loved you unconditionally yesterday, but what about tomorrow when you really blow it? That is why God emphasizes His absolute, uncompromising faithfulness throughout His Word. We need that assurance in order to know Him as God and to place our faith in Him.

In 1 Corinthians 1:9 we read, "God is faithful, by whom you were called into the fellowship of His Son, Jesus Christ our Lord." Your salvation is guaranteed, because He sealed your redemption at the cross. Let your heart rejoice and say, "Great is Thy faithfulness!"

Father, Son, Holy Spirit—triune God—You have ever been the same, unchanging. Thank You for Your faithfulness. I offer You my heart to mirror that faithfulness.

(PATHWAYS TO HIS PRESENCE)

The Mind of the Father

SCRIPTURE READING: JOHN 14:16–18
KEY VERSE: JOHN 14:26

*The Helper, the Holy Spirit, whom the Father will send in My name,
He will teach you all things, and bring to your remembrance all things
that I said to you.*

The natural or unsaved man does not have the ability to discern God's
ways. Only the person who has accepted Jesus Christ as his Savior can
know the mind of God, and even then there is a limitation to the knowledge given. We cannot really know all things about God. Jesus told His
disciples that there are some things the Father has kept unto Himself.

Perhaps God does this because He knows that our limited, earthbound minds could not understand the vastness and power that are His.
In this way, we do not need to understand all that God knows. But we do
need to know Him as our personal Savior and loving Lord.

He has given us the Holy Spirit so that we might know Him better. Over the course of your lifetime, God will reveal many things about
Himself. One thing you can be sure of, He will never withhold His loving
care from you. He is present with you today, through the life of the Holy
Spirit. You can pray to the Lord and know He hears you.

Even when you don't know what to pray, God is aware of every need
and will minister His hope to your heart so you will not become tired or
weary. God's Spirit is there, conveying His love and truth each moment.
You are held safe in the arms of Christ because the Holy Spirit stands
guard over your soul. Praise Him for His goodness and mercy!

*Lord, I am so thankful that I am held safe in Your arms. Thank You
for setting the Holy Spirit as a guard over my soul. Thank You for Your
goodness and mercy!*

(SEEKING HIS FACE)

A Path to His Presence

SCRIPTURE READING: JOHN 1:1–9
KEY VERSE: PSALM 32:5

I acknowledged my sin to You,
And my iniquity I have not hidden.
I said, "I will confess my transgressions to the LORD,"
And You forgave the iniquity of my sin.

Do you know people who attend church every Sunday and profess the love of Christ, yet do not express His love to others? Could one of those people be you? It is easy to embrace the intellectual theology of Christ's love, but quite another thing to let that love flow in and through your heart to a needy world.

One of the primary reasons people fail to experience God's love flowing through them is that a barrier of bitterness and resentment obstructs it. When you are bitter, you build a wall around your heart to protect yourself from pain. If you build it high enough, you may become entirely isolated from the world. Safe, but isolated. Your protective mechanism eventually leads to loneliness and ineffectiveness.

The root of this condition sometimes can be traced to an unforgiving spirit. When you enclose yourself in a cell of unforgiveness, you work, fellowship, and even worship behind bars. But this need not be the case. We know from Scripture that Jesus came to set the captives free. He did so through a divine act of love and forgiveness.

The power of Christ's strength to forgive even the most degenerate is available to you, if you are willing to accept it. If you are captive to your own anger and hostility, allow the Lord to exchange those attitudes for the love you need in order to forgive. In doing so, you yourself will experience the love of your heavenly Father and will, at the same time, become a vessel for sharing it with others—even those who hurt you.

Forgiveness is a pathway into the presence of God.

Dear Lord, give me the strength to forgive. I refuse to be held captive to
anger and hostility. Give me the love I need in order to forgive others.

(PATHWAYS TO HIS PRESENCE)

Preparation by Prayer

SCRIPTURE READING: PSALM 31:1–5
KEY VERSE: PSALM 31:1

In You, O LORD, I put my trust;
Let me never be ashamed;
Deliver me in Your righteousness.

When you hear the word *preparation*, what comes to your mind? Do you think about life insurance, studying for a test, or maybe even packing all the necessary equipment before a camping trip? Of course, all of these things are acts of preparation.

When we prepare beforehand, we consider all possible outcomes and make sure that we will have what we need when the time comes. We explore any potential problems and arrive at a solution "just in case." After all, no one wants to be caught up in an unexpected situation with no idea of what to do.

Yet do we approach our spiritual lives with the same forethought, or do we tend to take more of a haphazard approach? All too often, we overlook "gearing up" before heading into unknown territory. If it makes sense to prepare for a simple camping trip, how much more important it must be to prepare for our very lives!

We make this preparation by spending time with the Lord. Too many people call upon the name of God only in times of stress; however, if you want to be ready for crisis, then you must seek the Lord when there is no problem at all. In these precious moments of prayer and reflection, we have the opportunity to calmly dwell in the Word, focusing on an intimate relationship with our heavenly Father. These are the occasions for girding up our strength and laying a solid foundation in the Word that will provide sure footing later on when troubles come our way.

Lord, help me to draw aside each day to spend time with You. I want to be prepared for this life and eternity.

(PATHWAYS TO HIS PRESENCE)

The Voice of the Shepherd

SCRIPTURE READING: JOHN 10:1–5
KEY VERSE: JOHN 10:4

*And when he brings out his own sheep, he goes before them; and the sheep
follow him, for they know his voice.*

Have you ever seen a child who cannot find his mother in a crowd?
Although she may be out of sight, the little tyke may still hear her voice. It
is almost as though his inner radar scans the sounds around him, looking
for that one familiar tone. Did you know that Jesus encouraged His hearers to have that same familiarity with the voice of God?

In today's passage from the gospel of John, Jesus likens His followers
to sheep under the direction of the Great Shepherd. In this parallel, we
see that only the shepherd can approach the flock without causing alarm.
If an unknown intruder were to come near, the sheep would immediately
sense danger, and the doorkeeper would not open the stable door. Also,
we see that the sheep follow the shepherd wherever he leads because they
know his voice. Just like a child listening for his mother, sheep instantly
recognize the shepherd by his voice.

Why is this analogy important to us today? It is because we are the
sheep and Jesus is the Shepherd. He has entered our "flock" by stepping
into human history, and He calls us to Himself by word and deed.

Can you hear the word of the Lord? He desires to make Himself
known in your life. If you have trouble hearing His voice, stop and pray
for help in quieting the noises of the world so that you can focus intently
on the voice of your Great Shepherd.

*Lord, when I can't discern Your voice, help me not to ask You to speak louder
but, rather, to spend more time listening for it.*

(PATHWAYS TO HIS PRESENCE)

Listening for God's Voice

SCRIPTURE READING: MATTHEW 6:5–13
KEY VERSE: MATTHEW 6:6

But you, when you pray, go into your room, and when you have shut your door, pray to your Father who is in the secret place; and your Father who sees in secret will reward you openly.

Imagine yourself standing in the middle of a full auditorium, with thousands of people surrounding you. If every person there was speaking at the same time, would it be possible to hear any individual in the great crowd? More than likely, you would never be able to distinguish one voice from another.

This same principle holds true for our prayer lives. In our normal, everyday lives, we are surrounded by countless voices in need of our attention. Our children cry for it, our employers demand it, and our loved ones yearn for it. With all of these calls, is it any wonder that God's voice sometimes seems so muffled or distant?

Effective meditation demands seclusion. If we do not make an effort to find a moment or two to escape the demands of our daily lives, then our ability to hear God's voice will be weakened.

Jesus was well aware of this need for isolation. In teaching the disciples' how to pray, Jesus told them to go into their rooms and close the door behind them. He knew that it was vital to take a break from the demands of life in order to truly commune with the Father.

The modern world works against this need, however. Mobile phones, e-mail, and other technological advances have brought us the blessing—and the curse—of constant communication.

At some point today, turn off the television, cell phone, and computer, and simply listen for His voice. Your schedule will not surrender time easily, so make a decision to claim a block of time for the Lord.

Lord, I am surrounded by countless voices in need of my attention. Help me to stop, listen, and hear Your voice today.

(PATHWAYS TO HIS PRESENCE)

Praying to Your Father

SCRIPTURE READING: MATTHEW 6:9–13
KEY VERSE: MATTHEW 6:9

In this manner, therefore, pray:
Our Father in heaven,
Hallowed be Your name.

On the subject of prayer, A. B. Simpson wrote:

The first view given of God in the Lord's Prayer is not His majesty but His paternal love. To the listening disciples this must have been a strange expression from the lips of their Lord as a pattern for them. Never had Jewish ears heard God so named, at least in His relation to the individual. . . . No sinful man had ever dared to call God his Father.

They, doubtless, had heard their Master use this delightful name of God . . . but that they should call Jehovah by such a name had never dawned upon their legal and unillumined minds. And yet it really means that we may and should recognize that God is our Father.

The entire idea of Jesus addressing God as Father is one of personal love and devotion. You cannot know a person unless you love him. And you certainly cannot love God unless you know Him and realize He is intimately in love with you.

The idea of God as your Father is one of extreme love. Regardless of what your earthly father was like, God is a Father of love, and He cares for you. His parental love offers security, encouragement, and nurturing. Therefore, know that He has the ability to step aside from the occupation of the world's demands to listen to your heart. For the believer, prayer is a lifeline of eternal love and hope.

Listen to my heart today, Father. You are my lifeline in the midst of the storms of life.

(INTO HIS PRESENCE)

Give It to God

SCRIPTURE READING: PHILIPPIANS 4:6–9
KEY VERSE: PSALM 55:22

Cast your burden on the LORD,
And He shall sustain you;
He shall never permit the righteous to be moved.

That gnawing feeling of anxiety can grow from what we call the butter-flies to full-blown panic if left unchecked. The Lord knows how critical it is that you get rid of anxiety. It destroys your peace, clouds your perception, robs your joy, and consumes your thinking.

Have you ever worried about something and then, after a time of mental agony, finally handed the concern over to God? The relief you felt was indescribable. What's amazing is that the next time a worry threatens to dominate, you are equally reluctant to let go.

Why? As human beings, we relish the sensation of being in control. We somehow feel that by pondering a problem continuously, thinking through all the options and possibilities, we will come up with good answers. That may be true sometimes, but the process saps all our energy. And when we rely on our limited resources and understanding, we discount completely the wisdom and sovereignty of God.

God wants you to give Him your perplexities, fears, worries, and impossible situations. He is the only One who can handle them, and He knows what is best for you. God has the big picture—you don't—and trying to manipulate things results in further confusion and anxiety.

If you're ready to trust Him, He is ready to listen. Pour out your heart to the Lord, and He will lift the burden. Give it to God.

Lord, I'm ready to trust You. Take my burdens, fears, and impossible
situations. Give me confidence that You know best.

(INTO HIS PRESENCE)

You Are Forgiven

SCRIPTURE READING: COLOSSIANS 3:5–9
KEY VERSE: ROMANS 5:8

God demonstrates His own love toward us, in that while we were still sinners, Christ died for us.

Many people quake in fear after reading the list of sins in 1 Corinthians 6:9–10. Others read the list and breathe a sigh of relief, because their sins are not on the list. Unfortunately, the apostle Paul continued his list of vices in Galatians 5:19–21, Ephesians 5:3–5, and Colossians 3:5–9.

When these passages are seen together, it becomes very clear that every believer has some aspect of sin in his or her life. Clearly, Paul took a very hard view of sin. In many of these passages, he refers to the sinners listed as those who will not enter the kingdom of God. This is the ultimate punishment, and this is what we each deserve.

However, the hope offered to the Corinthians is still our hope today. We are washed in Jesus' blood. It has removed the stain of our sin; we are sanctified because our union with Christ has drawn us into the people of God; and we are justified by Christ's work on the cross that has drawn us into a restored, personal relationship with the Creator God.

There is joy in knowing that we have been forgiven. We must remember that our sin does not surprise God; on the contrary, "while we were still sinners, Christ died for us" (Rom. 5:8). Knowing who and what we are, our loving Father sent His Son to save us. Ask God to help you forgive yourself, just as He has already forgiven you in Christ.

Lord Jesus, through Your death and resurrection You have washed my soul and removed the stains of sin. Thank You.

(PATHWAYS TO HIS PRESENCE)

Facing Life's Mountains

SCRIPTURE READING: ZECHARIAH 4:6–10
KEY VERSE: ZECHARIAH 4:6

So he answered and said to me: "This is the word of the LORD to Zerubbabel: 'Not by might nor by power, but by My Spirit,' says the LORD of hosts."

The Bible uses the word *mountain* to mean different things: a geographical location such as Mount Zion (Ps. 2:6); an example of stability (Ps. 30:7); and a barrier, hindrance, or obstacle (Zech. 4:7).

As a disciple of Christ, you are not guaranteed an easy life. You may face many mountains—trials, difficulties, and hardships—throughout your life. How do you respond when facing what appears to be an overwhelming obstacle or problem? Do you panic? Do you feel discouraged? Do you feel like giving up?

When God calls you to a task, He assumes the responsibility of removing the hindrances that would keep you from succeeding. "Not by might nor by power, but by My Spirit" (Zech. 4:6).

What do you feel is looming before you like an impossible mountain? Work, relationships, finances, health, the future?

Isaiah 41:10 provides words of comfort for us to hold close to our hearts: "Fear not, for I am with you; be not dismayed, for I am your God. I will strengthen you, yes, I will help you, I will uphold you with My righteous right hand."

No matter what you are facing or how easy or difficult the task may be, always look toward God for victory. He is your eternal, unfailing hope (Ps. 123:2).

Lord, help me to see that the mountain I consider impossible to climb is the one that You see as an opportunity for a better view.

(PATHWAYS TO HIS PRESENCE)

A Candle of Hope

Scripture Reading: Genesis 39; 41
Key Verse: Genesis 45:5

Do not therefore be grieved or angry with yourselves because you sold me here; for God sent me before you to preserve life.

Many times in our spiritual walk with the Lord, we do not know where He is leading or why. Often we may misunderstand why He has allowed certain circumstances to invade our otherwise safe and appointed world.

More than likely, Joseph did not understand why God allowed his brothers to treat him with such deep animosity. He had faithfully worshiped the Lord, yet God did not save him from the trial of being sold into Egyptian bondage. Once Joseph was there, his life became a drama of ups and downs, good and bad. If we think about it, Joseph's story may remind us of our own lives at times.

Because he could not escape captivity, he was forced to trust God throughout his Egyptian days. Think about it; he never again walked through his beloved homeland of Canaan. Even after God blessed him and Pharaoh appointed him over all the land, Joseph remained in Egypt. But God had a plan. He used Joseph's banishment to save Israel from starvation when a famine struck.

Had Joseph not gone into Egypt, Israel would have perished. God used Joseph's suffering to bless others. The years from the time of his arrest until the time of his family's arrival were not explained in detail to Joseph. God's servant walked through the darkness with only one candle of hope—his faith in a changeless God. And guess what? It was more than enough light!

Master, help me walk through the darkness with the candle of hope—my faith in a changeless God. Your light is enough for my journey.

(On Holy Ground)

Running from Corduroy

SCRIPTURE READING: PSALM 56:1–4
KEY VERSE: PSALM 56:4

In God (I will praise His word)
In God I have put my trust;
I will not fear.
What can flesh do to me?

An older pastor remembers a time when, as a boy, he took a shortcut across a vacant field. His mother had warned him not to cross the field after sundown. But knowing he was late for supper, he ignored her words.

Halfway through his journey, he noticed the wind picking up. Bare tree limbs waved against the night sky, frightening him. As he wondered what lurked in the darkness, he began walking at a very brisk pace. Then he heard footsteps coming up behind him.

He turned to look, but no one was there. The moment he resumed walking, the steps returned. He tried walking faster, but the steps kept coming, right in cadence with his own. He even tried running, but that, too, was futile.

By that point he was besieged with anxiety. There seemed to be no escape! Suddenly a thought occurred to him: *Could I be imagining an evil intruder?* When he turned and looked, no one was there. Then he heard the noise again, but it came only when he moved his legs.

Looking down, he realized he was wearing corduroy pants. It was the rubbing back and forth of the material that made the sound he thought was footsteps.

Are you running from corduroy? Put your anxieties aside. Jesus is committed to protecting you.

Dear heavenly Father, take my fears and anxieties. I thank You that You are committed to protecting me.

(SEEKING HIS FACE)

Doing the Best He Can

SCRIPTURE READING: COLOSSIANS 2:3–6
KEY VERSE: GALATIANS 5:16

Walk in the Spirit, and you shall not fulfill the lust of the flesh.

Many people think that life will be easy after they get saved. Instead, they frequently find they seem to have even more struggles than before. We should not be dismayed, however; this is the normal Christian life. Before we met the Savior, we were walking aimlessly; but upon our salvation, we commenced a journey that would take us through rough terrain and high mountains.

In the epistle to the Galatians, the apostle Paul warned us not to use our newfound freedom in Christ as an excuse to revert—instead of drifting back into our aimless ways, we must take the yoke of Jesus and learn to walk in the Spirit. Paul specifically said "walk" (Gal. 5:16) because the Christian life has direction. We are climbing new heights toward a specific goal, and climbing means struggling.

Every day we grapple with jealousy, lust, and pride because we live in a world filled with such things. At the same time, we can learn to walk by the Spirit and rise above our temptations and enemies. Yes, it is tough to be in a perpetual fight, and many people have no stomach for such constant exertion. When they see the high standard of Jesus' example, they sometimes drop out of the contest and settle for doing the best they can in their own strength.

But doing the best we can is exactly what Paul said will not work—it simply isn't good enough. That's why the Holy Spirit came. By fully submitting to Him, we can learn to let the Spirit of God do the best *He* can. Then we will walk in victory.

Lord, I want to walk in victory, not just do the best I can. Do the best You can through me.

(PATHWAYS TO HIS PRESENCE)

Surrendering to God

SCRIPTURE READING: ROMANS 12:1-5
KEY VERSE: ROMANS 12:1

I beseech you therefore, brethren, by the mercies of God, that you present your bodies a living sacrifice, holy, acceptable to God, which is your reasonable service.

When many people hear the word *surrender*, images of conflict and over-powering forces come to mind. In contrast, the act of surrendering one's life to God is a beautiful and peaceful experience.

Why, then, are we so afraid to hand over the reins of our lives to God's omnipotent leadership? The answer lies in our self-oriented nature. We live in a world that encourages us to take pride in what we have accomplished and accumulated. The concept of surrendering these things to God is unthinkable for most people.

As a believer, however, God has called you to a higher standard of living. He wants to help you reach the goals that He has set for your life. Yet, in order to fulfill His plan, we must choose to lay our selfish desires before Him.

Until you make this important step toward God, you will find your-self in a state of unrest and uncertainty. However, once you surrender your life to God, He will unleash the storehouse of blessings waiting for you.

In Romans 12, God specifically asks you to present yourself as a living sacrifice to Him (vv. 1–2). God wants to guide, direct, and bless you. Do not let disobedience stand in the way of His plan for your life.

Lord, I present myself as a living sacrifice. Help me understand Your good and acceptable will.

(PATHWAYS TO HIS PRESENCE)

Tools for Growth

SCRIPTURE READING: 1 PETER 5:6–10
KEY VERSE: 1 PETER 5:10

May the God of all grace, who called us to His eternal glory by Christ Jesus, after you have suffered a while, perfect, establish, strengthen, and settle you.

Imagine being forced to leave your home and live in a land far from those you love. Some of us find this hard to visualize, while others have experienced this very trauma. In recent years, we have witnessed entire ethnic groups being forced to flee their homelands for fear of annihilation.

That was the same dilemma facing the early church in Jerusalem. Nero, the Roman emperor at the time, blamed the Christians for a fire that burned a large portion of Rome. Believing Jerusalem was the hub of Christian activity, Nero sought to disperse the early church and crush it by forcing its members to leave the city.

Nero's persecution of Christians was both relentless and hideous. Yet he could not stop the early church from growing. In fact, though they were forced underground, the church grew at a rapid rate. Today we see this same thing taking place in China and other parts of the world where there is severe persecution. Trial and persecution cause those who suffer to run to God.

Peter reminded the early church that the outcome of their faith would produce results. No matter what you are facing, you can trust that God stands beside you, and He will take your difficulties and persecution and bring a tremendous sense of victory out of each one. Let Him show you how to use life's difficulties as tools for tremendous spiritual growth and witness to others.

Lord, please teach me how to use life's difficulties as tools for spiritual growth and witness to others.

(SEEKING HIS FACE)

The Light of God's Love

SCRIPTURE READING: PSALM 27
KEY VERSE: PSALM 27:1

The LORD is my light and my salvation;
Whom shall I fear?
The LORD is the strength of my life;
Of whom shall I be afraid?

The Tybee lighthouse near Savannah, Georgia, has seen many storms. Hurricane-force winds have threatened its existence. Gale-driven rains have bludgeoned its walls, and yet it survives. Even when floodwaters cover the roadway that leads out to the island on which it stands, the lighthouse remains a beacon of hope.

David declared,

> The LORD is my light and my salvation; whom shall I fear? The LORD is the defense of my life; whom shall I dread? . . . Though a host encamp against me, my heart will not fear; though war arise against me, in spite of this I shall be confident. One thing I have asked from the LORD, that I shall seek; that I may dwell in the house of the LORD all the days of my life, to behold the beauty of the LORD, and to meditate in His temple. For in the day of trouble He will conceal me in His tabernacle; in the secret place of His tent He will hide me; He will lift me up on a rock. (Ps. 27:1, 3–5 NASB)

More than once, King David found himself in a hopeless situation. He would have given up were it not for his hope in God. Instead of becoming angry and bitter, he chose to cling to the goodness of God even in harrowing circumstances. The storms of life will drive you to the light of God's love and care, or they will force you to retreat in sorrow.

Father, let the storms of life drive me to the light of Your love and care. I don't want to retreat in sorrow.

(SEEKING HIS FACE)

How to Treat Unbelievers

SCRIPTURE READING: COLOSSIANS 4:5–6
KEY VERSE: COLOSSIANS 4:5

Walk in wisdom toward those who are outside, redeeming the time.

Many people have become Christians due to the influence of a Christian friend or coworker. If you ask them what was the predominant characteristic of the individual who attracted them to Christ, most would allude to a keen, unworldly sense of love and acceptance.

Treating the unbeliever in a biblical fashion is not easy for some Christians. We operate on such different standards and think on such contrasting wavelengths that compatibility can be quite difficult. Despite such differences, God often uses ordinary Christians as His instruments to proclaim the gospel of Christ.

The non-Christian is just like you before you were saved, dead in sin and separated from God. The love of God can be clearly communicated to the unbeliever through upright conduct, positive conversation, and a servant spirit.

Don't judge those around you who are not Christians. Focus instead on releasing the love of Christ through your daily lifestyle.

Everybody needs the Lord—even people who seemingly resist all overtures. The love and grace of God expressed through your words and deeds can be amazingly used by Him in a most wonderful way.

Lord, help me to express Your love and grace through kind words and deeds today.

(SEEKING HIS FACE)

Stimulated to Action

SCRIPTURE READING: ACTS 17:22–31
KEY VERSE: ACTS 17:16

While Paul waited for them at Athens, his spirit was provoked within him when he saw that the city was given over to idols.

In Acts 17:16, we read that as Paul waited for the arrival of Silas and Timothy in Athens, he became "provoked" at what he saw. The city was filled with images of idols. Men had erected statues and monuments to gods that did not exist—the evidence of an inner need to worship something or someone greater than themselves.

Being "provoked" as the apostle Paul was did not mean being angry as we know it. Here the word *provoked* means "stimulated to action." At the sight of the spiritual ignorance of the Athenians, Paul was provoked to speak the truth concerning Christ and His messiahship.

Because Paul, a scholar in his own right, knew that words delivered in anger are rarely worth considering, he challenged the Athenian philosophers to a debate. He was amazed at their attempt to worship every god imaginable, even to the point that they made sure they did not leave one out.

Warren Wiersbe comments on Paul's effort: "Paul's message is a masterpiece of communication. He started where the people were by referring to their altar dedicated to an unknown god. Having aroused their interest, he then explained who that God is and what He is like. He concluded the message with a personal application that left each council member facing a moral decision, and some of them decided for Jesus Christ."

Dear Lord, stimulate me to action in behalf of lost souls. Provoke me to respond.

(SEEKING HIS FACE)

A Bowl of Hot Soup

SCRIPTURE READING: JAMES 2:14–20
KEY VERSE: JAMES 2:20

Do you want to know, O foolish man, that faith without works is dead?

While believers realize good works do not bring salvation, we all some-times act as if we don't realize salvation should bring good works. You were saved by grace through Christ's sacrifice on the cross. You didn't work for it and could not have earned it if you tried. However, you can offer expressions of gratitude to God with your conduct and character. Scholar Warren Wiersbe shares a wonderful example:

> A pastor friend told about a Christian lady who often visited a retirement home near her house. One day she noticed a lonely man sitting, staring at his dinner tray. In a kindly manner she asked, "Is something wrong?"
>
> "Is something wrong!" replied the man in a heavy accent. "Yes, something is wrong! I am a Jew, and I cannot eat this food!"
>
> "What would you like to have?" she asked.
>
> "I would like a bowl of hot soup!"
>
> She went home and prepared the soup and, after getting per-mission from the office, took it to the man. In succeeding weeks, she often visited him and brought him the kind of food he enjoyed and eventually she led him to faith in Christ. Yes, preparing soup can be a spiritual sacrifice, a good work to the glory of God.

Good works often leave someone indebted enough to lend you his ears.

Lord, show me ways to do good to those in need around me.

(SEEKING HIS FACE)

An Act of God's Will

SCRIPTURE READING: MATTHEW 28:19-20
KEY VERSE: JOHN 6:27

Do not labor for the food which perishes, but for the food which endures to everlasting life, which the Son of Man will give you, because God the Father has set His seal on Him.

Remember how you felt the last time you helped someone? Maybe you helped a stranded motorist. Maybe you joined a neighbor for a home repair job or took on a task that was burdensome and you were glad to eventually complete it.

Whatever the circumstance, you probably were warmed by the fact that you had performed an act of goodwill. But what about doing an act of the Father's will? Often our deeds are only for temporal benefit. Have you ever considered extending your efforts to eternity?

Our best labor is to accept and honor the words Jesus spoke as He prepared to return to heaven. He commanded us to make disciples of all the nations.

This means whether at home or abroad we are to share the gospel of Jesus Christ. We can't all ship off to a distant land, but we can put our arms around a hurting family member, friend, coworker, or stranger and say, "You know, Jesus loves you, and so do I. I'll pray for you. Is there anything else I can do?"

Jesus commanded all believers to take Him and His Word seriously in our approach with others. When you honor His command, you will honor God. The result of your love and obedience is an inexpressible appreciation of the fruit of the Spirit. People notice when we share the love of Christ.

Give me a heart of compassion, Lord. Help me to reach out to people in need.

(SEEKING HIS FACE)

God's Guarantee

SCRIPTURE READING: REVELATION 21:1—7
KEY VERSE: HEBREWS 11:13

These all died in faith, not having received the promises, but having seen them afar off were assured of them, embraced them and confessed that they were strangers and pilgrims on the earth.

Have you ever known the frustration of canceled hotel reservations? Sometimes even the "guaranteed late arrival" system isn't foolproof. You hustle through two airports, fumble with bags all the way, grab a rental car, drive through unfamiliar territory, and finally make it to the hotel, only to hear the clerk say, "I'm sorry, but no rooms are available."

When Jesus told His disciples about His impending departure, He gave them special assurance for the future: "In My Father's house are many mansions; if it were not so, I would have told you. I go to prepare a place for you" (John 14:2). This promise was not for the disciples only; it is for everyone who accepts Jesus as Savior and trusts Him for salvation.

Your name is written in the Lamb's Book of Life, and it cannot be erased (Rev. 21:27). Your reservation in heaven can never be changed, and the place Jesus is making ready is custom-made just for you. In fact, you are supposed to consider heaven your real home; earth is a mere way station.

Hebrews 11:13 notes that the heroes of faith regarded themselves as "strangers and pilgrims on the earth" because they were so focused on the end of their temporary journey here. You have God's guarantee: no mansion on earth can compare to the eternal home waiting for you.

Dear Father, thank You for the guarantee of a place reserved for me for eternity. I'm on my way!

(INTO HIS PRESENCE)

Our Heavenly Home

SCRIPTURE READING: REVELATION 22:6–21

KEY VERSE: 1 CORINTHIANS 2:9

Eye has not seen, nor ear heard,
Nor have entered into the heart of man
The things which God has prepared for those who love Him.

In *The Pilgrim's Progress,* a spiritual allegory written in the mid-1670s, the characters Christian and Hopeful finally get a glimpse of their heavenly home. Here is John Bunyan's vision of what they saw when they arrived:

> Now they went along together toward the gate. Though the Celestial City stood on a great high hill, the pilgrims went up the hill with perfect ease because of the two heavenly ones leading them by the arms. . . . They ascended through the regions of the air, joyously conversing as they went. . . . Their conversation was about the glory of the place, which the shining ones termed inexpressible. . . .
>
> When they drew near the gate, they were met by a company of the heavenly host. . . . The heavenly host gave a joyous hallelujah, saying, "Blessed are those who are invited to the wedding supper of the Lamb!" There also came out several of the king's trumpeters to welcome the pilgrims with heavenly music. Then they walked on together to the gate.
>
> When they came to the gate leading to the City they saw written over it in letters of gold: "Blessed are they that do His commandments, that they may have the right to the tree of life, and may go through the gates into the city."

Human words are inadequate to describe the matchless joy God has for you now and in eternity.

O Lord, I am looking forward to what You have planned for me in the future. Thank You for the joys that lay ahead.

(INTO HIS PRESENCE)

The Good Things to Come

SCRIPTURE READING: I THESSALONIANS 4:13–18
KEY VERSE: I THESSALONIANS 4:16

The Lord Himself will descend from heaven with a shout, with the voice of an archangel, and with the trumpet of God. And the dead in Christ will rise first.

Did you know that when Jesus comes back, you'll get a new body? It's true; in a flash, in the "twinkling of an eye," you will receive a new body, a special and fresh creation of God (1 Cor. 15:52). If you're frustrated with physical problems right now, imagine the liberating feeling of a restored body.

Christian author and speaker Joni Eareckson Tada, paralyzed as a teen in a diving accident, talks about some of her physical and spiritual struggles in her book *Heaven.* She explains how her suffering today prepares her heart all the more for that glorious day, the moment when she can look her Savior in the face.

Surprisingly, though, she doesn't want to forget her infirmities here:

I wish I could take my big old, tattered wheelchair to heaven. I would stand up in my new, strong, bright, beautiful, glorified body—brilliant and powerful and full of splendor—and I would point to the empty seat and say, "Lord, for decades I was paralyzed in that thing, but it showed me in a very small way what it must have felt like to be nailed to a cross. My limitations taught me about the limitations You endured." Then I might say, "The weaker I felt in this chair, the harder I leaned on You."

That's the right way to anticipate the good things that God has ahead for you, in this life and the life to come.

Dear Lord, I am really looking forward to all the things You have prepared for me in the future.

(SEEKING HIS FACE)

The Glory to Come

SCRIPTURE READING: REVELATION 22:1–5
KEY VERSE: JOHN 14:27

Peace I leave with you, My peace I give to you; not as the world gives do I give to you. Let not your heart be troubled, neither let it be afraid.

You may not consider yourself to have a very active imagination, and fantasy stories may hold little attraction for you. But the scene unfolded in this passage of Revelation is no fairy tale. Heaven, a place of such wonder and beauty, may be beyond your immediate comprehension, but it is as real as the chair you are sitting in right now.

Every detail is worth savoring, even though this picture is only a shadow of what you will experience. There will no longer be the loneliness that comes from darkness, the curse of sin, tears shed, pain felt, or the anxiety of fear. Jesus will be your Light and secure comfort. He will wipe away every tear and end all anxious thoughts.

Heaven is the absolute, unending presence of almighty God: "There shall be no night there. They need no lamp nor light of the sun, for the Lord God gives them light. And they shall reign forever and ever" (Rev. 22:5).

It may not seem relevant to dwell on the glory to come, but you need this hope to keep your perspective. When you have "heavenly vision," then heartache, disappointments, and difficulties assume their place—under the light and authority of an eternal Lord who lives in the lives of those who believe in Him through the power of the Holy Spirit. Be at peace today because He is with you.

You are with me today. I am at peace. Thank You, Father.

(INTO HIS PRESENCE)

The Exalted Lord of Revelation

SCRIPTURE READING: REVELATION 5:1–14
KEY VERSES: 1 PETER 1:18–19

You were not redeemed with corruptible things . . . but with the
precious blood of Christ, as of a lamb without spot or blemish.

Lambs were significant for the people of Israel. When they fled Egypt, they put the blood of lambs on their door frames as a sign of belonging to God (Ex. 12). They had to kill a perfect lamb as a sacrifice for certain sins.

Sheep were stock animals, common, somewhat dirty, and not known for their intelligence. Many must have reacted with surprise when John the Baptist said to Jesus, "Behold! The Lamb of God who takes away the sin of the world!" (John 1:29). He did not look like a lamb, and few understood at that point that Jesus Himself would die as a sacrifice for sin.

Revelation 5 describes an even more amazing picture of the Lamb: "And I [the apostle John] looked, and behold, in the midst of the throne and of the four living creatures, and in the midst of the elders, stood a Lamb as though it had been slain, having seven horns and seven eyes, which are the seven Spirits of God sent out into all the earth" (v. 6).

This image is beyond our human understanding; it is full of awe-inspiring power and mystery and might. The Lamb who died is now glorified, reigning over all His creation as its true Master. Christ the Lamb is to be worshiped and revered. It is no wonder that hosts of angels praise Him, saying,

> *Worthy is the Lamb who was slain*
> *To receive power and riches and wisdom,*
> *And strength and honor and glory and blessing!* (Rev. 5:12)

You are worthy, O Lord, to receive power, riches, wisdom, strength, honor,
glory, and blessing!

(INTO HIS PRESENCE)

The Perfect Savior

SCRIPTURE READING: LUKE 2:25–32
KEY VERSES: LUKE 2:30–31

For my eyes have seen Your salvation which You have prepared before the face of all peoples.

To the other people in Bethlehem, there was nothing magical about the day. There was nothing extraordinary about the child who was receiving the ritual circumcision. Yet Luke 2:30–31 reports that Simeon exclaimed, "My eyes have seen Your salvation, which You have prepared in the presence of all peoples" (NASB).

The Lord sent Jesus to be the perfect sacrifice for humanity. When Jesus comes again, He will come as a great warrior and king, not a baby. So why was Jesus born the first time? Why did Christ leave His throne in heaven to work as a carpenter? Why didn't He come as a thirty-year-old man? Wouldn't three years of sinlessness have been sufficient?

In order for Christ to be the Son of man, He had to endure everything from birth to death. In order for Him to share in our humanity, He had to encounter every part of it. There was nothing extraordinary to the people in Bethlehem, because Christ was experiencing what they encountered every day. Yet consider the miracle that the God with perfect power, understanding, and love has participated in every aspect of human life and sits on the throne of grace as He intercedes for you.

Jesus did not miss one moment of knowing what your life is like. In God's wisdom, He truly became the perfect sacrifice and Savior.

Lord Jesus, You humbled Yourself to a life of lowly humanity in order to raise me to the life of a child of the King, through Your death and resurrection. No words can express my gratitude.

(PATHWAYS TO HIS PRESENCE)

The Message of Christmas

SCRIPTURE READING: LUKE 2:1–13
KEY VERSE: LUKE 2:10

The angel said to them, "Do not be afraid, for behold, I bring you good tidings of great joy which will be to all people."

For the shepherds watching their sheep outside Bethlehem one evening, the sudden sight in front of them was terrifying. A glorious angel shining brightly in the sky was enough to make anyone rub his eyes and take a second look . . . and run.

But the first words from the angel's mouth were words to calm their frightened hearts: "Do not be afraid" (Luke 2:10). One of the messages that we learn from the Christmas story is that of peace. While God might appear overwhelming at times, He always wants to give us the assurance that with Him, peace reigns, even in the announcement of His Son's birth.

The peace we receive from the Christmas message calms our hearts, letting us know everything will be all right as long as we trust God. However, it also includes a message of peace that assures us that Jesus and His methods of teaching were all designed to draw us to the heavenly Father. The same is true of His birth. There was no need to fear; salvation would soon be realized for all mankind.

Some people have never heard the message of Christmas. When we tell them why Christ came, they might get frightened. However, there is no cause for alarm. The gospel is good news, and God will give them the peace they need to submit to Him.

Dear Father, You laid Your mighty plan of salvation before a humble band of shepherds. Thank you that those who humble themselves before You receive those same good tidings today!

(PATHWAYS TO HIS PRESENCE)

God's Awesome Love

SCRIPTURE READING: LUKE 2:15–20
KEY VERSE: LUKE 2:20

The shepherds returned, glorifying and praising God for all the things that they had heard and seen, as it was told them.

With great awe and in complete reverence, the shepherds looked upon the baby Jesus. It was true. Everything. All the words spoken to them by the angel in the sky were truth! The Savior had arrived!

And almost instantly, the shepherds realized that this kind of news didn't need to be hidden. Others needed to know that the Savior had arrived—even more prophecy was about to be fulfilled. Were these the first missionaries? No, these were the first witnesses, who understood that along with the knowledge of this great information came the responsibility to tell others.

As we grow in our relationship with Christ and deepen our knowledge of Him through intimacy, there is no need for us to keep this information to ourselves. In light of what Christ has done for us—through not only His birth, but also His death and resurrection—we should desire to share this with others.

Our method of sharing the good news with others might vary. But regardless of the method in which we proclaim Christ, the message of Christmas—God's awesome love for mankind—is a story that warrants being told again and again.

Lord, we are Your witnesses on earth as surely as were the shepherds of Bethlehem. Help us to announce the Christmas message with the same enthusiasm and urgency.

(PATHWAYS TO HIS PRESENCE)

A Personal Promise

*In My Father's house are many mansions; if it were not so, I would
have told you. I go to prepare a place for you.*

Jesus came to earth with the view of offering you salvation. He wanted
you to have a restored relationship with the Father, a relationship that
was so close, so intimate, that you would have your special place in the
Father's house (John 14:1–4). In John 14:2, Jesus said, "In My Father's
house are many mansions; if it were not so, I would have told you. I go to
prepare a place for you."

Christmas is the holiday that we celebrate God coming to make His
home with us for a season, so that He could make our eternal home with
Him in heaven. In the hymn "Hark the Herald Angels Sing," Charles
Wesley described the relationship Jesus came to establish:

*Hail the heaven-born Prince of Peace! Hail the Sun of righteousness!
Light and life to all He brings, Risen with healing in His wings.
Mild He lays His glory by, born that man no more may die,
Born to raise the sons of earth, born to give them second birth.
Hark! The herald angels sing, "Glory to the newborn King."*

Christ's birth was God's reaching out to you. Celebrate the season.
Rejoice in the knowledge that God loves you so much that He left all
the glories of heaven in order to build a loving relationship with you.
Christmas means you have an eternal home waiting for you. That should
make more than the angels sing!

*Lord, I am so grateful that through the death of Your Son, Jesus, my
relationship is restored with You and I have an eternal home waiting for me.*

(PATHWAYS TO HIS PRESENCE)

The True Colors of God's Nature

Scripture Reading: John 1:1–24
Key Verse: James 1:17

Every good gift and every perfect gift is from above, and comes down from the Father of lights, with whom there is no variation or shadow of turning.

For years, poinsettias have been a favorite plant at Christmas. But in order for their brilliant color to be revealed at just the right time, nursery growers make sure the plants spend a certain amount of time in darkness. When the plants grow to maturity, large amounts of light are then introduced into their environment.

The poinsettia is native to Florida. Even in its natural environment, the poinsettia must be planted in the right location in order for the plant's leaves to turn a brilliant color. Again, the secret lies in the amount of sunlight the plant receives. The more sun at the right time, the more brilliant the color.

God calls us to be lights in a world of darkness. However, we can never forget that He is our Source of light. Without the light of His presence, we become dull and colorless. Christ said, "Let your light shine before men in such a way that they may see your good works, and glorify your Father who is in heaven" (Matt. 5:16 NASB).

The true colors of God's nature are released within us by spending time in His Word. If we fail to read and study His principles, our lights will never reflect the brilliance of His love, forgiveness, and grace to others. We must have contact with the Father of lights in order for our light to have purpose.

Precious heavenly Father, the true colors of Your nature were reflected in Your Son, who came to this earth to share Your light. Let my life be a reflection of Your divine gift of love.

(On Holy Ground)

Setting Goals by Faith

SCRIPTURE READING: ROMANS 8:28–30
KEY VERSE: PROVERBS 16:9

A man's heart plans his way, but the LORD directs his steps.

God reminds us that He has a plan for our lives (Jer. 29:11). This is an important word of encouragement. But often we worry what His plan is and how we can achieve it. While goals are very important because they help to set a positive tone for our lives, they should never take the place of true love and devotion to the Savior.

Establish your goals with God in mind. In Romans 8:28–30, the Lord underscores the fact that He truly has His eye on our lives. Every detail is woven together so that the outcome will be beautiful.

Sorrows, heartaches, and failures play an important part in your life, as do the times when you achieve great accomplishments. Set your goals and live by faith in God. Trust Him to guide you as you dream of good things for the future. Be sure each goal you set is something He would approve.

Prayer is vital to goal setting. When you talk to the Lord, ask Him to make you sensitive to His desires for your future. If you find yourself doing something that is not in keeping with His plan for your life, abandon it immediately.

Be encouraged! God will never leave you without direction and hope. Seek Him, and He will guide you. Remember, some goals take a long time to achieve. But the Captain of your soul is a God of love, who has wonderful blessings in store for you!

Heavenly Father, I praise You for the blessings You have in store for me!

(INTO HIS PRESENCE)

How to Walk with God

SCRIPTURE READING: PSALM 12:1–8
KEY VERSE: PSALM 12:6

The words of the LORD are pure words,
Like silver tried in a furnace of earth,
Purified seven times.

To find a cause that we will stand behind, fight for, live for, and die for requires complete agreement with its principles and the people in leadership. How willing would we be to defend something that does not stir us with passion? How eager would we be to risk anything for a cause that merely piqued our interest?

Living in agreement with God and His Word is something we must learn if we truly desire to walk with Him. Keeping in step with God proves more than challenging if our hearts are not unified with His. After we have reconciled our relationship with God by accepting His Son, Jesus Christ, as our Lord and Savior, we must learn to trust Him by living a life in agreement with His principles and precepts.

What God says about His Son, His church, His Word, and sin are all of utmost importance for us. If we think that some biblical principles are false or unreliable, how can we walk in step with what God desires for our lives?

When the leadership of an organization and the body of people within it are in disagreement, their collective effectiveness is reduced. How hard will people work to advance a cause they do not support? So it is with our Leader and us. We must submit more of our lives to God, so that our wills are broken to the point that they are in complete agreement with His plans for us.

Heavenly Father, I submit my life anew. Break my will so I can easily submit to Your will for me.

(PATHWAYS TO HIS PRESENCE)

Focus on the Finish Line

SCRIPTURE READING: 1 CORINTHIANS 9:24–26
KEY VERSE: 1 CORINTHIANS 9:24

Do you not know that those who run in a race all run, but one receives the prize? Run in such a way that you may obtain it.

A key to living above your circumstances is leaning on the faithfulness of Christ while refusing to be caught up in the instability of your surroundings. Paul used the analogy of a runner to explain how you are to respond to life's circumstances (1 Cor. 9:24–26).

You are to fix your gaze on the finish line and race with all your might toward that goal. Once God places a goal in your heart, never give up. Instead, move toward it with swiftness and courage.

Paul's goal was to take the gospel message to Asia. Three completed missionary journeys proved he had a plan and purpose. Personal testimonies bear witness that he achieved his goal, but not without cost. No one completes the race of life without facing many trials and tribulations.

Paul had a wonderful system for bypassing negative thinking and potential defeat. He looked beyond his circumstances to the sovereignty of God. He focused on the positive results of his ministry, not the personal pain.

In the end, the trials of Paul matured and strengthened his spiritual walk. Even though you are hard-pressed on every side, Jesus will bring light to all you are facing. Trust Him, and you will see His victory.

Dear God, fix my gaze on the finish line. Help me race with all my might toward the goal. I rebuke negative thinking and potential defeat. I will finish my journey in victory.

(ON HOLY GROUND)

The Challenge to End Well

SCRIPTURE READING: PHILIPPIANS 1:3–6
KEY VERSE: PHILIPPIANS 1:6

He who has begun a good work in you will complete it until the day of Jesus Christ.

A writer once penned a story about Hudson Taylor, the great missionary to China. He reported that the government of China commissioned a biography to be written portraying the missionary negatively. Yet the purpose of the assignment backfired: "As the author was doing his research, he was increasingly impressed by Taylor's saintly character and godly life, and he found it extremely difficult to carry out his assigned task with a clear conscience. Eventually, at the risk of losing his life, he laid aside his pen, renounced his atheism, and received Jesus as his personal Savior."

Taylor followed Christ faithfully, diligently carrying out the mission given to him. Like the apostle Paul, he experienced intense persecution but stayed focused on introducing men and women to Jesus. As a result, even after his death, Taylor's life testifies of God's goodness.

You are challenged to end well so that God's grace will show itself in you. As Paul and Taylor did, lead a godly life that will influence future generations. People will hear of your faithfulness and believe in God.

Philippians 1:6 says, "He who has begun a good work in you will complete it until the day of Jesus Christ." Live in courageous godliness to the end.

Dear heavenly Father, thank You for Your loving care throughout this past year. Give me courageous godliness so that I can end not only this year properly but my time on earth as well.

(PATHWAYS TO HIS PRESENCE)

Beginning a New Adventure

SCRIPTURE READING: ISAIAH 60:1–3
KEY VERSE: PSALM 31:3

You are my rock and my fortress; therefore, for Your name's sake, lead me and guide me.

Remember the last time you began a new adventure? Maybe it was to visit a faraway city or to fulfill a desire you longed to achieve, such as riding horses, learning how to play tennis, writing poetry, studying watercolor painting, or climbing mountains. How did it feel to approach a new beginning? You were probably filled with hopeful anticipation.

In contrast, think about the last major disappointment you experienced. The loss of a job, the grief of betrayal, or the shock of a friend's rejection can leave you feeling hopeless. The last thing you want to do is take another risk.

Before he became president of the United States, Abraham Lincoln lost four elections in twelve years. The last public office he held before being elected to the nation's highest office was a seat in the U.S. Congress in 1846. It was not until 1860 that he was elected president. Despite the defeat he experienced, Lincoln refused to give up.

What has you discouraged today? God wants you to know whatever your situation, He is aware of it. He is your constant Source of encouragement. His strength is released in your life when you make a conscious decision to continue in faith. If there is darkness, pray for His light to rest over your life, guiding you into a new season of hope and revival.

Dear heavenly Father, let Your light rest over my life, guiding me into a new season of hope and revival. I am ready to begin a new adventure with You!

(SEEKING HIS FACE)

Personal Notes

About the Author

Dr. Charles Stanley is pastor of the 16,000-member First Baptist Church in Atlanta, Georgia, and is head of the international In Touch Ministries. He has twice been elected president of the Southern Baptist Convention and is known internationally from his radio and television program *In Touch*. His many best-selling books include *When the Enemy Strikes, Finding Peace, Landmines in the Path of the Believer, Enter His Gates, The Source of My Strength*, and *How to Listen to God*.

OTHER BOOKS BY CHARLES STANLEY
PUBLISHED BY NELSON BOOKS

THE IN TOUCH STUDY SERIES